REVOLUTION, ARMIES, AND WAR

Jonathan R. Adelman

REVOLUTION, ARMIES, AND WAR

A Political History

Lynne Rienner Publishers, Inc. • Boulder, Colorado

Published in the United States of America by
Lynne Rienner Publishers, Inc.
948 North Street, Boulder, Colorado 80302

Library of Congress Cataloging-in-Publication Data

Adelman, Jonathan R.
  Revolution, armies, and war.

  Bibliography: p.
  Includes index.
  1. Military art and science—History. 2. Revolutions.
3. Military history, Modern. 4. Armies. I. Title.
U39.A34 1985   322'.5   85-19668
ISBN 0-931477-53-0

Distributed outside of North and South America and Japan
by Frances Pinter (Publishers) Ltd, 25 Floral Street,
London WC2E 9DS England. UK ISBN 0-86187-590-7

Printed and bound in the United States of America

For Nancy

Contents

Tables

Preface

It is always a pleasure to acknowledge the obligations incurred in the course of writing a book. My intellectual debts are owed to two people whose books have greatly influenced me. I first encountered Barrington Moore while I was an undergraduate in Columbia College in the late 1960s. As a graduate student at Columbia in the early 1970s, I was deeply impressed and even enchanted when I first read his *Social Origins of Dictatorship and Democracy*. At my comprehensive exams I blithely declared it to be my favorite book. In the late 1970s, while teaching at the Graduate School of International Studies (GSIS) at the University of Denver, I read Theda Skocpol's *States and Social Revolution*, which represented a major advance in the field of comparative revolution. Her encouragement with regard to my work is much appreciated.

Another major influence has been the "Comparative Revolutions Seminar" that I have taught at GSIS over the years. The three colleagues who have team-taught this course with me—Peter Van Ness, Arthur Gilbert, and Alan Gilbert—have contributed immeasurably to my thinking on the subject. All three have graciously given of their time by reading and critiquing parts of this manuscript. They and the students in the seminar will doubtless recognize themes developed over time in the classroom. The students too have helped with this book, and I would like to recognize three in particular. Jennifer Bailey and Lucy Rugh have penetratingly analyzed possible flaws in the arguments of this volume. Nancy Richler, my research assistant, has carefully and assiduously scoured the manuscript with a knowing eye for the inconsistencies in logic and presentation that inevitably crop up in such a work.

I would also like to acknowledge the efforts of Mike Ward, James Mittelman, and Franklyn Margiotta, who have all contributed to this book. And, of course, in the time honored mode of academia, I exculpate all of the above readers for any errors or problems that may exist in this manuscript.

And finally, I wish to thank my parents, Benjamin and Kitty Adelman, my wife, Nancy, and my son, Joshua, for their aid in this lengthy process.

CHAPTER 1
Introduction

Imprinted on our historical consciousness are the indelible images of triumphant revolutionary armies sweeping inexorably to great victories: Cromwell's New Model Army crushing its enemies at Naseby, Dunbar, and Drogheda; Napoleon's army driving all before it in Europe at Marengo, Austerlitz, and Jena; Russia's Red Army destroying the Whites in the civil war and storming Berlin, Prague, and Vienna in World War II; and the People's Liberation Army (PLA) marching across China in the civil war and then ousting the Americans from North Korea in the Korean War. This hard-earned glory won on the battlefield was all the more remarkable in that it was won by new armies in states that had lagged noticeably, and even badly, behind in the international political and military arena. For the England of the Stuarts had been decisively routed in the European expeditions of the 1620s and the two Bishops' Wars of 1639 and 1640. The France of Louis XV and XVI had lost badly in the Seven Years War and various non-American campaigns of the 1778–1782 war with England. The Russia of Tsar Nicholas II had faced disaster in the Russo-Japanese War (1904–1905) and in World War II, especially against the Germans from Tannenberg to Riga. And the China of the Manchus and Chiang Kai-shek had known a century of humiliation and degradation, from the first Opium War (1839–1842) and Sino-Japanese War (1894–1895) to the Boxer Rebellion (1900), Japanese conquest of Manchuria (1931–1936), and second Sino-Japanese War (1937–1945).

This volume addresses the question of how these major changes could occur in the international system, especially given systemic constraints against such rapid changes. Other nations, such as the

1

United States, Germany and Japan, have gained preeminence in the international system, but they have done so through a lengthy historical process reflecting secular trends of industrialization, modernization, and nation-building. How could these revolutionary states in a matter of a few short years burst through all the constraints that had condemned their countries to an inferior position in the international arena and win great victories that restored their countries to positions of power redolent of the distant glory of Queen Elizabeth, Louis XIV, Peter the Great, and the Middle Kingdom?

In order to answer this question, we need to look at the complex interrelationship of revolution, armies, and war. The relationship is unusually complex since all three can be independent and dependent variables in politics. Military failure, for example, can both reflect domestic social conditions and impact domestic politics at the same time. War and revolution have had at times an almost reciprocal and symbiotic relationship, with each spurring on the other. Given the centrality of the international political system for the continued viable existence of states, dire and repeated failures in the military sphere have often caused domestic crises and strained internal structural relationships. Repeated English and French military failures contributed to the development of the English and French Revolutions. The Russian defeats in the Sino-Japanese War (1904–1905) precipitated the 1905 Revolution. Defeat in World War I caused the disintegration of four dynastic empires (Tsarist Russia, Imperial Germany, the Austro-Hungarian Empire and the Ottoman Empire), while World War II brought the destruction of fascism in Germany and Italy. Manchu military failures contributed to the 1911 Revolution, while Kuomintang failures in the war with Japan paved the way for the success of the Chinese Communist Revolution.

That violent international conflicts (wars) should breed violent internal conflicts (revolutions) is hardly surprising. In states lagging behind in the intensely competitive international system, military failures have been highly visible symbols of the ineptitude of the regime. In contrast with the victories of former glorious rulers of the states, these defeats have dealt a serious blow to the legitimacy of the regime at home. The extraction of resources for war has aroused strong popular resistance. Furthermore, sharp military reversals have undermined the armed forces, a crucial pillar of regime support. Military reversals directly disintegrated the army (Russia in 1917); considerably undermined army morale (China before 1911 and in the 1940s, France by 1789); or revealed the total importance of armed force (England in 1640). Given the important role played by armies in maintaining domestic control, any significant disintegration and wavering of the armed forces must affect the survival of the state. Charles Tilly has observed,

> What is more, the armed forces have historically played a large part in subordinating other authorities and the general population for the state. They backed up collection of taxes, put down rebellions, seized and disposed of enemies of the crown, literally enforced national policy.[1]

Furthermore, as in England and China, the perceived weakness of the military machines, accompanied by weakness in civil government, encouraged revolutionary forces to raise their own armed forces. Overall, war pitilessly has revealed the strengths and especially the weaknesses of the regime (as reflected in mass opposition to the regime) and forced the regime to attempt mobilization of capabilities usually beyond its strength. Theda Skocpol put the relationship cogently,

> Rather revolutionary political crises, culminating in administrative and military breakdowns, emerged because imperial states became caught in cross-pressure between intensified military competition or intrusions from abroad and constraints imposed on monarchical responsibility by existing agrarian class structures and political institutions. The old regime states were prone to such revolutionary crises because their existing structures made it impossible for them to meet the particular international military exigencies that each had to face in the modern era.[2]

If failures in wars create a powerful but not sufficient condition for revolution, then revolutions often, but not always, promote wars. Revolution in a major state in the international system poses a serious threat to other states in the system. The genuine hatred of the English, French, and Russian revolutions by leaders of other states was deep-seated, as was fear and loathing of the Chinese Revolution in Asia and the United States. According to Elbaki Hermassi,

> The world-historical structure of revolutions means, among other things, that they introduce new political ideals and principles of legitimacy which threaten existing power arrangements by their explosive novelty or demands for societal restructuring. They exert a demonstration effect beyond the boundaries of their country of origin, with a potential for triggering waves of revolution and counterrevolution both within and between societies.[3]

The mutual distrust and hatred unleashed by revolution and

counterrevolution and attempts made to find a new international equilibrium have often led to war. From 1792 until 1814 varying coalitions of European states struggled to subdue revolutionary France until success was achieved. From 1918 to 1920 all of the major powers, including England, France, Japan and the United States, intervened to varying degrees in the Russian Revolution attempting to crush the Bolsheviks. In China the United States extended significant support (over two billion dollars in aid) to Chiang Kai-shek until 1948 when it became apparent that the war was lost. Only in the English Revolution was foreign intervention relatively minimal and indirect since at that time Europe was embroiled in the Thirty Years War and also because of England's physical separation from Europe. In general, then, revolutions often promote wars and intervention by external powers.[4]

Perhaps more importantly the fate of all major revolutions has ultimately been decided on the battlefield. Although the first phase of a revolution may be relatively bloodless (France 1789-1791, Russia 1917), as the revolution becomes more radicalized and the forces of counterrevolution organize (often with external aid), a showdown becomes inevitable. Often the result is a protracted and bloody civil war. While in England in the 1640s three civil wars claimed 100,000 lives, both the Russian civil war (1918-1920) and final Chinese civil war (1946-1949) claimed millions of lives. Even in France the suppression of the Vendee and other Royalist revolts required the liberal application of force.

The central roles of the military and war in determining the fate of the revolution are thereby manifest. Without the creation of a strong and capable revolutionary army (as in Germany from 1919 to 1923 or Spain from 1936 to 1939), the fate of the revolution is sealed by the army of the old order. The triumph of the revolution over domestic counterrevolution (whether the English Royalists, French Vendee, Russian Whites, or Chinese Kuomintang) and foreign intervention is in the first instance the military triumph of a new army and a new order. Furthermore, in a revolution the role of the army goes beyond crushing its foes on the battlefield and protecting the state in a hostile external environment. Given the disintegration and reconstruction of societies undergoing revolution and the greater than normal need for force to rebuild societies, the armies generally play a major role in consolidation of the new order. This may take the form of military rule (as Cromwell and Bonaparte in the English and French Revolutions) or, as with the advent of mass mobilizing parties in the twentieth century, the army may become a strong political force (China, 1949-1954). Finally, there often remain significant external tasks to be performed by the army. The revolutionary state may seek by force to reclaim outlying territories that took advantage of the chaos of the civil wars to achieve independence. Thus the New Model Army reclaimed Scotland and Ireland (1649-1652) for England, the Red Army retook the Ukraine and Belorussia (1920) and the Transcaucasus (1920-1921) for Russia and the People's Liberation Army occupied Tibet (1950) and prepared to invade Taiwan for China. Or, as in the case of France after 1792 and Russia in the 1920 Polish Campaign, the new republic may seek to export revolution in its army's bayonets. Thus, to the new army falls a series of important contributions to the revolution.[5]

Given the centrality of the armed force in the revolution and the emergence of the military as one of the more modern institutions of the new regime, study of the military inevitably reveals a great deal about the nature of state and revolution. Armies do not and cannot exist in total isolation from society. Rather their structures and capabilities tend to reflect those of their nation. Especially given the broadened scope of warfare inherent in revolutions, the military capability of a nation depends on the capabilities of that nation's governmental apparatus, and its political and economic strengths, as well as on purely military factors. And these capabilities in turn significantly reflect the degree of social support for the regime.

Furthermore, the army itself, as an important total institution created by the state to serve as the ultimate protection from domestic and foreign threats, represents a microcosm of society. A comparative study of armies in prerevolutionary and revolutionary states can thereby tell us a great deal about the impact of revolution on states. The effectiveness of armies is usually highly reflective of overall societal capabilities. Means of recruitment into the officer corps and relations between officers and soldiers often reveal the nature of class divisions in society. The nature and extent of the mix of mechanisms of control (normative, utilitarian, and coercive) employed to motivate soldiers tells a great deal about the relationship between the government and its citizens and that government's capacity to mobilize the population. The style of war adopted in battle is frequently a telling indicator of the morale of a society. A study of armies in four major revolutions will thereby reveal much about the ultimate impact of revolution in society.

And yet, despite the centrality of military affairs in the course of revolution, the subject has been largely ignored in the literature; as early as 1902, Charles Firth (1902) observed that "the political histories of the period and standard histories of the English army left many things unexplained."[6] More recently, Richard Hamilton (1982) noted that "for the most part the army, despite its massive size and manifest power, is an institution that is regularly omitted from discussions of macro theory."[7]

Indeed, there exist only a precious few works that deal at all with the subject of armies and revolution in any comprehensive fashion.[8] Notable among these is Theda Skocpol's *States and Social Revolution* (1979), in which she stressed that the state and the international political and military environment are key factors influencing the nature and outcome of a revolution.[9] By so doing, she indicated the important role of military affairs in the course of a revolution.

Although the bulk of the literature on comparative revolution and military history shows little interest in the interrelationship of revolutions, armies, and war, it does provide a solid basis on which to ground our study in each area. The military history of the four revolutions to be discussed is fairly comprehensive. For the English Revolution we have many works on Cromwell's army and the battles of the English civil war.[10] The sources are even better and more voluminous on the French Revolution.[11] And there is equally good material available for Russia and China.[12]

From this wealth of work on military history and the equally strong work done on political and social history, it is indeed possible to proceed to a comparative analysis of the military aspect of these four key revolutions. In a basic sense, these great revolutions have had a significant impact on the course of modern history. Each produced a dramatic impact on the governing structure of its respective society. And each entailed the violent destruction of the old autocratic political order and the creation of a new, authoritarian, and more modern political order. All the revolutions occurred in large states with significant economic and political resources. They are rare and epochal events in the history of each country.[13]

One could easily argue that a number of factors make it difficult or even undesirable to carry out such a comparison. After all, the English and French Revolutions are often (somewhat inaccurately) labelled bourgeois, while the Russian and Chinese Revolutions are called socialist. The two earlier revolutions lacked any modern parties and resulted in military rule while the two twentieth-century revolutions were guided by mass mobilizing political parties that avoided military domination. These four revolutions took place at different periods in history each with very different international systems, levels of technology, and political consciousness. Too, there is a great difference between the primitiveness of Cromwell's and Napoleon's armies, in which cavalry charges often carried the day, and modern warfare of the twentieth century with its tanks, aircraft, and mechanized infantry.

The striking aspects are the uniformities, not the differences, among the four revolutions in their military histories. Facing armed domestic counterrevolutionary elements (often led by military generals) and foreign military threats, the new revolutionary regimes, seeing their fates decided on the battlefield, built up new, strong, and capable armies. Furthermore, in many ways the new armies over time became among the most distinctive and modern institutions in those societies in terms of their organization, style of warfare, and indubitable success. The length of time necessary to carry out this transformation varied considerably among the revolutions—a few years in France (1789-1799) and England (1642-1645), one or two decades in Russia (1918-1940) and China (1927-1945). Factors such as access to state resources, retention of professional cadres from the old army, level of technology, and nature of the revolution were quite important in determining the length of the transition period. But in the end, in a world in which military changes are usually slow and incremental, the sudden emergence in each instance of a powerful, offensive-minded new army was an event of the first magnitude, securing for the revolutionary states a strong position in the international political order.

In a fundamental sense this volume is most concerned with the relationship between revolutions and power. The most permanent effect of revolutions historically has been to expand state power. While Bertrand de Jouvenel has argued that "the true historical function of revolutions is to renovate and strengthen Power," Franz Borkenau almost 50 years ago noted ironically that revolutions "begin as anarchistic movements against bureaucratic state organizations which they inevitably destroy; they continue by setting in its place another, in most cases stronger, bureaucratic organization, which suppresses all free mass movements."[14] Over time each of the four great revolutions succeeded in erecting a state power greater than that created by the preceding revolution. The power of Napoleonic France greatly exceeded that of Cromwell's England, while in turn Lenin's Russia was notably more powerful than either state. And Mao's China in the 1950s erected state power at a rate far faster than in Lenin's Russia.

My concern, then, is with revolution as a distinctive form of social change. While most theorists of revolution have been preoccupied with the causes and processes of revolution, I am concerned primarily with the impact of revolution on state power. It is in this area that were seen the permanent impact of revolutions. Studying revolutions both within and between states over time should provide a broad perspective on the relationship between states and revolutions.

For over 150 years, from the time of the French Revolution until World War II, there was a strong and positive appreciation of the impact of revolution on states and society. But the rise of fascism in the interwar period and the development of the cold war after 1945 led to a dissipation and even disappearance of these traditional views. The new totalitarian theory explicitly denigrated any such linkage. A strong counterrevolutionary movement and even concensus emerged in western scholarship in the postwar era. This was especially true with regard to the socialist revolutions, which were denied linkage with the revolutionary tradition extending back to the English and French revolutions and which were not given credit for any positive accomplishments. Stephen Cohen, in his fascinating new book, *Rethinking the Soviet Experience,* reflected that during the cold war,

> the purpose of counter-communism, therefore, was to refute every historical and contemporary aspect of Soviet ideology and propaganda. Simple anti-Communism—the assertion that 'Communism is evil'—was not enough. The larger scholarly purpose was to show that the evil had unfolded inexorably at every historical turning point since 1917 and that professed Soviet achievements were not only empty but the antithesis of real progress. Most Sovietologists probably saw no conflict between that missionary work and scholarship. America's cold war concensus often fused the two.[15]

Although the matter improved somewhat during the era of detente in the 1970s, the resurgence of the cold war in the 1980s and official denunciation of the Soviet Union as the "evil empire" has in many aspects set the clock back to the 1950s.

This volume then seeks consciously to redress the balance and attempts to examine the Soviet and Chinese experiences in light of their revolutionary traditions. In order to move away from predominantly ideological and subjective interpretations to more objective considerations (to the extent that it is possible), it is necessary to find ways to measure the impact of revolution by relatively concrete standards. It is here where the comparative study of armies at war over time becomes especially valuable. For through the comparison of the accomplishments of the armies of the prerevolutionary state and revolutionary state, the validity of many arguments about revolutionary states can be tested and observed. Furthermore, armies in battle in major wars provide clear, definable, and comparable measures, both qualitative and quantitative, of the effectiveness of a social system. Moreover, the outputs are precise in that battles and wars are won or lost, as opposed to the vagueness of many indicators of social change. Beyond the realms of data and material generated by the traditional and revolutionary states on their major war, there exists valid western material on Russian involvement in the two world wars and Chinese participation in the Sino-Japanese War and Korean War. Thus, unlike in many areas of study of Communist states, we are not data poor but rather data rich on this vital topic. Our judgments can be based on a plethora of available materials in assessing the impact of revolution on Russia and China.

In examining each of the revolutions I will begin with a comparative analysis of the military fate of the country during and before the revolution. Then I will look at the military, political, social, and economic factors that may help explain the sudden increase in military capabilities of the state. I will contrast and compare the prerevolutionary and revolutionary armies, governments, and economies. Striking differences particularly in the nature of armies and in the greatly enhanced capacity of the state to extract resources from society to support the new revolutionary forces will become apparent. I will look at the entire revolutionary period for the four countries, but focus primarily on the latter consolidation phase, in which the greatest military gains are made and the army is most completely transformed (England from 1645, France from 1799, Russia from 1940, and China from 1946). Finally, I will assess the limitations of the impact of each revolution after a generation of change, whether by monarchical restoration of the old order (England 1660, France 1814/1815) or waning of the revolutionary impulse (Russia 1956, and China 1976).

I am not attempting a comprehensive military history of the four countries, but rather my intention is to highlight critical changes over time in each country. This accounts for the almost complete omission of any discussion of the Russian and Chinese civil wars or the insurrection in the Vendee, events which merit a separate volume and are only touched on briefly in the conclusion. Nor am I attempting a comprehensive political history of the four revolutions in order to formulate a new theory of revolution. Nor for that matter am I focusing significantly on the political role of the armies or trying to establish new facts about these individual cases. Rather I am looking at the critical intersection of revolution, armies, and war in order to establish key relationships in this important but neglected field of study.[16]

In the following pages I begin with a relatively short study of the English Revolution, comparing Cromwell's army with Charles I's army, and the French Revolution, comparing Napoleon's army with Louis XV and Louis XVI's army. The inclusion of these two earlier nonsocialist revolutions makes it possible to demonstrate the validity of many of the relationships among revolution, armies, and war in spite of difference in time, place, and ideology. After demonstrating the relationship of revolutionary dynamics with the radical changes in English and French military capabilities, I move on to a more detailed analysis of the Russian and Chinese Revolutions. Given the strong Western tendency to deprecate Russia's military role in World War II, I make an extended examination of Russia's military capabilities in World War II as compared with World War I. As with the English and French Revolutions, I see great improvement in the army on the battlefield and locate the sources of these changes both in the 1917 October Revolution and Stalin's "third revolution" of the 1930s. Finally, I turn to China, whose military capabilities also have been significantly denigrated by Western scholars. Making a detailed comparison of the performance of the People's Liberation Army in the Korean War with the performance of the Kuomintang army in the Sino-Japanese War, I again note a strong improvement in Chinese military capabilities and relate this improvement to changes brought by the revolution. Finally, in the conclusion I will bring together the multiple ties binding revolution, armies, and war.

PART **1**
The English and French Revolutions

CHAPTER **2**

The English Revolution

In this section the relationship between the armed forces and the English and French Revolutions will be examined. In both revolutions the emergence of powerful armed forces—the New Model Army and ocean-dominating navy in England and the revolutionary and Napoleonic armies in France—was one of the most distinctive features of both revolutions. Suddenly the full resources of these two countries were mobilized for warfare and the extent of the resultant successes amazed and even shocked the world. This section seeks to understand what military and nonmilitary forces immanent in the revolutions were responsible for these outcomes. I will conduct a comparative analysis of each old regime and new revolutionary state to see precisely how these revolutions transformed the armed forces.

Interestingly, although the English Revolution was less outwardly revolutionary in certain aspects (most notably in social change) than our three other revolutions, it manifested especially striking changes in the role and power of the military. Under the Stuarts, the glories of the Tudor past gave way to an English passivity and even relative insignificance in European, and hence world, affairs. Charles Firth in his classic work on Cromwell has observed:

> It is difficult to realize the military impotence of England under the rule of James the First and his successor. . . . the intervention of James and Charles in the European struggles of their time was feeble and futile, not only because there was no consistency in their policy and no skill in their diplomacy, but because the material force at their disposal was insufficient to strike an effective blow.[1]

England's powerlessness forced it to the sidelines while the face and fate of Europe were being decided in the Thirty Years' War. By the late 1620s "neither France nor Spain was greatly interested in Britain. She was neither valued as an ally nor feared as an enemy."[2] By 1640 the Venetian ambassador in London could pithily conclude that "England . . . has become a nation useless to all the rest of the world and consequently of no consideration."[3] By the eve of the civil war in 1642, English influence on the Continent was negligible, except in the United Provinces.

The record of the English military in the 1620s and 1630s, both at land and at sea, was appalling and even disgraceful. The 1620s in particular saw a whole series of military disasters piled one on top of the other. James I's attempt to restore the Prussian husband of Charles' sister to his Palatinate throne in 1624 and 1625 was a dismal failure. Indeed, the German mercenary Erich von Mansfeld set sail for Breda in January 1625 with 12,000 unwilling conscripts and by June had 600 left! The 1625 campaign against Cadiz involved 15,000 soldiers and sailors who, under Sir Edward Cecil's command, did not even carry out a serious assault on Cadiz before evacuating back to England. The 1627 Buckingham expedition against the French fortress of Ile de Rhe, which guarded La Rochelle, wasted 6,000 soldiers in a four-month siege of a third-rate fort. When the English decided to lift the siege and return home, the French added insult to injury by destroying the rear guard, allowing only a minority of English soldiers to make it home. Perhaps the penultimate disaster came in 1628 when repeated assaults against La Rochelle were abandoned with the English expedition having returned without firing a shot and the Huguenot center having surrendered to Richelieu. Truly, as Denzil Holles wrote to his brother-in-law Sir Thomas Wentworth about the La Rochelle disaster, "since England was England it received not so dishonorable a blow."[4]

Although England was at peace in the 1630s and Charles I endeavored to build up her navy, England's sovereignty was flagrantly violated by other nations. While North African Barbary pirates carried off seamen to slavery even in the English Channel and Dunkirk pirates looted the Kent and Sussex coasts, English merchants were driven out of the East and West Indies. The ultimate insult came in 1639 when the Dutch won a naval battle over the Spanish fleet in English waters and then mockingly lowered their flag to sneer at English sovereignty over the sea. Surely English sea power had reached a nadir at the point where it could not even protect its own waters.[5]

The end of the 1630s confirmed a similar impotence on land in the two campaigns against Scotland known as the Bishops' Wars of 1639–1640. The problems with Scotland began in 1637 when Charles I tried to impose his Book of Common Prayer on the Scottish Kirk. In response in 1638 the Scottish Kirk assembly in Glasgow defiantly took an oath to defend its Presbyterian faith and swept away both the prayer book and the bishops. When Charles I tried to raise an army to subdue the Scots, who were under the experienced professional leadership of Alexander Leslie, he ran into numerous problems. Without the active support of the nobility he found it hard to raise men, and without convening Parliament he lacked the money for an army. Nevertheless, undeterred by these obstacles or by his own lack of military experience, he conceived an elaborate fourfold campaign against Scotland. For commander of the navy he chose the Marquis of Hamilton, who said he knew nothing about ships. For general of the horse he chose the notoriously incompetent but favorite of the queen, the Earl of Holland. As supreme commander he chose the Earl of Arundel, who had an antiquarian view of war. Only his assistant, the Earl of Essex, could be considered a competent, professional soldier. The 15,000 soldiers, generally poorly paid, armed, and supplied, were mainly raw and indifferent men who, having been pressed by force into service, plundered the countryside and deserted en masse. By May 1639, Leslie's experienced force had already seized Aberdeen and Edinburgh Castle, while Charles I was still advancing toward York. Soon thereafter the English army advanced a few miles beyond the Tweed, met the Scots in full battle array, and fled back to England having fired barely a shot. Charles I was forced to sign the Treaty of Berwick whereby he accepted the abolition of the episcopacy in Scotland and agreed to call the English Parliament and Scottish Kirk into session, leaving the hostile Earl of Argyle in control of Scotland. Too, both sides agreed to disband their armies. This humiliation was forced on Charles I by the egregious failure of English arms. Sir Edmund Verney, the king's knight marshal of the household, wrote in May 1639:

> Our army is but weak, our purse is weaker, and if we fight with these forces and early in the year, we shall have our throats cut. . . . Our men are very raw, our arms of all sort naught, our victuals scarce and provisions for horses worse. . . . I daresay there was never so raw, so unskillful and so unwilling an army brought to fight.[6]

The second Bishops' War in 1640, despite greater English preparation, was even more humiliating for England. When the Short Parliament refused to pay for a large army, Charles I dissolved it and mobilized by summer over 18,000 soldiers, largely pressed men from the south of England and trained bands from the north. Under the command of the Earl of Strafford, who lacked any military experience, the sullen and raw soldiers mutinied, plundered, and deserted in large numbers. Before this rabble of an army could move north, Leslie's force of 25,000 Scots crossed the Tweed in August 1640 and advanced to Tyne without opposition. At Newburn the Scots effortlessly routed the English army, sending the inexperienced English cavalry fleeing in panic to Durham and the scattered remnants of English infantry fleeing to Newcastle. Durham and Newcastle were shortly taken by the Scots. With most of the north of England, as well as the bulk of Scotland (including Edinburgh castle) under Scottish control, Charles I now had to sue for a humiliating peace. Under the Treaty of Ripon, the Scots remained in occupation of northern England; suffering the ultimate indignity, the English agreed to pay 850 pounds per day to the Scots until a final agreement could be worked out in London.[7]

Thus, on the eve of the English Revolution, the military fortunes of England had sunk to a very sad state. The once-proud English navy could not even prevent pirates from raiding its coast or foreign navies from invading its waters, let alone carry the battle to distant shores. Its army not only lacked any ability to intervene effectively in Europe but could not even protect England from its weaker neighbor to the north.

What a difference a revolutionary decade made. By 1652 Oliver Cromwell's New Model Army had decisively defeated the Royalists in three civil wars, forcibly united Scotland and Ireland to England, and emerged as a significant European force. And during the 1650s it would wrest Dunkirk from the Spanish. Perhaps it was the poets who said it best. Marvell eulogized Cromwell, writing that "he once more joined us to the Continent"; Sprat proclaimed that Cromwell had woken the British lion from his slumbers; and Dryden added that Cromwell had taught the lion to roar.[8]

Naturally, as in France and Russia, the creation of a triumphant revolutionary army took time. Parliament's advantage in having control of the fleet, the major ports and arsenals, London, and the financial (City of London) and governmental centers of the country were offset by its indecisiveness, the support of much of the wealthier gentry for the king, and the natural tendency of the people to follow the monarch whatever his faults. After the inconclusive battle at Edgehill in October, the year 1642 marked the opening round of the first civil war; Parliament was able to stave off Charles I's march on London through popular mobilization of citizens, militia, and trained bands at Turnham Green in November 1642. The year 1643 saw a number of Royalist victories, especially in the north and west, but Parliament again staved off a final defeat, though its numerous forces were contentious and in poor shape. But in July 1644 at Marston Moor the Parliamentary and Scottish forces under Cromwell and Fairfax, by outnumbering their opponents three to two and by utilizing Cromwell's fine cavalry, decisively routed the Royalists under Rupert and Goring who enjoyed a strong defensive position. No less than 3,000 Royalists fell and 1,500 soldiers, including three major generals, were taken captive. This settled the fate of the war in the north.[9]

The formation of the New Model Army in 1645 and the rise of Oliver Cromwell marked the emergence of an ever-victorious revolutionary army and its indisputable leader. Finally an army had been created that could make full use of Parliament's considerable resources. In its very first battle at Naseby in June 1645, Cromwell, Ireton, and Skippon used a cavalry charge, numerical superiority, and immediate and thorough pursuit for 13 miles to decimate the more experienced Royalists and achieve their greatest success of the first civil war. At a cost of 200 Parliamentary fatalities, the New Model Army killed roughly 1,000 Royalists and took 4,000 to 6,000 Royalist prisoners. In the ensuing rout Cromwell's prizes included all the king's guns, 2,000 to 3,000 weapons, large quantities of food and ammunition, and the entire baggage trains of Charles I, Rupert, and other top commanders. Naseby, then, was the turning point that "gave this army its corporate existence, its baptism of fire" and saw the New Model Army become "a single superb fighting instrument."[10] After Naseby the New Model Army smashed Goring's forces at Langport in July (taking 1,400 prisoners), seized Bristol in September and Winchester Castle in October, and by April had occupied Exeter. With the triumphal march of the New Model Army in 1646, the civil war came to an end in June with the surrender of Oxford and flight of the king to the Scottish Army.

The new-found might of the New Model Army was demonstrated in the speed with which it crushed a Scottish invasion and English Royalist revolts in only five months during the second civil war in 1648. These victories were all the more impressive since for the first time Cromwell's forces were outnumbered two to one. Indeed at the decisive battle of Preston, the 21,600 man Scottish army (of which 4,500 did not participate in the battle) under Hamilton greatly outnumbered Cromwell's 8,600 men. But Cromwell brilliantly and daringly interposed his forces between Hamilton's forces and Scotland, launched a surprise flank attack and speedily carried out one of the most relentless pursuits in military history. In the panic that followed a staggering 2,000 Scottish soldiers were killed and 8,000 to 9,000 were taken prisoner, including the Duke of Hamilton and his top commanders (Langdale, Baillie, Callander, and Middleton). With only 7,000 Scottish soldiers left fleeing across the border and Colchester soon taken by Parliament forces, the Royalist uprising rapidly disintegrated and the second civil war came to a quick and successful end for Parliament.[11]

After the execution of Charles I in January 1649, the revolution further consolidated itself at home, while the New Model Army moved to reintegrate the United Kingdom. Most importantly this meant the conquests of Ireland and Scotland, tasks which had been beyond the scope of Charles I. Charles I, as we have seen, had failed miserably in his two campaigns against Scotland. Its fiercely independent character, its numerous natural obstacles, and numerically superior army under professional military commanders made its conquest a daunting task, which no English government had even attempted for a decade. If Scotland had been in open revolt since 1637, then Ireland had technically been in revolt since the days of Elizabeth, with its most recent period of semi-independence dating from the revolt of 1640.

With the civil wars now safely over, Cromwell prepared to bring these recalcitrant independent nations back into the fold. He carefully utilized political and military measures. In his campaign against Ireland in 1649, he faced numerous problems including many natural and artificial obstacles, fortified cities with strategic value, mountains and bogs ideal for guerrilla warfare, an unhealthy climate, a hostile populace, and the lack of local supplies. This forced the New Model Army to resort to a war of sieges, forays, and marches in which it was unable to bring the enemy to bay and defeat in a single great battle. Too, the fleet was especially important for providing supplies and securing seaports and rivers.

By 1649 Ireland had no less than five armies with over 35,000 men in the field representing Parliament, English Protestant Royalists, English Catholic Royalists, Ulster Catholics, and Ulster Scots. Arriving in September 1649 with 12,000 soldiers in the wake of Jones' success over the Royalists at Rathmines, Cromwell landed in Dublin and within a month had stormed and captured the east coast strongholds of Drogheda and Wexford and the town of Cork. Although badly outnumbered by Ormande's English Protestant Army and O'Neill's Ulster Army and with his own forces reduced to 5,000 men as a result of military action, sickness, disease, and the need to leave men behind for garrison, Cromwell pressed on at the end of 1649. Bringing in the reinforcements from England and pursuing an unusual winter campaign, he renewed his campaign in the south. By March 1650 Cromwell had been so successful that only Waterford and Limerick held out. By the time he left in May, Royalist resistance had been broken, and matters of dealing with scattered resistance could safely be turned over to his lieutenants. Henry Ireton, Edmund Ludlow, and Charles Fleetwood in turn steadily reduced Irish resistance until with the seizure of Limerick in 1651 and Galway in 1652 English control was secure, albeit at the cost of enormous bloodshed.[12]

If subduing the rebellious Irish weren't enough, Cromwell immediately turned his attention to the militarily powerful Scottish forces and their ally, Charles II, in the third civil war. At this point the Scots wanted Charles II as their king and the imposition of Scottish Presbyterianism on England as their price for supporting him. In August 1650 Cromwell crossed the Tweed with 16,000 men against a Scottish force under Leslie that numbered 30,000 to 40,000 men. At first the war went badly as David Leslie maneuvered brilliantly along his inner lines of command and behind impenetrable defense lines. By September Cromwell's forces were reduced to 11,000 men while Leslie had 22,000 men. But at Dunbar, Cromwell maneuvered Leslie's forces into battle and once again the New Model Army devastated its enemies. Taking advantage of a weak Scottish defensive disposition, Cromwell launched a surprise attack early in the morning in bad weather with overwhelming force at the weakest part of the Scottish line. His forces smashed the Scottish right then rolled up the center while the infantry were penned between hill and a ravine. Using his cavalry in relentless pursuit of the broken Scots, Cromwell's forces killed 3,000 to 4,000 Scots and took 10,000 prisoners with only minimal losses. No less than 15,000 small arms, 30 cannon, and 200 colors were seized in this magnificent victory. In the aftermath of Dunbar the English army occupied Edinburgh in September, Glasgow in October, and by December all of Scotland south of the Clyde and Firth.

After recovering from a serious illness, Cromwell launched a spring campaign with 16,000 to 18,000 men. By June 1651 the New Model Army had control of most of the Lowlands, and in July Lambert routed the Scots at Inverkeithing. This set the stage for the final act in which Cromwell lured the Scots into an invasion of England that led to their ultimate destruction. By September Cromwell's forces enjoyed a two to one advantage (60,000 versus 30,000) over Charles II's Scottish army cooped up at Worcester. A strong New Model Army assault combined with a vigorous pursuit resulted in the killing of several thousand Royalists and the taking of 8,000 to 9,000 Scots prisoners. In Scotland, General Monck rapidly mopped up the Scottish resistance, taking Stirling in August, and Dundee in September (with the bulk of the political leaders in tow). By May 1652 the last Scottish fortress had surrendered to Monck. Thus, by the summer of 1652 the three kingdoms had been forcibly reunited, and Charles II had fled to France. His prospects were bleak:

> He left little hope behind him. Three civil wars had taken their toll of the men who were fitted by military experience or social status to raise armies for him. Conversely the raw material for Royalist forces no longer existed. . . . The English Royalists had been bled white at Marston Moor and Naseby and the Scots had suffered cruelly at Preston and Dunbar. Worcester had wrung the last drop of blood from the King's military power; after it any hope of resistance to the New Model could be no more than a wishful illusion. Well might Cromwell term Worcester, his last and final battle, a crowning mercy.[13]

The remaining years of the 1650s saw the New Model Army maintain and extend its ever-victorious reputation. A brilliant campaign under Monck, utilizing swift marches, cavalry sweeps, good intelligence and political persuasion, destroyed a major Scottish rebellion in the mountainous and roadless northern highlands in 1654 and achieved total peace (in combination with political concessions) in 1655. That same year the army easily crushed the Penruddock Royalist uprising in England. In 1657, an army of 6,000 English troops fought well with French troops against Spain in the Netherlands. And especially impressive was the great French-English victory at Dunkirk in 1658, which brought that major port under English control.[14]

But if the New Model Army had fewer opportunities to shine after 1652, the opposite was true of the navy. In the 1650s the English navy shed its incompetent Royalist past and suddenly and brilliantly projected English power to the four corners of the globe.

These sweeping changes began in the 1649–1652 period when the new regime, in the wake of Charles I's execution and consolidation of its position at home, turned its attention to the sea. In 1649 Admiral Blake's fleet blockaded Prince Rupert's Royalist fleet in Kinsale to prevent interference with Cromwell's campaign in Ireland. When Rupert's ships escaped in March 1650, Blake trapped them in the mouth of the Tagos, and when they escaped again Blake's fleet destroyed or captured most of Rupert's ships off Malaga. During 1651 Blake attacked and seized the Isle of Man, Jersey, and Guernsey, the main centers of Royalist privateers. Thus by the spring of

1652 the navy had secured the homeland by sweeping Royalist privateers from the British seas and the Mediterranean. The navy then
turned its attention to the Royalists in the colonies, as Sir George
Ayescue's fleet seized Barbados and the West Indian islands in
January 1652 and Virginia and Maryland in March 1652. Then cap-
ping this phase, the English navy under Blake flexed its new-found
muscles by dispersing the French fleet sailing to relieve Dunkirk,
thereby ensuring the surrender of the port to Spain in September
1652.

But it took the Anglo-Dutch War (1652-1654) for the English
navy to show that it had truly come of age. For in Holland the English faced a powerful mercantile rival with the largest merchant
marine in the world and a larger and more powerful navy than
England had possessed for the past 50 years. But under Admirals
Robert Blake, George Monck, and Richard Deane the new English
navy regained control of the English Channel and decisively defeated
the powerful Dutch navy. In a series of eight major battles, from
June 1652 to December 1653 at places such as Portland (February
1653), Gabbard (June 1653) and Schweningen (August 1653), the
English captured over 1,000 Dutch merchant ships and 120 men-
of-war, in action from the Baltic and Mediterranean to the East and
West Indies. The English navy was so successful in its tactics, firepower, chain of command, and administration that it dictated the
April 1654 Treaty of Westminster. By this treaty the beaten Dutch
formally acknowledged English supremacy in English waters, agreed
to compensate damage to English merchant ships, acquiesced to
England's Navigation Act, expelled English Royalists from Holland, and excluded the Princes of Orange from any position of military command. With a touch of pomposity, Oliver Cromwell could
tell the Dutch in 1654: "The Lord has declared against you. After
the defeat you have undergone, your only recourse is to associate
yourself with your formidable neighbour."[15]

With arguably the best navy and one of the best armies in the
world, England under Cromwell proceeded to project its power in
every area of the known world. Apart from a failed expedition
against Hispaniola in 1655 (which did at least take Jamaica), its
efforts were crowned with success everywhere. The British flag
became feared in the Mediterranean when Blake in 1654 and 1655
won key victories over the Barbary pirates and destroyed the fleet of
the Bey of Tunis and burned his castle. The war with Spain (1656-
1658) was largely triumphant as the English navy destroyed and
seized large treasure fleets from America, blockaded the Spanish
coast, and facilitated the seizure of Dunkirk. Furthermore, the Por-

tuguese, overawed by Blake, signed a 1654 treaty with England giving English merchants access to the vast Portuguese Empire and European markets. Thus with the Barbary pirates subdued, the Dutch and Spanish beaten, and the Portuguese cowed, Brittania now ruled the waves.

How did these enormous changes in military capabilities occur? How did England in the space of a decade go from a relatively impotent fleet and almost nonexistent army to a mighty fleet and an ever-victorious army? The remainder of this chapter examines the changes in military, foreign, and domestic policies from Stuart to Cromwellian England that made these changes possible.

MILITARY POLICIES

The essential impact of the English Revolution on the military arena was the creation of a more modern army under Cromwell that easily destroyed the neofeudal forces of Charles I and the old order. This modern army, aptly entitled the New Model Army (1645-), represented significant modernization of the older armies in four key areas: (1) officers, (2) soldiers, (3) organization, and (4) style of warfare.

Perhaps nowhere were the changes so evident as in the officer corps of the two armies. In the armies of James I and Charles I, reflecting the monarchical nature of the regime, the leading officers tended to be drawn from a very thin stratum of wealthier nobles in favor with the court and without any military capabilities. Furthermore, the courtiers around the king often agitated against truly talented commanders out of fear that they might displace them in the king's favor. Hence men with a genuine flair for war, as Prince Rupert, found their way often blocked by the jealousy of other commanders and the courtiers. In this milieu where birth, connections, and wealth counted for more than talent, mediocre commanders such as Lords Wilmot, Percy, and Byron came to the fore, as did steady but less than brilliant commanders such as Lord Astley.

Inevitably, too, (as happened later in Tsarist Russia) the monarch would retain the option of being commander in chief even if, as in the case of Charles I, he was uniquely unsuited for the position (which should have gone to Rupert). Although personally brave, Charles I was fatally indecisive, excessively cautious, and unable to or unwilling to give strong direction to the war effort. His confused and complex war command was unable to exercise control over the numerous, semi-independent armies raised by his aristocratic squires. This was the natural result of the neofeudal nature of the monarchy. Charles I, "hedged about with localism and hamstrung by feudal hierarchy, had neither the opportunity nor the inclination to reform the 'rabble gentility' which marched beneath his banner."[16]

Furthermore, given the limited appeal of the monarchy to the middle classes, the rest of the officer corps was heavily drawn from two very limited strata of population—professional mercenaries and Catholics. The mercenaries fought for hire and the Catholics out of appreciation of the tolerance shown them by the king. In six northern counties in 1642 no less than one-third of all regimental officers were Catholics. However, the use of these two elements posed serious problems for the armies. The mercenary officers were often of limited military value, "with a reputation of drunkenness, swearing, quarreling and a readiness to draw their swords at any imagined affront." Their arrogance led the populace, who formed the bulk of the soldiers, to cordially despise them.[17] As to the Catholics, they provided a number of good officers, but their enlistment alienated large segments of the populace and soldiers who were vehemently anti-Catholic at this time.

In short, European armies at this time bore many traces of their origins as privately raised mercenary companies. William McNeil's summary of the nature of the officer corps of such traditional armies is apt:

> As a result, proprietary rights often conflicted with bureaucratic rationality in matters of recruitment, appointment and promotion. Professional skill competed with patronage and purchase as paths to advancement while both were tempered by the principle of seniority on one hand and by acts of valor in battle on the other. Appointments and promotion often reflected the king's personal choice or those of his minister of war.[18]

By sharp contrast in the more modern New Model Army, Oliver Cromwell replaced the standards of birth and privilege with efficiency and merit in recruitment and promotion of officers. By the late 1640s the commanders from the upper gentry (such as Essex, Manchester, and Waller) were gone, and those few that remained (such as Fairfax) were genuinely talented. The key to success was the recruitment of talented officers from all classes and religious persuasions, not simply from a thin noble stratum, and the open rejection of professional mercenaries. Cromwell made these principles, revolutionary for their time, clear on a number of occasions. In a famous August 1643 letter responding to concerns of the Suffolk committee that a new troop commander was not a gentleman, he wrote, "I would rather have a plain russet-coated captain that knows what he fights for, and loves what he knows, than that which you call a gentleman and is nothing else."[19] In September 1643, in response to other complaints that an officer was not a gentleman he wrote:

> If these men be accounted troublesome to the country, I shall be glad you would send them all to me. I'll bid them welcome . . . (for) better plain men than none, but best to have men of patient wants, faithful and conscientious in employment, and such, I hope these will approve themselves to be."[20]

Finally in March 1644, in response to complaints that a lieutenant was an Anabaptist he wrote:

> Ay, but the man is an Anabaptist. Are you sure of that? Admit he be, shall that render him incapable to serve the public? . . . Sir, the State in choosing men to serve them, takes no notice of their opinions, if they be willingly faithful to serve, then, that satisfies.[21]

The bulk of the capable colonels and generals in Cromwell's army came from classes well below the traditional ruling elite of Stuart England. Men such as Oliver Cromwell, John Desborough, John Lambert, Charles Fleetwood, Henry Ireton, Robert Blake, and Richard Deane came from the lesser gentry and richer merchant stratum of the rising middle class. A surprising number, given the prevalent illiteracy and prejudice, were recruited from the lower classes, including Thomas Kelsey (buttonmaker), John Barkstead (goldsmith), Thomas Harrison (butcher), James Berry (clerk), Thomas Pride (drayman), and John Hewson (cobbler).

With regard to promotions, merit, tempered by seniority and a limited degree of favoritism, was the norm under both Fairfax (1645-1649) and Cromwell (1649-1658). The commander in chief did not have incompetent generals thrust on him for political reasons, could dismiss or promote anyone he liked, and was not obligated to fight battles or hold positions for political reasons. The pay was quite decent and regular, plus Parliament was generous in rewarding top commanders from lawful plunder and confiscated Royalist land. Both infantry and cavalrymen without high birth, wealth, or connections, but with proven talent and courage, could rise from the ranks, as did Browne, Okey, Rainsborough, Blake, Haselrig, and Harrison. Indeed no less than 6 of the 12 officers on the Hispaniola campaign were former privates. At the same time a leavening of professional soldiers, such as Philip Skippon and George Monck, found their talents rewarded. Thus, the quality of Cromwell's officers, as epitomized by the brilliance of Cromwell himself, was markedly superior to that of the traditional armies.[22]

A similar comparison could be made between the soldiers of the two armies. In traditional armies of the period in general and in the armies of Stuart England in particular the view prevailed that, given the high expenses of war, the productive classes of society needed to be exempted from service in the army. Thereby the bulk of soldiers were drawn from largely illiterate thieves, rogues, and vagabonds who lived in the margin of society and had to be forcibly impressed into the army by local constables. Unwillingly dragged into service, such men lacked any normative motivation to fight or any utilitarian concerns. The pay was low and irregular and opportunity for advancement virtually nonexistent. Only coercion, drill, liquor, and rigorous isolation from society could make these men fight.

The consequences of using such soldiers were profound. They frequently mutinied and deserted in large numbers at the first opportunity. When the 1627 expedition to the Isle of Rhe faltered, for example, many soldiers simply abandoned their officers. Both in the 1620s and 1640s the soldiers frequently plundered the local population. In December 1624 when soldiers were forced to wait for ships at Dover, they so terrorized the town that martial law had to be proclaimed. Similarly during the civil war the poorly paid Royalist soldiers often took out their anger on local inhabitants and went unpunished.[23]

Worst of all, such men were often almost useless in battle. At Cadiz in 1625, the soldiers, a high percentage of whom were lame and handicapped, were often drunk and ill-disciplined. When a small force of 300 Spaniards attacked them, most fled immediately. Sir Edmund Cecil has related that the soldiers "were so ill exercised that when we came to employ them, they proved rather a danger to us than a strength, killing more of our own men than they did of the enemy."[24] In 1627 at the Ile de Rhe, Buckingham "found his pressed half-mutinous soldiers more or less useless, this time overcome by French instead of Spanish wine."[25] And in 1628 the Earl of Lindsey found his crews "lethargic and mutinous" and his soldiers "unwilling and untrained."[26]

The contrast with the soldiers of the New Model Army was telling. Although the Parliamentary armies from 1642 to 1644 had a large number of pressed men and the New Model Army had some pressed men, the number declined from 1645 to 1650, and after

1650 only volunteers were taken into the army. Cromwell strongly encouraged freeholders and their sons to enlist as a matter of conscience. Furthermore, rather than the mass enrollment of soldiers as in traditional armies, entrants to the New Model Army were carefully screened to eliminate vagabonds, criminals, and mercenaries. Cromwell stressed the importance of moral character and religion in new recruits. Furthermore, capable soldiers of whatever background were encouraged to enlist, and by 1647 no less than 4,000 former Cavaliers formed 20 percent of the army.[27]

With the emphasis on the volunteer came a far more complex and effective system of control and motivation. Utilitarian motives were especially strong as talented soldiers could expect to rise from the ranks into the officer corps. Pay was far more decent and regular than in the old armies and based directly on monthly county assessments. Adequate uniforms were provided the soldiers. Funds were voted to provide for maimed and old soldiers, while discharged soldiers, who in the past often became beggars or highwaymen, now were encouraged to take up trades. As a consequence, desertion was significantly lower than in the Royalist forces. Thus many incentives designed to turn the army into a means to a career rather than jail were instituted.[28]

With the development of decent treatment for soldiers, it became possible to lay the groundwork for effective discipline, which is so crucial a part of the coercion necessary for an effective army. Both Fairfax and Cromwell rigorously stamped out plundering and maintained strong control on the march. All punishments were publicized with mutineers shot, plunderers whipped, and drunkards sent to the stockades. Even swearing was fined. These rules were also applied on foreign expeditions. The result was "an army whose order and discipline, whose sobriety and manners, whose courage and success made it famous and terrible all over the world."[29]

Perhaps most striking was the existence of a strong normative commitment to the revolution among many officers and men, which gave the New Model Army a fighting zeal and corporateness so conspicuously lacking in traditional armies. The men of the New Model Army saw themselves as free men consciously motivated by their beliefs rather than professional soldiers driven by mercenary and coercive considerations. Increasingly, over time the men and officers were deeply moved by both fundamentally political and religious beliefs, often inextricably linked.

Politically the army came to see itself as the symbolic representative of the English people, standing against monarchical tyranny and private interests and proclaiming the liberties and freedoms due to

Englishmen according to Parliamentary law. This politicization grew stronger after 1646 and after the failure of Parliament to secure peace and dissolve the army. In the famous manifesto issued at St. Albans in August 1647, the newly united army declared:

> We were not mercenary soldiers, brought together by hopes of pay and the fortunes of war; the peace of our country, our freedom from tyranny, preservation of due liberty, administration of judgment and justice, the free cause of the laws of the land, preservation of the King, privilege of Parliament and liberty of subject were the main things which brought us together.[30]

Although the radical potential of such views would be repressed with the crushing of the Leveller revolt in 1649, the overall military leadership, under men such as Cromwell, Ireton, Harrison, Okey, and Rainsborough, would instill a sense of national and social mission that gave the New Model Army "a political direction and coherence that had been lacking in all previous armies."[31]

Of course much of the normative motivation in the army came from the religious beliefs of the Puritans and various Independents, who were protected and encouraged by Cromwell. As early as 1643, Baxter relates that Cromwell and his officers in the Ironsides cavalry had proposed to make their troop into a "gathered Church."[32] Cromwell actively and openly recruited his East Anglia regiments from "men of spirit" on the grounds that such men would make better fighters. Indeed in 1650 he made the famous comment that "Truly I think he that prays and preaches best will fight best."[33] Overall, the Puritan spirit was especially strong in the officer corps, among men such as Oliver Cromwell, Charles Fleetwood, Thomas Pride, and John Hewson, and perhaps 25 percent of the men. These men, much like the Communists in the Russian and Chinese armies, were a strong minority that provided the ideological and revolutionary leaven and dynamism in the army.[34]

To aid them in their work were the seventeenth-century version of modern commissars, the chaplains. Although Mark Kishlansky is correct that their numbers were small, their influence was significant in an army of only 20,000 to 40,000 soldiers where many were by definition receptive to their appeal. Just like commissars, the chaplains were attached at the regimental level; they gave sermons to the troops, and troop members often preached themselves as well. The chaplains and the officers instilled in the men a feeling that they were the second chosen people, shock troops fighting the Lord's battle for the creation of a reformed Church and a New Jerusalem.

Identifying the Church with the army, Puritan millenarianism united the army in a struggle against tyranny, the whore of Babylon, and the Antichrist. In 1644 Stephen Marshall preached before the two houses of Parliament, exhorting the soldiers, "Go now and fight the battles of the Lord . . . all Christendom . . . do now see that the question in England is whether Christ or Antichrist shall be lord or king."[35] Over time, as Michael Walzer has shown, the Puritan saints, interpreting the world in both cosmological and worldly terms, provided the seventeenth century with the same revolutionary dynamism that the Communists, whom Trotsky would label a "band of samurai" in the Russian civil war, would provide in the twentieth century. As Walzer has written:

> And so the spiritual soldier finally appeared on a real battlefield. . . .
> Christianity might produce a discipline and courage of its own. Braced
> by sermons of his chaplains, excited by mass prayer meetings, shouting
> hymns as he rode into battle, the pious Protestant warrior was not very
> far from a crusading fanatic.[36]

If we turn to the area of organization, we see similarly great differences between the armed forces of Stuart England and Cromwell England. The fundamental problem in Stuart England was its lack of any coherent military structure, either in peacetime or wartime. Indeed in peacetime there was not even a standing army, as the Stuarts relied instead on the ill-trained country bands and the recruitment of pressed men. The army suffered from benign neglect. By contrast, the Stuarts did of necessity maintain a navy and from 1635 to 1639 ship money was devoted to its improvement. But the navy suffered abysmally from many of the same faults that plagued the governmental administration. From 1604 to 1618 the navy was under the command of the Lord Admiral Earl of Nottingham and Sir Robert Mansell. Abuses and corruption were so bad that a 1618 commission of inquiry forced their ouster, noting that despite great outlays, "the fleet was in the greatest decay," with only 25 seaworthy ships. Yet little changed, for by 1623 another report found a recrudescence of various abuses and higher expenditures.[37] And, despite efforts during the 1630s, conditions in the fleet by 1642 were "wretched almost beyond description" with a very high rate of illness and mortality from terrible physical conditions. This gross neglect led every ship but one to declare for Parliament in 1642.[38]

In wartime the advanced state of disorganization of the Stuart military became all the more apparent. The attack on Cadiz in 1625 might have gone better if the soldiers hadn't been kept idle for three months due to lack of preparation for war and if they hadn't been provided with so many defective muskets. As Sir John Eliot wrote, "our honor is ruined, our ships are sunk, our men perished, not by sword, not by enemy, not by chance but by those we trusted."[39] The 1627 expedition to Rhe might have done better if the troops hadn't been so poorly supplied that when winds held the fleet up at Plymouth the men hadn't had to consume most of their provisions before reaching Rhe. Two local observers wrote that such "a rotten, miserable fleet set out to sea no man ever saw," and "there were no pikes, very few corselets, no match and most of the fleet poor rotten ships."[40] Similarly in the two wars against the Scots in 1639 and 1640 there were "serious shortcomings" in equipment and supplies, as well as in the Royalist war effort in the civil wars.[41]

The New Model Army was far better organized. Cromwell and the Parliamentary committees ensured a regular flow of equipment and supply to the army and ships to the navy. The army developed a powerful artillery, while the navy, between 1649 and 1652 alone, added 41 new men-of-war. All soldiers were equipped with regular uniforms and helmets. Men with practical military experience now were in charge. The provision of equipment was no longer an idiosyncratic issue but rather a matter of bureaucratic routine. The results were eminently noticeable on the battlefield, although in certain areas, as medical care, gross negligence continued.[42]

Finally, there was the question of the style of warfare adopted by the two armies. The Stuart armies had not been noted for their innovativeness or skill at the art of war. They preferred to view wars in the traditional way as a series of limited campaigns and endless maneuvers with stress on the defensive value of fortresses. Wars were seen as cautious, defensive, and relatively bloodless, indecisive struggles. During the civil war Prince Rupert did attempt innovative changes in cavalry charges, adopting the new Swedish system, but he was limited by the propensity of his troopers who after one charge turned to looting rather than returned to the field of battle.

By contrast, although there were no technical innovations in this period, the New Model Army successfully adopted aggressive infantry and cavalry methods. Even in approaching fortresses the army avoided slow sieges and long approaches, preferring to storm fortresses softened up by powerful artillery. But the key was the cavalry, which, on the Swedish model, Cromwell deployed for its shock effect backed by cold steel. Unlike Rupert's cavalry, Cromwell's cavalry charged slower but under more control and could regroup for a second charge. The cavalry invariably took the initiative, charging at a trot in close ranks with heavy horses and reserving fire until at close quarters. The cavalry was used as a compact battering ram operating with stern discipline. Much the same as Napoleon, Cromwell sought decisive results on the battlefield in short, swift strokes, followed up by a relentless pursuit of the beaten enemy. Destruction of the enemy armies, not occupation of places or protection of castles, was the key to the New Model Army. The results were overwhelming. The well-trained and disciplined troopers led cavalry charges with few parallels in the Thirty Years' War, showing that they "had become one of the most formidable body of fighting men in the British Isles, if not indeed in Europe or the world."[43]

Finally, changes in the navy paralleled those in the army. Under James I and Charles I the direction of the navy had been poor. With most positions in the navy for sale even in the 1630s, the quality of naval captains was unimpressive. Influence at Court and money counted for far more than merit. Fraud and embezzlement of funds were common. The treatment of sailors was incredibly abusive under the monarchy. Utilitarian and normative motives were virtually absent among sailors. Michael Oppenheim in his late nineteenth-century study of the Royal Navy said of the common sailor:

> All he could associate with the Crown were memories of starvation and beggary, of putrid victuals fraught with disease, and wages delayed, in payments of which, when he at last received them, he found a large proportion stuck to the hands of minor officials.[44]

By contrast, the Navy commissioners after 1642 were chosen for their business or military experience. Officers were chosen for their professional qualifications, and many were promoted from the ranks. Utilitarian considerations were advanced by raising the pay of sailors and captains and after 1649 giving them one-third of the value of a captured prize. With sailors being fed decently and paid regularly, the incidence of mutiny declined sharply. Clearly, the revolution had also come to the navy.

FOREIGN POLICIES

If we turn to foreign policies, we see a similar trend. Under the Stuarts, English foreign policy was sufficiently ineffectual that the country's international stature was at its lowest point. There was no consistency to English foreign policy, no attempt to match goals with means, and no integration of military, commercial, and governmental resources. Charles I conducted a foreign policy that was highly opportunistic, often seemingly more concerned with restoring the Palatinate to his family than to improving England's position in European politics.

A number of specific factors contributed to the failures of Charles I's foreign policies. The neglect of military capabilities inevitably sharply restricted England's potential in European politics. England could not even conduct a successful expedition, let alone a major campaign. English lack of interest in Europe was seen in the fact that in 1633 England had no foreign envoys in Europe except Constantinople—and that one was sent and paid for by merchants. Failure to participate in the Thirty Years' War, which was deciding the fate of Europe, epitomized England's weakness. At times English policy even seemed suicidal, as when Buckingham, with Charles I's consent, provoked a war in 1627 with France at a time when England was already at war with Spain. Often Charles alienated any possible domestic support for his policies by supporting Catholic Spain despite the virulent anti-Catholicism endemic among his subjects, and by his treatment of the Scottish Presbyterians.

By contrast, Cromwell ended England's isolation and made England a strong and respected actor in European politics. All of Europe, from the sultan of Morocco and Duke of Courland to the prince of Transylvania and Dutch Jews, sought his ear. The well-known Royalist, Clarendon, noted that "Cromwell's greatness at home was a mere shadow of his greatness abroad," and Godfrey Davis stressed that "during the Protectorate Cromwell restored English prestige to the height attained after Agincourt or the defeat of the Armada."[45]

Cromwell was so successful because he consciously pursued an energetic and consistent policy of enhancing England's world position. He built up England's military resources and aggressively used sea power on a global scale to further England's interest and even secure a foothold on the Continent in Dunkirk. He built up England's commercial resources through the 1651 Navigation Act, which created an imperial monopoly of trade and shipping. He signed treaties with a number of European countries that expanded England's trading possibilities. Cromwell was the first English ruler to systematically use power to increase and extend colonial possessions, especially in North America and the West Indies. He especially cultivated the New England colonists. He developed a coherent policy for Scotland and Ireland, with representation in Parliament, free trade, and proportionate taxation. Overall, means and ends were successfully matched, and English power greatly advanced.

There were some significant failures. The repression in Ireland and attempt to encourage active cooperation of the American colonists in English expansion were bound to fail in the long run. The stress on Protestant solidarity was outdated in an era in which national concerns were replacing religious concerns. And the failure of Cromwell to consolidate his rule meant that the restoration of the Stuarts was likely after his death. But, overall, Cromwellian foreign policy was markedly more successful than Charles I's foreign policy.

DOMESTIC POLICIES

Finally, there were some significant differences in domestic policies that had a direct impact on the armies under discussion and especially on the tax base to support them. For it was the ineptitude of Charles I (1625–1649) and his domestic policies that brought on the civil war and resultant revolution. He wanted his subjects to unquestionably accept his absolute authority, yet he worked only sporadically and indolently at his tasks, as he was often bored by the details of government. He wanted his people to follow him, yet he dissolved three parliaments and ruled without them after 1629. At the same time he was a remote king with a highly decorous and formal court, from which were excluded representatives of significant currents of public opinion.

The irony of the situation was that Charles I possessed great strengths in a number of areas other than politics. He had exquisite artistic sensitivities and was probably the greatest collector and connoisseur of painting ever to sit on the throne. He was a major patron of all the arts, including sculpture, poetry, plays, and masques. He possessed great personal courage and willingly shared the discomforts and dangers of his soldiers on the battlefield. Charles I was an intelligent, sober, and well-intentioned monarch in many ways. But these traits, while relevant to an overall appraisal of the man, could not compensate for his incompetence in the political arena.[46]

His problems to a great extent originated with the Court and advisors that surrounded him. The opulence of the Court, the endless quest for favors and sinecures, the strong Catholic element surrounding the Queen, and the sumptuous masques in celebration of imaginary deeds all set the Court apart from the people. The policies of many of his advisers, on whom he heavily relied, further alienated the country. Charles I's royal favorite, the Duke of Buckingham, through control of the Court and patronage and failed

foreign expeditions "brought the royal regime into hatred and contempt" until the duke's assassination in 1628.[47] Archbishop Laud,
with his relentless use of the Star Chamber to achieve a ceremonial,
uniform church, alienated Puritans, moderate Anglicans, and above
all Scots. While many able politicians, such as Richard Weston and
Francis Cottington, served the king, they were unable to keep the
split from widening between the Court and the country.

Not only was the Court inept and corrupt, it also could not manage to raise and spend the wealth and taxes of the kingdom in a
reasonably efficient and rational way. Worst of all was the massive
alienation of royal resources and authority to the peerage and royal
favorites. From 1603 to 1628 James I and Charles I had directly
given to the peers 2.7 million pounds in grants and favors (including
over 1 million pounds worth of crown lands), followed by another
400,000 pounds by 1642. Thanks to royal generosity, by 1641 it
is estimated that fully one-fourth of the capital assets of the top 121
aristocratic families had derived directly from the state. Of even
greater consequence was the astonishing fact that in the 1620s
unrecorded state income that passed directly to a small group of
courtiers and officials by means of fees and gratuities (bribes),
grants, exploitation of proximity to the throne (as rights to taxation
and regulation of the economy), and underassessments of rents
or taxes actually equalled total recorded state income (500,000
pounds)! And when to this figure (which averaged between 250,000
and 400,000 pounds in the 1630s) one adds roughly 300,000 pounds
paid out in the forms of wages, pensions, and allowances, the extent
of the problem is clear. This is especially true considering that in
1630, pensions cost the crown 125,000 pounds, of which over one-
third went to 22 noble families and the bulk of the rest to a few
hundred courtiers. Truly, as Lawrence Stone concluded, these pensions represented "an extravagant system of outdoor relief to a
minority of highly favoured noblemen" and reflected a "rickety
structure" of finance with "a huge annual drain."[48] Overall, only
6 percent of the gentry, or perhaps 1,000 families, gained 600,000
to 800,000 pounds a year directly or indirectly through office-
holding. And, they were often allowed to run up huge debts and
arrears to the Crown without repayment.[49]

Beyond the gross rapaciousness of such a system, there was the
simple fact that the Crown was thereby inevitably very short of
money for the traditional functions of government. To maintain
this extravagant style at Court was in the long run impossible,
even with the economies introduced after 1628. During the 1630s
yearly Crown revenues from ordinary sources were only 600,000

to 900,000 pounds, and even with extraordinary measures were 700,000 to 1,100,000 pounds, a figure representing only 2 to 4 percent of the national income. The state lacked any system of public debt and relied for tax collection on tax farmers, who contracted to pay the state a set price in return for collecting a particular tax for themselves. These venal office holders bought or inherited their offices. Reform and efficiency were impossible in a system where everyone was absorbed in exploiting public positions for private profit. By the 1630s the king's credit rating was minimal, and by 1635 his debts equalled two years income.[50] In a disintegrating environment the Crown exploited archaic fiscal privileges, such as compulsory knighthoods and forest laws, which brought in relatively little revenue and further alienated the populace. By 1640 the government was on the verge of bankruptcy, and some revenues had already been mortgaged to 1651. Charles Wilson has written:

> The poverty of the King was in part a product of inflation; much more, of his own extravagance and his obstinate refusal to retrench or reform. It was Stuart ineptitude in seeking a way out of the impasse thus created that led directly to methods of public finance no better than a racket. At Whitehall the royal household had become an administrative rabbit warren. Public business was turned into a Dutch auction that accentuated social tensions and set up favoured against unfavoured, family against family, faction against faction, court against country.[51]

The essential problem, of course, was the extraordinary weakness of the country's administrative system. England had very little government, no standing army or proper police force, a very small central bureaucracy, and limited local bureaucracies largely dependent on the voluntary cooperation of a hierarchy of part-time, unpaid officials. These officials, who gained their positions by patrimony, patronage, and purchase, treated their offices as private property and showed little loyalty to the Crown. The result was an ineffective, small government bureaucracy often impervious to reform.[52]

While the Parliamentary and Cromwellian governments were never terribly efficient by modern standards, they were markedly more effective than their predecessors. The change began at the top with Oliver Cromwell, who was a vastly more capable politician than Charles I, who didn't understand the nature of politics. Perhaps the greatest indication of Cromwell's abilities was his elimination of all bases of opposition to his rule, from foreign and domestic Royalists to Scottish Presbyterians and from Irish Catholics to radical Levellers. He uprooted the monarchy, unified England, Scotland, and Ireland, made England a strong state, and led Brittania to mastery of the seas. Unlike Charles I, he cultivated popular support and his vast personal network to expand his base beyond the army. His stress on religious toleration won him support among the Puritans, and his economic and political policies gained him support among the nascent middle classes. His conscious labors to rebuild the fabric of civil government and put the state on a new basis did quell active unrest after 1649. Yet he never forgot the importance of the armed forces and maintained them at a level of 30,000 to 50,000 men in the 1650s.

The key, of course, lay in taxation. Like all revolutionary governments, the new English government was far more effective in mobilizing and utilizing resources (especially for war) than its predecessor. With a ruthless efficiency the Cromwellian government raised an average of two million pounds in regular revenue a year from 1649 to 1658, a figure three times greater than Charles I's government's regular revenue in the 1630s. At the same time, its extraordinary income also greatly exceeded that of Charles I's government of the 1630s. Parliament and Cromwell expropriated land and possessions of the Royalists, Crown, and Church worth between six and seven million pounds. The land and customs taxes were collected more regularly, new taxes were added, including an excise tax on common commodities, and penalties were levied on lesser Royalists. Administrative efficiency was greatly improved by having the customs tax collected by commissioners, by regulating fees and increasing salaries, by greatly restricting the sale of offices, and by limiting life tenure and reversion of offices. Too, spending was greatly controlled in a conscious and deliberate manner by the relatively small expenditures made on Cromwell's household, minimal gifts to political favorites, significant reduction in fees and gratuities to officials, and free quartering of the army in return for promises of future payment. Although significant yearly deficits remained, as did corruption, and although efficiency was still limited, the Cromwellian government was "far superior to that of the governments it succeeded."[53]

Some similar points can be made about the government bureaucracy in general, which was significantly more modern than its predecessor. The business of government was pursued with energy, enthusiasm, talent, and even honesty by men devoted to public service. Gone were the courtiers and royal favorites; in their place came the Council of State, dominated by rural gentry with military and political experience, as well as by some able lawyers, merchants, and officers. Throughout the 1642-1658 era, government was conducted by committees and boards, both in London and the counties, which often sought the advice of outside experts. A rudimentary civil service emerged with fixed (and reasonable) salaries for government employees, an oath of loyalty to the regime, and significant reductions in bribes and sales of office. The elimination of the arbitrary and erratic monarchy and its prerogative courts allowed a more consistent and positive environment of government rule to develop. Although these developments were rudimentary and subject to reversal, Cromwell's government was unquestionably more able in administering the affairs of England than Charles I had been.[54]

The dramatic changes in England's military capabilities, then, clearly paralleled and reflected significant changes wrought by the revolution in other key areas of English government.

CHAPTER 3

The French Revolution

Many of the patterns seen in England reappear in France 150 years later. The glory of France as the dominant European power in the days of Louis XIV had faded under his heirs. Although France remained the most populous, culturally influential, and richest power on the Continent, its position in the European, and, hence, international state system had markedly deteriorated under Louis XV and Louis XVI. Nowhere had this been more visible than in the wars of the period, beginning with the War of the Austrian Succession (1741-1748), accelerating with the Seven Years' War (1756-1763) and ending with the Anglo-French War (1778-1782). In all these wars France obtained some successes on the battlefield but, especially in the latter two wars, they were overshadowed by sharp and serious defeats.

The War of the Austrian Succession ended in a stalemate and restoration of the status quo in the Treaty of Aix-la-Chapelle in 1748. During the war, France under Marshal de Saxe did win significant victories in the Austrian Netherlands (1745-1747) and under Dupleix took Madras from the English in India. More broadly, France's attempt to invade England was a total failure (1745-1746); French campaigns in Germany and Italy resulted in defeat (1745-1745); the main North American fortress at Louisburg fell to the British (1745); and French fleets off Quebec and the East and West Indies were scattered by the English (1747). In short, the record of French arms was hardly overwhelming.[1]

The Seven Years' War (1756-1763) was a major disaster for France and its armed forces. Both on and off the Continent the French war effort, despite considerable expenditure of resources, enjoyed few successes. On paper the alliance with Austria and its compatriot Russia should have easily smashed the smaller forces of Prussia and England. And an early French victory in Hanover in July 1757 seemed to presage this result. But at Rossbach in November 1757, the 22,000 Prussian troops of Frederick the Great with devastating artillery and cavalry charges routed the 34,000 mainly French troops. Prussian losses were 550 men; French losses numbered 7,000 men. After Rossbach, with few exceptions, the record was gloomy with defeats at Krefel (1758), Minden (1759), Fillingshausen (1761), Wilhelmshtal, and Lutternberg (1762). During this period after Rossbach, the French army was rendered so ineffectual in Germany by Prince Ferdinard of Brunswick's Allied "Army of Operations" that, as it states in the *Cambridge Modern History,* after 1757 "the French vanish almost entirely out of the sphere of Frederick the Great's military struggles; and on this account, they will not be mentioned again in the course of the present chapter, except in way of a single cursory reference."[2]

Even greater disasters loomed in the colonies. They were set up by two naval disasters in 1759—the defeat of the French fleet by Boscowen at Lagos in August and the defeat at Quiberon Bay by Hawke in September. This disrupted a planned invasion of England and left the French colonies exposed to the British. In Canada the British seized Louisburg and Fort Duquesne in 1758, and Wolfe defeated Montcalme on the Plains of Abraham to take Quebec in 1759. By 1760, with the surrender of Montreal, Canada was lost to France. Similarly in India the British fleet under Pocock devastated the French fleet off Negapatam. Clive's great victory at Plassey in 1757 virtually ended French claims to India and established British control of Bengal. In 1758 the French were driven from Calcutta, in 1759 from Pondicherry, and in 1761 the surrender of the forces of the Comte de Lally signalled the end of French rule in India. Finally in the Caribbean (West Indies) in 1762, Rodney conquered the French colonies of Martinique, Grenada, St. Lucia, St. Vincent, and St. John. "British success was everywhere apparent."[3]

The Treaty of Paris, which ended the Seven Years' War in 1763, confirmed the results of the war. France lost her colonial empire in Canada and India, except for some minor fishing rights off Newfoundland and a few trading stations in India. French colonial ambitions in North America were abandoned with the transfer of New Orleans and Louisiana to Spain. Furthermore France received no compensation in Europe, indeed having to dismantle fortifications at Dunkirk. In the Caribbean, France got back Martinique and Guadaloupe, losing the other islands to England. The *Cambridge Modern History* summed it up well.

> This Treaty, which secured the maritime supremacy of England and the military prestige of Prussia, was called in France 'the disgraceful peace.' It did in fact signify for France loss of her colonial empire, annihilation of her navy and ruin of her finances, and discontent created among all classes by so unparalleled a series of reverses was to prove a source of great trouble in the future.[4]

The French attempts to redress the balance by attacking England during the American War of Independence had only limited success, even though England was tied down in America and France was allied (formally after 1778) with the American colonists and Spain. There is no question that French arms and the French navy played a role in securing the final American victory at Yorktown in 1781. Overall, though, the efforts of the American colonists, the small size of the British army, the incompetence of the British government, the large American land mass, and huge distance between England and America were probably more decisive. All the major French initiatives during the war ended in failure. Although a Franco-Spanish fleet under Admirals d'Orvilliers and Cordova greatly outnumbered the British fleet under Admiral Hardy (60 to 30 ships) and was supported by a 40,000 man army at Brest and Dunkirk, the attempt to invade England and capture Portsmouth ended in disaster in 1779. When the fleet returned home to winter in Brest and Cadiz, it brought back nothing but a lone British ship that had mistaken the enemy fleet for its own fleet. Two French attacks on the island of Jersey, in 1779 and 1781, ended in abject failure. A second major attack, the 1779-1783 seige of Gibraltar, failed when the English valiantly held out against large enemy forces. And a third large expedition, the 1782 French armada under Comte de Grasse to the Caribbean, was defeated by an inferior force commanded by British Admiral Rodney and surrendered. While the 1783 Treaty of Versailles did secure American independence and a swap of territories, it did relatively little to restore French prestige. This was clearly recognized by the French government, for a 1783 French Foreign Office report declared that if France continued along its current path of making weak preparations of its army and navy for war and pursuing a passive foreign policy, "she will be what Lord Chatham wished her to be; a Power of secondary rank limited to Continental Europe."[5]

Further, the financial crisis that emerged from financing the American Revolution more than vitiated the impact of military reforms undertaken at this time and ensured continuing French military weakness and passivity in European politics. Nothing better illustrated this than the events of 1787-1788 in the Netherlands. In November 1785, France and the United Provinces signed a close defensive alliance. In May 1787, William of Orange, seeking monarchical power, attacked Utrecht, and in September a 20,000 man Prussian army under the Duke of Brunswick invaded the United Provinces, allowing William to triumphantly enter The Hague and then Amsterdam the next month. Although William was a British ally, and the Netherlands sat on the French frontier and had an alliance with France, France sat idly by. As Montmorency-Luxembourg wrote at the time:

> Abandoning the Patriots served to demonstrate the inexperience, the weakness and the incompetence of the first minister and foreign minister, prompting scorn for the alliance with France and disgust with her conduct; she was a plaything of the will of others.[6]

As in the case of England, the revolution transformed France from a weak and passive country to a strong and powerful one capable of sweeping all before it. No longer would France sit idly by while neighbors with whom France had an alliance were overcome by their enemies. The military aspects of the era can be traced in two phases: revolutionary France (1792-1799) and Napoleonic France (1800-1815). In both eras France enjoyed considerable military success and, indeed, the ultimate downfall of Napoleon is traceable in significant part to the fact that his successes were so great that he made the fatal error of aspiring to world domination.

The early successes of the revolutionary French army in the 1793-1795 period were especially impressive given the formidable odds surmounted by France. In the First Coalition arrayed against France were four major powers (Austria, England, Prussia, and Spain) and a host of smaller powers including Portugal and several Germanic (Baden, Hesse, and Hanover) and Italian (Naples and Sardinia) states. At the same time France, torn by Royalist revolts in the Vendee and Brittany, her finances in ruins, and the old army disintegrating, was seemingly in sad shape. And the failure of the spring 1792 French invasion of Belgium confirmed that all the pre-1789 military problems were merely being multiplied.

Yet France rallied under new revolutionary leadership to score impressive victories against all odds. At Valmy in September 1792,

Dumouriez and Kellermann's troops forced Brunswick's withdrawal. After some setbacks in 1793 (as at Neerwinden where Dumouriez deserted to the enemy), by the end of 1794 French troops under Pichegru, Moreau, and Jourdan had occupied Belgium, Holland, and the left bank of the Rhine. While events in 1796 went poorly for France in Germany, the brilliant 26-year-old commander of the Army of Italy, Napoleon Bonaparte, daringly drove the Austrians out of northern Italy and forced a peace treaty on Austria by advancing on Vienna. In the 1797 Treaty of Campo Formio, Austria ceded Belgium and Lombardy to France, accepted French control of the left bank of the Rhine, and recognized the French satellite state of the Cisalpine Republic in Italy. France in turn only gave up Venetian territory. By 1798 England and Portugal alone stood in the path of France. However some of the French luster was dimmed by the ill-fated, 1798–1801 Egyptian expedition in which, despite seizure of Malta, Alexandria, Cairo, and Jaffa, the French army was eventually forced to evacuate in 1801. Overall, though, the 1797–1799 period can be accounted as a significant, though not overwhelming, success. At the cost of 600,000 casualties, France by 1799 had annexed Belgium, Dutch Flanders, the left bank of the Rhine, much of Switzerland, and such key towns as Avignon and Nice.[7]

Under Napoleon, who became first consul in 1799, consul for life in 1802, and emperor in 1804, the greatest victories lay before France. He speedily prepared to defeat the Second Coalition (1798–1802), which included three major powers (England, Austria, and Russia) and a number of smaller powers including Portugal, Naples, the Ottoman Empire, and the Papal states. The early reverses of 1799 in Italy, Germany, and Holland were replaced by significant victories later in the year by Massena in Switzerland and Bruene in Bergen. Napoleon's spectacular 1800 victory at Marengo forced Austria to sue for peace in the Treaty of Luneville in 1801, which acknowledged French control of Belgium, the left bank of the Rhine, and a number of Italian republics in north and central Italy. In the 1802 Peace of Amiens, which ended the Second Coalition, England was humiliated, as it lost all bases except Malta, and France regained some of its colonies.

The pinnacle of French glory occurred by force of Napoleonic arms from 1805 until 1812 when France was the master of all Western and Central Europe, the center of the world at that time. The Napoleonic Empire, encompassing one-half million square miles and 44 million people, ran from Seville to Warsaw and from Naples to the Baltic. Only England remained unconquered and largely defiant, if impotent, most of this time. In 1805 and 1806 Napoleon's newly formed Grande Armee in only 13 months swept across the Rhine towards the Danube, smashed the three armies of the great powers in the Third Coalition (Austria, Prussia, and Russia), and pushed its border eastward 350 miles. It was truly one of the most phenomenal campaigns in the history of warfare.

The campaign began with Napoleon moving his army so rapidly (500 miles in 15 days) and masterfully that the bewildered and encircled Austrian General Mack surrendered with 16 generals and 33,000 men at Ulm in October 1805. Following this great blood-less victory, Murat's troops took Vienna in November, only to be faced by a large Russian army moving in on them from the east. In December at Austerlitz the French army was outnumbered signifi-cantly by the Austro-Russian force (85,000 to 67,000), but Napo-leon maneuvered his forces well, smashed in the enemy center, held the wings, and put the enemy to flight. In the rout that followed, France took 11,000 prisoners and forced on Austria the Treaty of Pressburg, in which a prostrate Austria sued for peace and lost its Italian and German territories to France and French allies. In the fall of 1806 it was Prussia's turn. In remembrance of past glories under Frederick the Great, Prussia recklessly sent France an ultimatum. In a lightning campaign lasting only a few weeks, the French army annihilated the vaunted Prussian army, even though the two armies were roughly of the same size. At Jena and at Auerstadt (where the French were outnumbered two to one), the French army in October 1806 shattered three Prussian field armies and, in a relentless pursuit led by Bernadotte and Murat, bagged over 25,000 prisoners, 200 guns, and 60 colors and standards. Wiping out the stain of Rossbach, the French moved rapidly into Berlin, the Prussian capital. By late November the French army was in Warsaw, as 125,000 Prussian troops were taken prisoner, and nearly all of Prussia's fortresses sur-rendered without a shot. In the aftermath Prussia ceded half its pop-ulation to France, agreed to support a garrison of 150,000 French troops, and limited the size of its army. Rarely had a triumph been so sudden or complete.

There remained only the Russians in the way of the Napoleonic dream of a continental empire. In February 1807 at Eylau, the French won a bloody battle in terrible weather, as Bennigsen's Rus-sian forces left them in battered possession of the field. But four months later at Friedland the Russians lost 20,000 men, and only fragments of the Russian army retreated to Tilsit with the French in pursuit. Fearing a French invasion of Russia, Tsar Alexander met Napoleon at Tilsit and reached an agreement that sealed French con-trol of the Continent. Russia agreed to ally itself with France, join the Continental System against England, send the Russian navy to help France take Gibraltar, and create a Grand Duchy of Warsaw under French influence and garrison. All Prussian territory west of the Elbe was given to the Kingdom of Westphalia to be ruled by Napoleon's brother Jerome. Russia in turn was to be given a free hand against Finland and Turkey. Thus at Tilsit, Napoleon reached a peak of power unmatched since Charlemagne, with Austria, Prussia, and Russia crushed, and the empire extending 900 miles from the Pyrenees to the Elbe, south to the boot of Italy, and east to the Dalmatian coast.[8]

From 1807 until 1812 Napoleonic France was the undisputed master of Europe. During this time France created the Continental System to attempt to bar English goods from the Continent, improved its hold over Italy, and annexed Holland, the North Sea littoral, and parts of Italy and Dalmatia. France beat off English attempts to gain a foothold in northern Europe, as in the 1809 bid to seize Antwerp. And when Austria launched a surprise attack across the Bavarian frontier with 300,000 men in April 1809, Napoleon's army retaliated quickly, seizing Vienna in May, and defeating the Austrian army at Wagram. In the ensuing treaty in October, Austria ceded to France Salzburg, Trieste, parts of Croatia, and Dalmatia (territory with three million people) and Austria agreed to pay a large indemnity and to limit its army to 150,000 men. After this treaty peace reigned everywhere except on the Iberian Peninsula. There, although France from 1808 to 1812 poured in over 500,000 troops and took Lisbon in 1807 and Madrid in 1808, Napoleon was unable to gain a final victory against local and British forces. This front was to prove a costly drain over time, and by 1811 France had retreated from Portugal.[9]

By 1812 France stood at the zenith of its power with an empire of 44 million people and the satellites—the Confederation of the Rhine, Italy, Switzerland, and Poland—largely docile. Only England remained defiant, while Denmark, Austria, and Prussia, even though outside direct French control, were relatively compliant. While there were strong centrifugal forces within the system, it clearly could have survived, had it not been for the Russian campaign that made it suddenly vulnerable to other challenges. But in Russia, Napoleon had attempted something far beyond the technical capabilities of his day, unless the Russians were foolhardy enough to risk all their forces in battle. Indeed, in truth, the campaign saw not a single Russian victory, as the French army won at Borodino and entered Moscow. But while Napoleon entered Russia with 614,000 men in June 1812, he had only 100,000 men left by the time he entered Moscow in September, and only between 30,000 to 60,000 made it back to France by December. In this campaign Napoleon lost 570,000 troops (of whom 370,000 died of battle injuries, illness, and exposure, and the rest were captured), 200,000 trained horses, and 1,050 cannons. Interestingly Russia suffered over 450,000 casualties and had only 40,000 troops left to chase Napoleon in November. The causes of the French disaster were numerous: the impossible logistics of feeding and equipping 600,000 troops in a hostile land with only a minimal number of poor roads, the inability to force a major battle, the unreliability of the non-French half of the army, the attempt to wage a two-front war with 200,000 French troops in Spain, and Russian capabilities.

After this Russian disaster, the end came quickly as the numerous enemies of France were galvanized into action. And yet, even facing impending defeat and decimated by the Russian campaign, the French army put up a good fight against great odds. In May 1813 French victories at Lutzen and Bautzen resulted in the June armistice of Pleischwitz. And in August the Napoleonic army scored a notable victory at Dresden though outnumbered three to two. But, Wellington triumphed in Spain, and by the summer of 1813, Russia, Prussia, Sweden, and Austria put over 500,000 men in the field. At the climactic battle of Leipzig in October, the French army was outnumbered almost two to one (342,000 versus 195,000). Although inflicting more casualties on the enemy than it suffered, the French army was defeated by the allies. The French Empire was destroyed east of the Rhine, and by December only 80,000 weary troops were left to defend the eastern frontier against 300,000 allied troops.

Even then, the French army did not fold. In January, Napoleon scored victories at Brienne and La Rothiere and in February at Champaubert, Montmirail, and Vauchamps, and in March at Rheims. However, 75,000 French troops could not forever hold off 200,000 allied troops, and in early April the allies entered Paris and Napoleon capitulated. In the famous One Hundred Days of Napoleon's return in 1815, Napoleon would pit his 124,000 French troops against 208,000 allied troops in Belgium and 320,000 troops elsewhere. Although he scored a notable victory at Ligny in June, he met his final defeat at Waterloo, which brought his tumultous reign to an end.[10]

The final defeat clearly showed the ultimate limitations on any army in general and the revolutionary army in particular. While Napoleon was exhausting French resources and the army from too many wars, other countries were mobilizing their resources and remodeling their armies on the French system. His numerous enemies were roused to a new-found nationalism by the Continental System, Napoleonic delusions of grandeur, excessive demands for men, money, and munitions, and the despotic nature of Napoleon's rule. At home the endless fighting drained war enthusiasm and manpower resources, diminishing popular support. His army increasingly suffered from overcentralized command, declining quality of soldiers, avarice of his marshals, and inability to adapt to large theaters of operations in poor areas. And yet, given all this, and especially the united opposition of the other four great powers of Europe, what is remarkable is not the inevitable tragic denouement but the fact that for 22 years France had been the dominant, hegemonic power in brilliant contrast to the decay of French power before 1789. Or, as Charles de Gaulle aptly put it, no doubt Napoleon in the end struck too hard and too strong but what was everlasting was "the mighty reputation won for his country."[11]

MILITARY POLICIES

How did France transform itself from the beaten, disputed power of the Seven Years' War, the power that had failed both in its actions against England (1778-1782) and in its action in Holland (1787), into one of the greatest powers in world history? How had it recaptured the glorious days of Louis XIV? We obviously need to begin by looking at specifically military features. Not surprisingly many of the features noticeable in England resurface in France. It is important, though, not to stereotype French power and the armed forces before 1789. Unlike England, France remained quite respected and even feared in Europe and had some recent victories to its credit in America and India. If French power had declined significantly, France retained great potential as the largest and richest European state with a proud military tradition. We begin by comparative analysis of officers, soldiers, and style of warfare in the two armies.

Perhaps most importantly, in the wake of the Seven Years' War, there was a series of reforms initiated by such war ministers as Choiseul (1761-1770), St. Germain (1775-1777), and Puysegrin (1788-1789). Over time progress was made in improving the training of officers and quality of arms, fixing the number of regiments, improving conditions for soldiers, regularizing abolition of the proprietary rights of officers over units, and slashing excessive officers from the payroll. Men such as Marshal de Broglie and Comte de Guibert worked diligently at modernizing the armed forces. But with 12 war ministers in the last 30 years of the ancien regime, much ground was gained only to be lost. And the fundamental defects of the armed forces could not be remedied under Louis XV and Louis XVI.[12]

The French army was a faithful reflection of ancien society in its traditional conservative nature. Despite the progress made by reforms in the post-1763 era, the aristocratic reaction had chained the officer corps ever more tightly to the exclusive rule of the aristocracy. In the military schools, proof of nobility was required to attend the Ecole Militaire by 1751, Artillery Schools by 1772, and Engineering Schools by 1776. By 1781 the Edict of Segur eliminated formal certificates and required original papers to prove 16 quarterings of nobility. From one-third of all officers in 1750, nonnobles were reduced to only 10 percent by 1789.[13]

But not even all 400,000 nobles were created equal. The higher nobles presented at court dominated the upper reaches of the officer corps, while the lesser nobles languished in the lower ranks. By 1789 the 11 marshals consisted of 5 dukes, 4 marquises, 1 prince, and 1 count, while 187 of 196 lieutenant generals, 760 of 950 lesser generals, and 194 of 200 regimental colonels were titled aristocrats. The lower ranks of captain and lieutenant were dominated by lesser nobles. A court noble could expect to become a general officer, regardless of talent by age 39, a provincial noble by age 58. And, having spent one-fourth the time (8 years versus 31 years) in the army, the court noble would expect to receive more than four times the pay. Merit and experience counted for little in promotion to the higher ranks for, "With or without merit it was traditional that a young court noble, after a few years as a nominal captain, for form's sake, should be appointed colonel and have a regiment."[14]

Under these circumstances little could be done to promote professionalism in the officer corps. The noble officer viewed his position as a traditional birthright over which only he and his peers were fit to establish the conditions of service. He did not view it as a vocation and often took extensive leaves beyond the seven and one-half month paid leave to which he was entitled every two years. When not on leave he did little training or interacting with his soldiers, preferring instead to carry on his supervision of estates and family businesses and performance of social obligations. Officers frequently fought duels, flouted regulations with impunity, and lived a luxurious life-style with as many as 40 servants to a regiment. The state supported this extravagance, as in 1787 the 18 French marshals received as much money (nearly two million livres) as all Prussian and Austrian generals combined.[15]

In this system merit, talent, experience, and even seniority often took second place to other considerations. Noble birth, and especially high noble birth, was the most important attribute for promotion and appointment. Without high noble birth a provincial noble, as Napoleon Bonaparte who was commissioned as an officer in 1785, could have expected to spend 30 years as a lieutenant and captain. Regardless of his talents, he would have considered himself lucky to become a major and retire on a miserable pension in his early 50s. Those without any noble birth had no chance for appointment or promotion. Money was important for the purchase and inheriting of posts, as well as for spending on the luxuries that were integral to the life of a proper officer. And favoritism and patronage, based on connections at Court, were especially important in this system.

Not surprisingly, the overall quality of officers under this system was quite poor, as seen in the Seven Years' War. With top commanders appointed through Court influence, the high command was in constant flux with no less than seven commanders-in-chief during the war. Of them only two (d'Estree and Broglie) were considered competent commanders while others, as Count Clermont and Soubise, were noteworthy mainly for their obedience. Marshal Richelieu, who replaced the victorious d'Estrees through intrigue, was known as the "Old Plunderer," while army commander St. Germain simply abandoned his soldiers during a retreat. The generals were afraid of taking any initiatives for fear of alienating the Court and feuded among themselves rather than working together. Duc de Broglie argued that the failures of the Seven Years' War came from the complete ignorance of officers at all levels of their duties, while Comte Guibert wrote in 1772 that the ministers "prefer to entrust their troops to mediocrities incapable of training them ... instead of the superior men who might gain too much credit and resist prevailing opinion."[16]

The officer corps, segregated by social strata, saw bitter internal feuds and lacked any social cohesion. The lesser nobles resented the higher nobles, who banned them from high ranks and feared wealthy commoners. Middle-class commoner elements resented their exclusion from advancement past noncommissioned officer and junior officer status. Lower-class elements were upset that they could not move beyond corporal. In short, the aristocratic reaction had created a straightforward class conflict in the army.

Finally, up until a few years before 1789, the army had a vast oversupply of officers that hindered creation of a professional officer corps. In 1763 there were 650 generals and 16,000 active officers for an army of 200,000 men. Every regiment had up to 10 colonels who took turns commanding for a day while their mass of personal baggage clogged the supply lines. Even by 1775 the army had 10,000 active officers and 50,000 inactive officers, whose pay (47 million livres) cost more than the rest of the army (44 million livres). There were 2,200 colonels and 1,200 general officers for 200 regiments. Under these conditions most officers lived frivolously in society rather than spending time with their men.[17]

Just as with England, some of the most revolutionary changes came in the officer corps of the French army. The basic principle of aristocratic exclusivity was swept away in 1790 by decrees abolishing the hereditary nobility and opening all ranks to commoners. With the rationalization and professionalization of the officer corps and increasing radicalism of the revolution, by the summer of 1792, 50 percent of the officer corps, including 6,000 noble officers, had abandoned the army. At the higher levels there was almost a clean sweep. In February 1792, only 5 of over 200 marshals and lieutenant generals of 1789 and 46 of over 900 brigadier and major generals of 1789 remained in the army. In their place came convinced political adherents of the revolutionary regime, often with real talent, military adventurers, and solid professional soldiers. The remaining, largely provincial nobles representing only 10 to 20 percent of all officers, rose so quickly that in 1793, 70 percent of all generals were nobles, and 96 percent of them had 15 years of military service. Promotion from the ranks was so strong that in 1793, 85 percent of all lieutenants were former sergeants of 1789, and a phenomenal 70 percent of all regimental officers were former soldiers.

Nowhere was the revolutionary principle of merit—regardless of class, age, or money—enthroned more strikingly than in the array of brilliant new revolutionary generals named in 1793. The eight new generals averaged 33 years of age and included such luminaries as the 24-year-old Hoche who had been a sergeant in 1792, the 34-year-old Jourdan who had also been a sergeant in 1792 and haberdasher in 1789, the 39-year-old Moreau who had been a notary clerk, and the 24-year-old Napoleon Bonaparte who had been a lieutenant in 1789.[18]

The Napoleonic armies retained this revolutionary principle. Of the 18 marshals created in 1804 there were only 3 nobles, 4 from the lower classes and 11 from the bourgeois middle classes. And the 14 active marshals among them had a median age of 37, while regimental colonels averaged 39 years of age. With merit, bravery, and success the keys to promotion, it is hardly surprising that fully 50 percent of all officers were former soldiers, which meant they were largely of lower-class origin. Indeed after each battle the colonels promoted men who had distinguished themselves to replace the fallen. The system rewarded daring and merit. The officers often paid a high cost, as 219 generals were killed from 1792 to 1815, and 15,000 officers alone were killed during the Napoleonic era. As Georges Lefebvre has written, "Like the armies of the Convention and Directory, the Napoleonic army drew its main strength from the social revolution which had opened careers to talent."[19]

At the same time, the revolutionary army retained a strong professional core. In the 1790s, as already mentioned, experienced provincial nobles dominated the officer corps. By 1805, 25 percent of Napoleonic officers similarly had been officers in the French army of 1789. Too, Napoleon founded schools such as St. Cyr (1802), which produced 4,000 cadets by 1815, and L'Ecole Polytechnique, which produced many gunnery and engineering officers. Emigre officers were welcomed back into the army. The courageous but untutored officers from the ranks were complemented by the existence of a solid professional cadre element.[20]

A similar, sharp contrast can be seen between the soldiers of Royalist France on one hand and revolutionary and Napoleonic France on the other hand. In the traditional professional army of prerevolutionary France, as in England, soldiers came from the lowest classes and were harshly despised by civilians. Soldiers were classed as "the vilest and most miserable citizens" as reflected in signs in Parisian public gardens on the eve of the revolution that prohibited "dogs, street-walkers, lackeys and soldiers."[21] Foreigners were heavily recruited (forming 10 to 20 percent of the army). All means, including persuasion, deception, intoxication, and intimidation, were used in recruitment, with bounties provided to professional recruiters. The army attracted men seeking to avoid bondage, famine, and psychological misery. Recruiters were given wide latitude, as seen in the Louvois order that "His Majesty finds it good that small irregularities be concealed. Only violence and kidnapping from fairgrounds and markets are forbidden."[22] Thus, the French army consisted largely of pressed Frenchmen and foreign mercenaries.

The situation of soldiers in the army was very poor. Utilitarian aspects were weak as the pay was so low that, even if a soldier saved it for a whole year, he would have enough only for a suit of clothes. Food and housing were wretched, and the soldier had few rights and no hope for promotion into the noble-dominated officer corps. He had no normative commitment to a regime that treated him as a feared alien or to noble officers who disdained him. Louis XVI's war minister, Comte de Guibert, bluntly observed that "In most European countries, the interest of the people and those of the government are very separate; patriotism is merely a word; citizens are not soldiers; soldiers are not citizens; wars are not the quarrel of the nation; they are that of the ministry and sovereign."[23] Control, therefore, was preeminently by strict, cruel discipline and harsh corporal punishment. Men were marched into battle, and they fought in tight formations under the closest supervision of their officers.

Under these terrible conditions the conduct of soldiers inevitably left much to be desired. Rowdy behavior, gambling, stealing, and drunkenness were the norm. In a typical year, a combat unit lost a staggering 20 percent of its strength to desertion and illness. And in wartime desertion could reach "appalling proportions," as during the Seven Years' War when 12,000 French deserters in 1760 took refuge in neutral Netherlands. Maltreated and ignored by the army and society, the soldiers fought with minimal enthusiasm for a regime that ignored their interests.[24]

By contrast, the French armies after 1789, in the spirit of the revolution, showed much concern for the soldiers, and the soldiers responded in kind. The rate of desertion declined markedly from its pre-1789 levels. Soldiers now were viewed as proud citizens of a country fighting for the survival of the revolution and France against the despotic old order of Europe. Now, in the 1790s there were a significant number of volunteers, as well as the establishment of the *levee en masse*. Afterwards from 1800 to 1815, 1.5 million men were conscripted into the army. Under the laws of 1798 all 20 to 25-year-old males were liable for service, but exemptions and substitutes made only the poorer 40 percent of the eligible males truly vulnerable, especially with the large-scale drafting of foreigners. The modern principle of universal conscription though had been established, and it was carried out locally by a staff of professional civil servants, thereby representing a major advance in the system.[25]

Now there was for the first time a strong normative commitment by many soldiers, who felt they were fighting for France and the revolution. The French army had become a politically conscious national force inspired by a new sense of patriotism. Katharine Chorley has put the matter nicely.

The French private realized that for the first time in his long history he was being exhorted to spend his blood in his own cause, for the sake of the country in which he and his friends and his relatives in the towns and villages all had a share, a country which at last had won the right to ask him for his life. And his answer was almost always loyal and unhesitating.[26]

Also, Napoleon, through his frequent visits with the soldiers, inspired a romantic heroic ideal in his troops.

Now, too, there were strong utilitarian motives. With half the officers coming from the ranks, the ambitious soldier could feel that a marshal's baton might be in every knapsack. For the striving soldier, glory on the battlefield could bring membership in the elite Guards with better food and barracks, weapons of honor, double pay, bonuses, and even a knighthood. Plunder, loot, and glory would all be rightfully his. And when he retired the army would provide a pension, employment, and even housing for the handicapped. All this was a far cry from the circumstances that existed before 1789.

Coercion was much reduced over the earlier years, reflecting both the closer officer/soldier relationship and the effectiveness of other means of control. The French army was often quite insubordinate off the field of battle. But in battle, discipline and coercion did work with reasonable effectiveness.

If we turn to style of warfare, similar sharp changes are evident, even if there were no significant changes in technology. The monarchist army, like other European armies, fought in a very traditional and stylized manner that reflected the nature of the international system. With soldiers representing a relatively expensive and unwilling commodity that was hard to replace, commanders preferred to avoid battle. On the road they could move slowly in file on a single road, and they were chained to a series of huge supply magazines. Once in battle the reluctant soldiers had to be deployed slowly in a compact, controllable line formation. Mobile activities or vigorous pursuit were impossible since large numbers of troops would defect. Defense, not offense, was the predominant motif of the day. Under these conditions the system clearly encouraged smaller armies, few battles, light casualties, and the avoidance of destruction. All these attributes were reflections of the objective conditions under which the armies operated before 1789.[27]

The revolutionary armies of France in over two decades smashed the old style of warfare and created a new, more modern style of war, which in many ways foreshadowed the wars of the twentieth century. Now that soldiers were plentiful and at times even eager to fight and officers were equally motivated to fight, the social revolution allowed the sweeping away of all the restraints on warfare. After

1792 the French commanders eagerly sought battle and exerted their utmost to destroy enemy forces. In the process they took heavy casualties in repeated battles, but could afford to do so now that conscription made manpower cheap and replaceable. With willing soldiers, the commanders could move with a mobility and decisiveness heretofore unknown and without fear of mass desertion. Banking on short and decisive campaigns, they could live off the countryside, freeing themselves from reliance on a chain of supply magazines.

Napoleon brought these revolutionary features to their peak of perfection. When he went to war, he moved all his resources to the front, leaving behind minimal reserves of manpower, supplies, and equipment. As he moved he used his agents and cavalry to gain good intelligence on the enemy, while deploying a dense cavalry screen to protect his own freedom to maneuver. His mobility was ensured by rapid, forced marches (often 10 to 12 miles a day) of large self-sufficient units and living off the land. All the threads of the campaign were in his hands, ensuring a unified command. Once he determined the enemy's intentions and dispositions, he usually developed a plan for the rapid deployment of his columns to achieve a decisive victory. Massed artillery prepared the way for the infantry. Ever seeking to seize the initiative, he relied on speed, mobility, audacity, rapid concentration of forces, and an unexpected avenue of attack to destroy the enemy with shock tactics. Once he gained the upper hand, he sent in the cavalry to pursue the enemy relentlessly and vigorously to achieve complete psychological and physical destruction of his enemy. In all, there was much that was quite modern in the Napoleonic style of war. It was not devoid of problems—overcentralized command, poor logistics and communications, weak discipline—but its central features reflected the revolutionary changes in French society and brought victory to France on a scale not seen since Charlemagne.[28]

DOMESTIC POLICIES

A brief survey of the domestic policies of prerevolutionary and revolutionary France shows significant differences that help explain the great successes of revolutionary armies as compared with the failings of prerevolutionary armies. The government of Louis XVI was shackled in many areas by outmoded social structures and privileges that were so deeply implanted in the nature of the system as to make the system itself relatively impotent. The French government before 1789 did not even possess undivided control over its own territory. Rather, reflecting the gradual assimilation of feudal principalities by inheritance, marriage, and conquest on negotiated terms to the royal domain around Paris, the French political map of the eighteenth century was one of unbelievable complexity. With many citizens possessing greater loyalty to their provinces or areas than to France, many felt that the unity of the kingdom was little more than a convenient myth. Mirabeau went so far as to call the French an "aggregate divided people."[29]

Numerous forces of tradition and privilege separated the king and his government from the people. Within France there were enclaves owned by the pope (Avignon) and the Dutch House of Orange. A number of cities, such as Marseilles and Dunkirk, had acquired a certain degree of independence from the Crown, while no less than seven provinces had their own estates in which clergy, the nobility, and the bourgeoisie met every one to three years. The governmental structure was also redundant with the intendant, the king's agent in the provinces, overlapping with the lieutenant generals of the provincial governments. The legal structure was unbelievably complex with 360 different legal codes and a division of the kingdom into a southern region governed by a code derived from Roman law and a northern region governed by customary law. Furthermore, there were many overlapping systems of civil law, church law, seigneurial courts, and administrative departments with judicial functions. Taxes varied widely from one area to another, with some areas exempted from a tax while other areas were hit hard by the same tax. Overall, there is little question that with no constitution to clarify matters, as Olwen Hufton has asserted:

> the king was hamstrung in the imposition of a central policy. His 'despotism' was hedged about with rules and regulations, and where his authority began and those of provincial laws and institutions ended was almost impossible to define, a factor which monopolizes the political history of eighteenth century France.[30]

Furthermore, as in prerevolutionary England, the success of absolute monarchy depended heavily on the accidents of heredity in providing an effective and capable monarch. But neither Louis XV nor Louis XVI could be so described. Louis XV's indolence, lethargy, and slothfulness by the end of his reign led French government "to become arbitrary and administration incoherent and mechanical."[31] Similarly, Louis XVI also preferred hunting to politics, displaying limited intelligence or interest in politics while often being led by his ministers. Neither were strong, capable, or effective monarchs seeking to avoid the coming disaster or overcome the tangle of privileges that stood in the way of progress.

A serious burden was the poor organization and leadership of the governmental structure, which had not turned into a nascent government bureaucracy with a core of civil servants, as was developing in England and Prussia. With the domination of the Court and the state by the higher nobles, the monarchy was incapable of rationalizing itself due to its inevitable defense of aristocratic privilege. The state was heavily infiltrated by privileged groups who used government as a vehicle for their class interests. Appointments were made by patronage, influence, and money, which guaranteed aristocratic dominance due to influence at Court. The higher officials, having bought their offices, were independent of the Crown and often did not accept any salary. Instead there was vast corruption, as they received presents and gifts far above their salaries from towns, guilds, and individuals. Thus, except at the bottom of the hierarchy, there was no bureaucratic structure of rationality.[32]

The worst aspect of the system could be seen in the Royal Treasury. Louis XVI, who knew very little about finance, had no less than eight finance ministers (some quite good as Necker and Turgot) from 1774 to 1787—yet none could resolve the fundamental problems of the Treasury. There was no formal annual budget, no accounting of expenditures or gathering of revenues. The Royal Treasury accounts for 1769 and 1770 were not ready until 1781 and the 1781 accounts not until 1790. There was no central pool of funds, nor even any segregation of public and private funds.[33]

The worst corruption came in the collecting and spending of revenues by several hundred venal accountants and large tax farmers. The accountants, who paid huge sums for their offices, had only a contractual relationship with the Crown and were not subject to any bureaucratic control. They openly used public office for private gain, and their employees were responsible only to them. There were no salary scales or formal positions for a functional organization. Behaving more as private businessmen than public officials, the tax farmers leased the right to collect indirect taxes every six years. This system inevitably spawned corruption and great waste. Michel Vovelle has called the system "crude and unsatisfactory," depicting it as

> cumbersome and odious: the brutality of the agents of the fermiers generaux, the searches conducted by gabelous (collectors of the Salt tax), the way in which consumption was at once compulsory and re-

stricted: the abuses of the system were in inverse proportion to its prof-
itability.[34]

The corrupt mixture of public and private interest in the state started
right at the top. Fully 25 percent of all expenses, other than debt
interest and the military, went to support the king's household and
Court alone. The king could be very generous, as in 1788 when he
paid off 37 million livres of debt of two counts. The king could also
be very capricious, as when he kept two stables just to allow the
queen's favorite in 1785 to have something to do. Corruption started
at the top.[35]

The French Revolution burst asunder many of the social, economic, and political constraints that had prevented full mobilization
of France's human and material resources for war. All intermediary
bodies between state and citizen were abolished, along with the corporate privileges of nobles, clergy, towns, and provinces. The revolution destroyed the chaotic institutions and privileges of the old
regime. All feudal remnants and the privileged position of the Church
were destroyed. Napoleon institutionalized many of the modernizing
reforms of the revolution. He created a completely new Code Napoleon, which guaranteed equality before the law, liberty of the individual, freedom of work, private property, freedom of conscience,
religious toleration, abolition of serfdom, and civil rights for Jews
and Protestants. He unified the systems of justice and created a network of secular educational institutions. France now became a single
political entity with a unified justice system, single customs area,
national army, and strong national consciousness. This modern centralized state now could mobilize its new citizens directly and without intermediaries.[36]

In this context one of the great achievements of the revolution
was the creation of a single, streamlined government with a nascent
bueaucratic structure. The prefect system effectively projected central power into the most remote communes. Most importantly, government careers were made on talent, merit, and devotion to the
state, criteria that allowed the integration of men from diverse social
origins into a new bureaucratic stratum. Indeed, Napoleonic personnel were recruited solely on aptitude and talent, with even former
enemies of the state eligible for entrance. The Council of State could
draw on talented experts from all fields to serve the state. This led to
a new professionalism as seen in a study of 300 prefects, which
found that 40 percent had strong administrative experience. Many
ministers, such as Fouche (Police), Talleyrand (Foreign Ministry),
and Berthier (War Ministry) were very talented. A study of 26

Napoleonic ministers showed that fully 40 percent were lawyers, while only 10 percent came from the nobility. Those of bourgeois middle-class origin were the most numerous. There was a strong contingent of youthful, ambitious men with almost half the ministers under 45 years of age. Napoleonic government consisted thereby of an oligarchy of officials and experts working directly under the guidance of Napoleon. Overall, revolutionary France "created the most powerful instrument of bureaucratic control that the Western world has known since the Roman Emperor."[37]

In no more important area were these changes evident than in the crucial area of finances, which had been an immediate cause of both the French and English Revolutions. The revolution ended the private exploitation of the government's finances by nationalizing them and creating the beginnings of public administration. The Treasury finally became a bureaucratic instrument of state with the destruction of venal accountants and tax farmers in the 1790s. By 1794 there existed a national bureaucratic Treasury, composed of salaried officials performing their duties by a rational, functional plan and preparing full annual accounts. Guarantees existed against arbitrary ministers, and the bureaucracy was guided by a stringent set of charts and tables. Although Napoleon undid some of these progressive features through the venality of the new aristocracy, reliance on tycoons, and confusion of public and private interests, the essential elements survived, aided by creation of the Bank of France and maintenance of a sound currency.[38]

The creation of a strong administrative instrument, no longer hampered by internal tariffs, feudal dues, and fiscal exclusions of the old regime, had great impact on the military capabilities of France. As J. F. Bosher has commented:

> With its flexible hierarchy of command, its division of labor, its central records, its double entry book-keeping systems and its mechanical efficiency, the new bureaucratic administration was capable of mobilizing the financial resources of the nation to a degree Louis XIV could hardly have imagined. The French revolution built a national business machine out of men and paper, not the first in Europe, certainly, yet so far improved that it furnished the wealth necessary for 20 years of war against nearly all of Europe.[39]

A new rigor was manifested in the assessment and collecting of taxes and expenditures, which meant "there is no doubt that the regime continued to get the most effective use of an imperfect instrument by serious progress in financial management."[40] By 1813 the government was taking in close to one billion livres, or two to three times more income than before 1789, and 60 to 80 percent of it went for war. Under Napoleon, who managed a frugal administration, the stress was on indirect taxes, war indemnities from conquest, confiscation of feudal and crown properties, customs revenues, and taxes on occupied areas. Budgets were largely in balance with only a small debt extant by 1814. Overall, the impressive aspect was the vast expansion in French financial capacity in this era.[41]

While there were few economic innovations and limited economic progress, the French government did promote enough economic growth to support the war effort. The abolition of guilds, elimination of internal customs duties, reduction of tolls, introduction of a decimal system, creation of a unified national market, and promotion of technical progress all aided economic growth and induced a certain prosperity. So too did creation of a unified law code that protected property and led to the promotion of road building, formation of the Bank of France and Chambers of Commerce, abolition of serfdom and feudalism, and conversion of land to private property.[42]

Finally, France in the 1790s, and even more so under Napoleon, saw the reconciliation of a wide variety of interests. Enemies of the regime were soothed by Napoleon's 1801 Concordat with the pope, his 1804 proclamation of the empire, his creation of a new service nobility, and his invitations for the return of emigres. He gained peasant support by confirming the revolutionary land settlement that eliminated feudalism and serfdom and improved peasant legal status. He wooed worker support through the promotion of full employment and urban spectacles. He wooed the middle classes with his financial reforms, emphasis on law and order, creation of a new legal code, and enhancement of secular education. Napoleon gained the active support of Protestants, Jews, and Freemasons, gratified by their new legal status. A masterful and hardworking if very egotistical politician, Napoleon successfully eliminated his Jacobin and Royalist enemies and created stability through raising France to hegemony in Europe and through his appeals to various strata of society. In the end, after 15 years of rule, external forces would be necessary to overthrow him.[43]

Napoleon especially pioneered such modern concepts as nationalism and propaganda to gain support for his regime. The revolution had laid the basis for these changes by transforming Frenchmen from subjects of Louis XVI into nominally equal citizens of a new political community. In this context Napoleon could consciously promote modern nationalism through the great war victories, service in the army, and a centralized, unified government. French nationalism could bind all Frenchmen together and especially appealed to the lower classes who formed the bulk of the population. Napoleon was also one of the first leaders to consciously use the machinery of government to systematically cultivate and control public opinion. Beyond traditional negative means such as censorship and press supervision, he stressed positive propaganda in the form of military bulletins, festivals, prizes, and subsidization of friendly newspapers. Robert Holtmann has analyzed this development of Napoleonic propaganda as a tool of modern politics:

> But Napoleon is important as being the first dictator to devote such a large share of his attention to public opinion. He spoke directly and frequently to his subjects, and not only fully exploited all existing media of communication but devised some new ones as well. He utilized existing tools of propaganda so extensively as to make control of military news in wartime a distinct and important arm of warfare. He did a remarkable job conducting his propaganda along lines which would make it most effective.[44]

FOREIGN POLICIES

Finally, a brief word should be added regarding foreign policy. The failures of French foreign policy before 1789 were quite evident. In the last 40 years of the old regime the influence and power of France underwent serious decline. Yet Louis XV and Louis XVI seemed often quite indifferent to these changes and incapable of doing anything to reverse the trend. French alliance policy with Austria proved quite disastrous and did nothing to prevent the partitioning of Poland, a French buffer, in 1772. The alliances with the American colonists in 1778 and Dutch Republic in 1785 merely showed the futility of French policy. The American alliance ultimately helped bankrupt France, while the Dutch alliance showed the impotence of France when it was unable to meet the terms of the treaty in 1787. French foreign policy under the last two monarchs was erratic, inconsistent, and ultimately a failure in preventing a significant decline in French influence.

By contrast, French foreign policy from 1792 to 1811 can be counted as quite consistent and successful in furthering French interests in Europe. After 1791 monarchist Europe was united in its implacable hatred of regicidal, revolutionary France. And if Europe could remain relatively united, it could foil French ambitions. Yet repeatedly France was able to pursue a policy of divide and conquer and reach agreements with various of its enemies. Only as Napoleon dismissed his more capable ministers and lost touch with reality in his Russian invasion did the quality of French policy decline significantly. And by the end in 1814 when Napoleon refused an allied offer of the 1791 borders, foreign policy totally lost any meaning. In general, there was a much more consistent and sophisticated rational thrust to foreign policy after 1789 than before 1789.

* * *

A number of critical similarities have emerged from the study of the English and French Revolutions. Both countries in the decades before the revolution had suffered a serious decline in their position in the international system. When major events occured on or near their borders, they were forced to remain idle by dint of domestic and military problems. Their military capabilities were openly called into question after a series of significant defeats at the hands of their rivals. Their traditional armed forces, dominated by aristocratic, nonprofessional officers, who used severe discipline over the lower-class soldiers, fought sluggishly and with minimal effectiveness. The absolutist regime, lacking a government bureaucracy or independent treasury, was thoroughly penetrated by aristocratic elements, who used their positions to drain state resources and defend their privileges. Under these conditions, the monarch, hedged about by numerous limitations on his ability to rule, was unable to mobilize significant resources for war beyond maintenance of a professional army, if even that.

The revolutions swept away the neofeudal obstacles to a more effective armed forces. Faced with domestic counterrevolution and foreign intervention, the new revolutionary regimes made their armies of necessity the first modern institutions. In the armies promotion was by merit and talent, and often from the ranks; officers were recruited from all classes; and the soldiers, also recruited from a wider base, now fought for a cause in which they believed. In short, the real social revolution first came in the army. Backed by a nascent government bureaucracy with far greater financial powers, the army adopted an aggressive and relentless mode of warfare that decimated more traditional armies. Its leaders became heads of their respective governments and consolidated the revolution by integrating aspects of the new and old order. The ever-victorious army was a key and necessary product of the revolution.

PART 2
The Russian Revolution

CHAPTER **4**

Russia and the Two World Wars

The comparison between the performance of the Russian army in World War I and in World War II is a fascinating one, made especially compelling by the numerous similarities between the two wars and the natures of Russia's armies. Both world wars saw the mobilization of tens of millions of men, deaths of millions of people, participation of dozens of countries, and universal development of war economies as part of "total war." In World War I and World War II an aggressive German-dominated coalition of European states (including Austria and Hungary) fought a losing battle against a disparate alliance of major powers, including England, France, Russia, and ultimately the United States. Both wars had a decisive impact on international politics. For Russia, World War I led to the demise of Tsar Nicholas II and the February and October Revolutions; World War II enshrined Russia as a new-found superpower sitting securely in the heart of Europe.

In the two world wars Russia yielded to no country in its mass suffering. Russia suffered the greatest number of soldiers killed and wounded, soldiers taken captive, and civilians killed of any nation in the conflicts. While the figures in table 1 represent only a rough approximation due to poor data collection and dissemination,[1] they nevertheless vividly show the massive level of Russia's losses. In both wars Russia lost two to four million soldiers and suffered seven to eight million casualties. Also, the losses in terms of prisoners taken were staggering, nearly three million in World War I and six million in World War II. Russia's total loss rate of 60 to 65 percent of its armies in both wars was enormous.

There is little doubt of the overall superiority of the German

TABLE 1:   Russian Military Losses in the Two World Wars (in millions)

	World War I	World War II
Killed	2.5	4.0
Wounded	4.7	5.0
Prisoners	2.9	6.0
	10.1	15.0
Total of Men Mobilized	15.8	22.4
Percentage Lost	63.9	62.5

SOURCES: Sovetskaya voennaya entsiklopediya (Moscow: Voenizdat, 1978),
v. 2, p. 65; G. I. Shigalin, Voennaya ekonomika v pervuyu mirovuyu voinu
(1914-1918) (Moscow: Voenizdat, 1956), p. 253; Major General Sir Alfred
Knox, With the Russian Army 1914-1917 (London: Hutchinson and Company,
1929), p. 542; Albert Seaton, The Russo-German War 1941-45 (New York:
Praeger, 1970), p. 586; and Norman Stone, The Eastern Front, 1914-1917
(New York: Charles Scribner's Sons, 1975), p. 215.

army in both wars. In World War I, nine Russians were taken captive for each German prisoner, in World War II, five Russians were
taken captive for each German prisoner. In 1914-1918, German
dead on both fronts (two million) were less than Russian dead on
one front. In 1941-1945 the number of Russians killed in action
(roughly four million) was double the number of Germans killed
on the eastern front (two million).[2]

During the first 16 months of World War I and World War II on
the eastern front, the Germans and their allies inflicted severe defeats
on the Russians and occupied significant Russian territory. In 1914
and 1915 the Germans thrust 150 to 350 miles into Russian territory, reaching near a line Riga-Minsk-Pinsk-Rovno-Czernowitz. When
in August 1914, two Russian armies invaded East Prussia with mar-
ginal superiority (18 Russian divisions versus 15 German divisions) to
help the French at the Battle of the Marne, the results were disastrous. Invading without adequate preparation, communication, or
supplies, the Russians were demolished at the battle of Tannenberg.
The Second Army disintegrated as its commander, General Sam-

sonov, committed suicide, over 60,000 Russians were taken prisoner, and 70,000 were killed or wounded.[3] Similarly, in the summer and fall of 1915 less than 40 German divisions, supported by several Austro-Hungarian armies, drove the numerically superior Russian army from Galicia, Poland, Lithuania, and most of Belorussia, land with 25 million citizens. This disaster cost the Russian army over 2 million soldiers killed and wounded and perhaps another 1.3 million soldiers taken captive by the enemy.[4]

Similarly, in World War II the German army, this time with three times the strength of World War I, struck deep into Russia. By the summer of 1942 they thrust near a line Leningrad-Moscow-Stalingrad, reaching 400 miles into Russia in the north, 600 miles in the center, and 900 miles in the south. This disaster cost the Russian army over three million casualties and nearly four million soldiers taken prisoner by the Germans. The land occupied by the Germans—primarily the Baltics, Ukraine, Belorussia, and Western Russia—held over 40 percent of the Soviet population (80 million people) and produced 33 percent of Soviet industrial production and 60 percent of Soviet iron and steel.[5]

And yet, despite all the failures suffered by Russia in the first 16 months of the two world wars, in both cases there were positive, significant achievements boding well for the future. In 1915 and 1941 Germany had tried to knock Russia out of the war—and had failed. In neither war did Germany come close to achieving its goals of capturing the requisite Russian territory for its "Mitteleuropa" dreams. In 1915 Germany fell short of capturing all the Baltics or penetrating purely Russian territory. The Russian army, while beaten, continued to fight on. In 1941, starting much further east, Germany dramatically failed to even come near to the line Archangel-Kazan-Kubyshev-Stalingrad-Astrakhan as envisioned in the 10-week, summer campaign of "Operation Barbarossa." Indeed, the Soviet Union successfully defended Moscow and Leningrad in the fall of 1941. By December, the Germans had suffered over 700,000 casualties.

Nor were the successes purely defensive in nature. In both wars the Russians scored localized but important successes during the first year. In August and September 1914, five Russian armies routed four Austro-Hungarian armies in Galicia, taking 100,000 prisoners. In December 1941 the Red Army's winter counteroffensive pushed the German army back as far as 100 to 150 miles from Moscow, the first major German defeat of the war. While neither victory was decisive, and the enemy was in a weakened state—for Austro-Hungary was inherently weak, and Germany's weakness was due to five months of arduous campaigning and long supply lines—the victories indicated that all was not necessarily lost for Russia.[6]

The war in the east acquired a special character in the two world conflicts. Winston Churchill's description of World War I would equally apply to World War II.

> The struggle upon the Eastern Front is incomparably the greatest war in history. In its scale, in its slaughter, in the exertion of combatants, in its military kaleidoscope, it far surpasses by magnitude and intensity all similar human episodes.[7]

In the two world wars similar factors helped produce early Russian defeats. The German enemy both times had the most powerful army in Europe. The top Russian military leaders (Yanushkevich and Grand Duke Nicholas in 1914, Voroshilov, Budenny, and Timoshenko in 1941) were ineffectual cavalrymen, captivated by the dogmas of past wars and uninterested in modern military theories. They lived and dreamed in the past. They inculcated and stressed a relentless offensive spirit, while mobile defense would have made more sense against the powerful German army. Both times war came to Russia while its armies were undergoing major modernization programs that would have the armies ready—but in 1917 and 1943.[8] Tsarist and Soviet generals both learned to trade space for time and use the harsh winter climate, thereby emulating Kutuzov in 1812.

In both wars there was a sharp misperception of Russian military capabilities at the onset of the war, at home and abroad. In 1914 the French relied on the Russian "steamroller" of seemingly inexhaustible manpower reserves to save them from the German onslaught. The Russian leaders, themselves, had visions of capturing Berlin, only 200 miles from their exposed Polish salient. In World War II both Germany and the Allied powers went to the other extreme, seriously undervaluing Russia. Looking at the Great Purges, failures in the Finnish campaign, and seeming peasant and nationality discontent, the Germans imagined they could destroy Russia in a 10-week, summer campaign. The British and French did not even bother to invite Russia to attend the Munich Conferences. For, as Albert Seaton has observed:

> The onset of the war saw Germany as the master of Europe at the peak of its fortunes, having established a New Economic Order which Hitler boasted was to last a thousand years. In comparison with Germany, the Soviet Union appeared a second rate power, so that Churchill, probably

counting on U.S. support, was to reckon in 1940 and 1941 that even if the USSR should enter the war on the side of Germany, Great Britain with its Commonwealth and Empire, would, in the final outcome, be victorious.[9]

And the Russians, no more realistic than they had been in World War I, dreamed in 1941 of a rapid march on Berlin.

After the enormous casualties, mass suffering, and serious defeats at the hands of the Germans in the early stages of the war, Russia faced very different fates in the last two years of World War I and World War II. In 1917 the Tsarist government and the successor Provisional Government were both overthrown, the Russian army disintegrated, and Russia was forced to leave the war through onerous peace terms at Brest-Litovsk in March 1918.

During 1917 the army's capabilities dwindled rapidly, despite a successful rearmament program and prospects for victory with America's entry into the war. The winter Mitau offensive near Riga failed to register any significant gains, despite a nearly two to one manpower advantage (184 versus 99 battalions) over the Germans. In April 1917 the Russian army, citing problems with discipline, transportation, food, and reserves, had to postpone a planned offensive promised the Allies at the Chantilly and Petrograd Conferences. As Commander in Chief Alekseyev told the war minister in March 1917, "The force of circumstances leads us to the conclusion that in the next four months our army must sit quietly, not undertaking decisive, broad scale operations."[10] When the new Commander in Chief, General Brusilov, launched an offensive against the failing Austro-Hungarian forces in late June, he scored initial successes, taking two towns and capturing 10,000 prisoners. Within a short time, though, the attack was halted by a German counterattack, and by August all Galicia was back in enemy hands. And in September a German offensive took Riga easily, with the loss of 15,000 Russians taken prisoner and 10,000 casualties.[11]

Hastened by unending Russian defeats, the revolution and a strong desire for peace, the army simply disintegrated. During 1917 alone 1.8 million men simply deserted the army.[12] Michael Florinsky has analyzed the process, especially in the wake of General Kornilov's failed coup attempt in August:

In the meantime the army was rapidly degenerating into an unruly mob which became the terror of the districts adjoining the front. It was accurately described in October 1917 as 'an immense, desperate and weary crowd of poorly clad and poorly fed men united by their common desire for peace and their disillusionment.' And we find its post mortem in the official reports of December 28, 1917 which estimated the fighting capacity of military units forming a Special Army *(Osobaya Armiya)* as 'equal to 0.' This was undoubtedly true of the Russian army as a whole.[13]

The final blow came in February 1918 when the Germans, tiring of peace negotiation talks, attacked the Russians in the north. Although the Russian army enjoyed a better than two to one numerical advantage over the attacking Germans and Austrians (173 Russian diversions versus 81.5 Central Powers divisions), it represented a "null quantity." Within five days the German army advanced 200 to 300 kilometers and rapidly seized Lithuania, Estonia, Dvinsk, Minsk, Rovno, Gomel, Pskov, Narva, and Revel.[14] So slight was Russian resistance that German General Hoffman noted, "This is the strangest war I've ever seen."[15] The supine Russian nation at Brest-Litovsk in March in March 1918 had to yield the Baltics, Ukraine, and part of Belorussia, while granting independence to Finland. The Germans seized almost one million square miles with nearly 50 million people, which represented one-third of the Russian population and 90 percent of the coal, 73 percent of the iron ore, and 54 percent of the railroads of Russia in 1914. The Red Army was to be demobilized while Russian ships had to stay in port or be disarmed by Germany.[16] Such were the costs of weakness.

And what was the performance of the Red Army? The last two years of World War II, 1944 and 1945, were years of glory purchased at a very high price. In the summer of 1943 the last major German offensive of the war in the east (in the battle of Kursk-Orel) had been decisively smashed. Early in 1944 the Red Army broke the siege of Leningrad after 800 days. By April, lead units of the Red Army were as close as 50 miles to the 1941 Russian-German frontier. By May the Soviet army had cleared the Germans from nearly all the Ukraine and was poised to push them from the rest of Belorussia and the Baltics and invade Poland. In August, after the Allied invasion at Normandy in June, the Red Army was at the gates of Warsaw and moving into Eastern Europe. By December 1944 the Red Army had freed all Soviet territory from the German invaders and liberated Hungary, Rumania, Bulgaria, and Yugoslavia.

And 1945 brought the ultimate victory, with the Red Army storming and taking Berlin and liberating Prague and Vienna. The Russian army, which in 1917 and 1918 had simply disintegrated and forced the new Soviet government to sue for a humiliatingly harsh, draconian peace from Germany, now in 1945 stood athwart Europe in Berlin, Prague, Vienna, Budapest, and Bucharest and received the German surrender. The Soviet army had become "a tremendously effective, competently and powerfully equipped army."[17]

This Russian turnabout in military capabilities was an important and rare event in twentieth-century military history. Chronically weak armies infrequently are transformed into powerful and capable forces. Most of the weak armies in World War I—Italy, Rumania, and Hungary (part of Austro-Hungary)—were also relatively ineffectual in World War II. Indeed, at Stalingrad in the winter of 1942 the Red Army started its offensive by attacking the armies from these countries. The Russian case stands out in stark contrast, even more so given the denigration of Nazi Germany, which felt it could conquer Russia in a lightning 10-week, summer campaign, and given that France and England failed to reach a military alliance with Russia and even excluded it from the 1938 Munich Conference.

SOVIET DISADVANTAGES IN WORLD WAR II

Furthermore, if anything, the Red Army in World War II faced a far greater German threat than the Tsarist army in World War I. While Imperial Germany only intermittently devoted its primary attention to the eastern front, Nazi Germany made the destruction of the Soviet Union its primary objective for almost four years. For three long years—from June 1941 to June 1944—there was no strong second front to draw off powerful German forces. And for two of those years, until the Allied landings in Italy in 1943, there was no second front at all in Europe.

The greatest loss was the defeat of France in 1940. In 1914 France had mobilized 3.8 million men (compared to the 3.9 million men mobilized for Germany), and by September 1917 had 4.4 million men in the army. Its overall military expenditures were roughly 80 percent of Germany's for the entire war. In World War I English and French troops had held down the bulk of Germany's army in the west. The destruction of the 5 million-man French army in May 1940 meant that this massive threat to Germany in the west had now been eliminated.[18]

Table 2 shows that in 1914 the Germans concentrated over 85 percent of their manpower in the west in a vain effort to implement the Schlieffen Plan against France. In the east a mere 15 German divisions (200,000 men), reinforced by 37.5 second-rate Austro-Hungarian divisions, awaited the expected Russian onslaught. Even in 1915, at the height of the German attempt to eliminate Russia

TABLE 2:   German Troop Disposition in World War I

Date	Number of German Divisions	
	Eastern Theater	Western Theater
8/14	15	86
12/14	36	81
6/15	66	83
9/15	65	85
2/16	47.5	111.5
7/16	42	108
1/17	64	129
3/17	78	147
8/17	84	148
12/17	74	194.5

SOURCES: Istoriya pervoi mirovoi voiny (Moscow: Nauka, 1975), vol. 2, pp. 252, 324; D. V. Verzhkovski and V. F. Lyakhov, Pervaya mirovaya voina (Moscow: Voenizdat, 1964), pp. 96, 86; I. I. Rostunov, Russkoi front pervoi mirovoi voiny (Moscow: Nauka, 1976), p. 385, and A. A. Strokov, Vooruzhennye sily i voennoe iskusstvo v pervoi mirovoi voinu (Moscow: Voenizdat, 1974), p. 445.
   Major General Sir Alfred Knox, With the Russian Army 1914-1917 (London: Hutchinson and Company, 1921), pp. 293, 551, 591; Norman Stone, The Eastern Front 1914-1917 (New York: Charles Scribner's Sons, 1975), p. 93; Marc Ferro, The Great War 1914-1918, trans. Nicole Stone (London: Routledge and Kegan Paul, 1973), pp. 129, 193; S. S. Oldenburg, Last Tsar: Nicholas II, His Reign and His Russia, trans. Leonid I. Mihalap and Patrick J. Rollins (Gulf Breeze, Florida: Academic International Press, 1978), v. 4, p. 151.

from the war, there were considerably more German divisions in the west (83 to 85) than in the east (65 to 66). And, after the failure of this attempt there were more than twice as many German divisions in the west (108 to 111.5) than in the east (42 to 47.5) in 1916. A similar pattern emerged in 1917. Overall, then, except for one campaign in 1915, German efforts were mainly directed toward the west, with 84 divisions in August 1917 representing its maximal and numerical height during the war.

World War II represented a very different story. Unlike in 1914, Germany in 1941 had destroyed France and conquered all of Western and Central Europe. Driven by Hitler's dream of smashing Bolshevik Russia, Germany in June 1941 could throw its full weight against Russia. Table 3 shows dramatically the impact of a lack of a strong second front.

From 1941 until 1944 the Germans concentrated 144 to 195 divisions on the eastern front, roughly a force three times their invading force of World War I. And in this effort they were reinforced by 45 to 60 allied divisions (mainly Austrian, Hungarian, Italian, and

TABLE 3: German Troop Disposition in World War II

Date	Number of German Divisions	
	Eastern Theater	Western/Other Theater
6/41	145	54
12/41	155	60
6/42	167	54
11/42	193	71
11/43	195	84
6/44	164	121
1/45	169	107
4/45	135	77

SOURCES: Istoriya vtoroi mirovoi voina 1939-1945 (Moscow: Voenizdat, 1982), vol. 12, p. 217; Sovetskaya voennaya entsiklopediya (Moscow: Voenizdat, 1978), vol. 2, p. 64, Istoriya vtoroi mirovoi voiny 1939-1945 (Moscow: Voenizdat, 1974, 1976), vol. 4, p. 272, vol. 6, p. 19.
     Albert Seaton, The Russo-German War 1941-1945 (New York: Praeger, 1970), pp. 62, 215, 270, 394, 458, 554.

Rumanian divisions), the same level of effort as in World War I. The efforts of Russia's allies, especially in the 1941-1943 period, did little to remove the military pressure on Russia, whose casualties were mounting into the many millions at this point. For the first 17 months of the Russo-German War, the Allies conducted only minor land fighting until November 1942, when Montgomery defeated Rommel at El Alamein. Even here the defeat of 12 Axis divisions (4 German, 8 Italian) entailed German losses of 13,000 men, at a time when Germany had roughly 3 million men on the eastern front.[19] The invasion of Italy did not prevent German troop strength from reaching a wartime high of 195 divisions in the east in November 1943. Only the Allied invasion of Normandy in June 1944 finally created a viable second front, which drained German forces from the east and led to rapid Allied victory within a year.[20]

A second major factor that made the plight of the Red Army in World War II considerably harder than the Tsarist army in World War I was the radical change in modern military warfare. While in World War I the defense, as epitomized by trench warfare, had gained supremacy over the offense, in World War II large-scale use of tanks and planes had restored primacy to the offense. Of course in the vast spaces of the east, trench warfare had not predominated in World War I. But mobility had been severely limited by minimal transportation, communication, and supply capabilities. The development of mobile warfare greatly aided the German army from 1939 to 1942, while it perfected blitzkrieg tactics to make the best use of its superior industrial capabilities and military leadership talents. By 1941 it was far more experienced in war than its counterpart of 1914. While the average soldier in 1914 used .3 horsepower and in 1918 1.5 to 2.0 horsepower, in World War II he used 20 horsepower. Similarly, the industrial base became even more important than in World War I. In World War II, yearly production by the main belligerents of airplanes was three times greater than in World War I (130,000 as compared with 45,000) and machine guns six times greater (1,660,000 as compared with 250,000).[21] Germany's advanced industrial base and conquest of Europe's industrial and natural resources by 1941 thereby acquired a far greater significance than Germany's lesser capabilities in World War I. While in 1937 Germany had 70 million people, by 1941 it ruled areas with 290 million people.

Third, military geography had changed for the worse for Russia between the wars. Tsarist Russia in 1914 had a strong foothold in Europe through its occupation of a 200-mile square Polish salient, which left the Russian army in peacetime only 200 miles from

Berlin. Offensively the salient posed a serious threat to eastern Germany and defensively it offered a major obstacie to any attack on Russia proper. By contrast, in 1941, having conquered Poland in 1939 (and traded Lithuania for Eastern Poland), German troops began their eastern campaign several hundred miles further east than in 1915.

Fourth, Tsarist Russia enjoyed a far better international position than Soviet Russia. A major partner in the Entente, Tsarist Russia in the years before 1914 had drawn up detailed war plans in close consultation with its allies, especially France. It could count on their close cooperation and aid in wartime. By contrast, Soviet Russia was diplomatically isolated in the interwar period and failed to conclude a strong military alliance with France and England. After the German invasion of June 1941, Stalin was uncertain and suspicious of Western aid and intentions. Relations among the Allied powers were strained and eventually paved the way for the onset of the cold war after the end of World War II.

As a result, Allied aid to Tsarist Russia surpassed that to Soviet Russia. Tsarist Russia was heavily dependent for its most basic needs on Allied aid during the war. During the war Tsarist Russia produced 3.3 million rifles, in addition to 4.7 million rifles it had on hand in 1914. It needed 17.7 million rifles and purchased abroad 2.5 million rifles, a number equal to 76 percent of its domestic production. It produced 28,000 machine guns at home and needed to purchase abroad 42,400 machine guns, or 150 percent of its domestic production. Tsarist Russia was not even self-sufficient in bullets, importing 983 million bullets, a figure equal to 25 percent of its domestic production. In more advanced weaponry, it lagged even further behind, ordering 8,930 planes and motors abroad, compared to a domestic war production figure of 4,898.[22] Thus, the Tsarist army was heavily dependent on Allied war supplies for its very existence. As Major General Alfred Knox, British military attache to Russia, wrote about the German occupation of Poland in 1915:

> [Germany] could not force Russia to her knees, and that if the Allies in the West were able to provide for its re-armament, the Russian army would once more take the offensive in spring, 1916. The main problem of the next six to eight months seemed to be the rearmament of Russia.[23]

By sharp contrast, the Red Army in World War II was only marginally dependent on Allied aid. The very sinews of infantry fighting—bullets, machine guns, and rifles—did not figure at all significantly in British and American aid to Soviet Russia during World War II. In more advanced weaponry, Allied aid played a role, but not a decisive one. Ten thousand Western tanks, 18,700 Western planes, and 9,600 Western artillery pieces constituted respectively 10 percent, 12 percent, and 2 percent of Russian war production—and their quality was not superior to Russian designs.[24] Colonel Albert Seaton, hardly a friendly observer of the Red Army, has commented, "the number of aircraft and tanks shipped to the Soviet Union, although of undoubted benefit, were probably too small to be of decisive importance. The same can be said for consignments of guns and small arms."[25] Only in the area of motor vehicles, airplane fuel, clothing, and footwear did the Allies make a significant contribution. Overall, then, Allied aid was a far more important contribution to the Tsarist war effort than the Soviet war effort.

Finally, Tsarist Russia in World War I could focus all its attention on the German and Austro-Hungarian enemies on the European front and the very weak Turkish enemy in the south. By contrast, Soviet Russia during World War II had a neutrality pact with a very dangerous and hostile Japan. From 1941 to 1945 Japan kept close to a million soldiers in Manchuria on the Russian border. The Russians in response raised their forces from 300,000 men in 1941 to 800,000 men in 1945. In 1945 they attacked and destroyed Japanese forces in Manchuria.[26]

Overall, then, Soviet Russia in World War II faced a far more dangerous and deadly Germany than Tsarist Russia had faced in World War I.

CHAPTER 5
Explanations

All of the factors analyzed in Chapter 4 reinforce the central question—if the Tsarist army was weak and ultimately ineffective in World War I and the Red Army suffered additional handicaps not encumbering the Tsarist army (lack of second front, modern military warfare, military geography, and foreign relations), then how did the Red Army manage to achieve such monumental victories in World War II? How did the Red Army, so maligned as a second-rate power after the Great Purges and Finnish campaign by both its friends (France and England) and enemies (Germany and Italy) before 1941, emerge as a superpower occupying all of Eastern Europe and part of Germany by the end of World War II?

In order to answer these questions, it is important to review the traditional scholarly assessments of Russia's role in World War II. There has been a strong tendency in Western scholarly literature to downplay the entire subject. Basil Liddell-Hart and J.F.C. Fuller devote less than 20 percent of their standard histories of World War II to the eastern front.[1] The standard explanatory variables usually cited for Russia's survival and victory—climate, geography, Allied aid, Russian nationalism, and German barbarism and mistakes—all have one thing in common: an ignoring of the positive impact of the Russian Revolution on Soviet society in the 25 years since the abdication of Tsar Nicholas II. I shall begin by analyzing these variables to see to what extent they can help explain the great improvement in Soviet military performance over Tsarist military performance.

Weather and geography, in the form of harsh climate, poor roads, and enormous spaces, are frequently cited as causes of Germany's ultimate defeat in the war, especially in 1941, and Russia's final victory. Adam Ulam has spoken of "Russia's great weapon, space" while Basil Liddell-Hart concluded that "space spelt first his [Hitler's] frustration and then his defeat."[2] As for weather, Colonel Albert Seaton has declared that "the part played by the Red Army in 1941 in halting the enemy advance has been exaggerated by Soviet historians. Success was due mainly to geography and climate."[3] And Major General J.F.C. Fuller, stressing that it was "the bogging of the transport behind the German front which saved Moscow," concluded that "the Russians had been dealt a staggering blow and but for the unexpected early winter would probably have lost Moscow. On December 6, 1941, the chances of victory or defeat were odds even."[4]

This explanation of natural causes has limited historical validity, especially in the twentieth century. The Tsarist army in World War I had the same beneficial value of natural causes as the Red Army in World War II, with the added value of less modern German capabilities to overcome. Both armies had to overcome the same natural obstacles in the course of World War II. From 1942 to 1945 the Red Army also had to traverse huge distances, forge broad rivers, and fight in bad weather. As James Lucas has cogently observed:

> It must not be thought that only Germans suffered during winter. The abnormally low temperatures affected both sides alike for it should not be believed that all Red Army soldiers had equal resistance to the cold or that each man was at ease in such conditions. It was training, discipline and upbringing that held Soviet units in the most appalling conditions of climate but German intelligence reports speak of many formations upon whom winter left its mark in a breakdown in military cohesion and a lessening in unit efficiency.[5]

And, similarly, Russian preparedness and German unpreparedness for the climatic and terrain conditions speak well for the Red Army.

Furthermore, the harsh winter climate and difficult terrain posed no serious obstacle to the Red Army, which launched major offensives during each of the four long winters on the eastern front during World War II. In the winter of 1941/42, the Red Army counterattacked the Germans on several fronts. In deep snow and mud the Red Army in December 1941 pushed the Germans as far as 150 miles back from Moscow. In January 1942 Meretskov began his Leningrad offensive in swamps and forests in waist-deep snow. Cavalry and sleds aided Russian progress. In bitter cold in November 1942, "Operation Uranus" was launched with great salvos of Katyushas. In January 1943 Rokossovsky's offensive seized the Stalingrad airfield in bitter wind and snow storms with a high temperature of minus 30 degrees Celsius. On February 1 1943, Stalingrad fell. In January 1943 fighting in minus 25 degrees Celsius, the Red Army took Voronezh, and Kharkov fell in February. Thanks to Soviet winter offensives the German Sixth Army was destroyed and the Caucasus liberated.[6]

A similar pattern emerged the next two winters. Despite the weather and strong defenses, Govorov in January 1944 smashed the German army, ended the siege of Leningrad, and took Novgorod. A December offensive seized Zhitomir, Berdichev, and Rovno and by February reached 100 miles beyond the Russian frontier. In the south, Konev in January launched his offensive in deep snow and even blizzards with minus 20 degrees Celsius and won the Dnieper battle and Ukraine west of the Dnieper, reaching Odessa. Overall, in the winter of 1943/44 Russian armies in three months recaptured 200,000 square kilometers of territory. And in the last winter of the war, in January 1945, a massive Russian offensive began in heavy snow, fog, and cold. In the first week the Red Army advanced 100 miles, soon taking Warsaw, East Prussia and Upper Silesia, laying the groundwork for the final spring attack on Berlin. Thus, the Red Army repeatedly launched major, successful offensives against often entrenched, well-prepared German defenses at the height of extremely difficult Russian winters.[7]

Indeed, given the Soviet penchant for offensives, one could even argue ironically that the weather actually helped the Germans. In the Moscow counteroffensive of December 1941, a partial thaw turned the roads to mud, bogging down the Russians and allowing the Germans time to build defense lines. The spring thaw with more mud finally stopped the Red Army by April 1942. In January 1943, Kleist's German army avoided encirclement in the Caucasus salient with a significant assist from the weather, for "Luckily for the Germans the desolate snow-covered country had limited even Russia's capacity to push beyond their distant railheads fast enough and in force enough to close the trap. But its jaws had only been held open by a narrow margin."[8] The deep snows at Millerovo helped save the Germans on the Lower Don and Caucasus. By January 1944 Seaton tells us, "Hitler was still relying on the mud and Soviet exhaustion to give him some respite."[9] In February 1945 the Russian offensive was hurt by a thaw that turned roads into a quagmire and a frozen Oder river into a significant obstacle.

It is thereby hard to see weather and natural difficulties as decisive factors in the ultimate Russian victory. That the spring and fall mud, the horrid heat of summer, and cold and deep snow of winter hindered operations on both sides is clear. At times, too, the freezing of winter roads could facilitate travel and advances on both sides. Whatever Soviet advantage garnered by better preparation the first winter was vitiated by the next three winters. The Germans, already used to cold winters and hot summers at home, adapted their army accordingly, especially in well-entrenched, defensive positions that were reinforced by the climatic problems. Both sides suffered equally.[10]

Next, we turn to the question of Allied aid to Russia in wartime. Authors such as Basil Liddel-Hart and Adam Ulam have stressed the great importance of such aid to Russia. Depicting "huge" war shipments, Ulam had declared them "a vital factor in Red Army victories from the winter of 1942-3 until the end of the war."[11] Ernest Dupuy has similarly argued that the Stalingrad campaign "could not possibly also have been mounted had it not been for equipment poured into the USSR by its Anglo-Saxon Allies."[12] But we have already seen that Allied aid cannot explain the differences in Russian performance in the two wars since Allied aid to the Tsarist army in World War I was far more significant than Allied aid to the Red Army in World War II. Too, as we have seen, Allied aid was not a significant element in Russia's supply of modern war material— cannons, rifles, machine guns, tanks, and planes. Only in areas such as footwear, airplane fuel, and trucks did the Allies make an important contribution.

It should be stressed that the Red Army was far more able to make use of Western equipment than the Tsarist army. Only 11 percent of total Allied aid (1.7 million of 15 million tons) arrived in 1941 and 1942. The Red Army, with its own capacity to produce massive quantities of modern military material, was able to rapidly integrate Western equipment into the army. The Allied trucks, locomotives, and railway cars were well used by the Red Army High Command to shuttle its reserve of 60 divisions from front to front. An efficient transportation system and port unloading system allowed significant cargos to reach the front from distant Vladivostok (8.2 million tons), Murmansk and Archangel (4.0 million tons), and Iran (4.2 million tons).[13]

By contrast, the Tsarist army had grave difficulties in using Allied aid. Its railway system was chaotic, and its ports often barely usable. Even though a German blockade of land routes to Russia in case of war was eminently predictable, Russia had no link to an ice free north port available in 1914. It continually postponed building a 700-mile rail link to Murmansk before 1914, and completed such a link only at the end of November 1916, even then with a small transit capacity. The direct link between Archangel and the center was finished only in 1916—and even then the rail link was so poor that other transportation had to be used. Archangel was the only key nearby military port, yet Duma leader Rodzianko has written "to it almost no attention was paid."[14] And the only other port, Vladivostok, was 8,000 kilometers from the center! Conditions at the two ports were so archaic and corrupt that "at both places enormous masses of materiel were piled up without hope of any early transport, so that they were even sinking into the ground."[15]

A third common explanation of Soviet victories is to attribute them to the errors made by Germany in occupation and military policies. Adam Ulam has emphasized that had the Germans pursued a more humane occupation "in the name of the true spirit of the Revolution" and declared the Ukraine, Belorussia, and Baltics independent, then "the effect of their occupation would become a danger to the Soviet system even after the invasion was chased back."[16] German Field Marshal Erich von Manstein has blamed Hitler for his lack of military experience, ignorance of Russia, and obstinate rigid defense policy.[17] Basil Liddell-Hart has stressed the role of German mistakes, such as the two-month pause in front of Moscow in 1941, splitting objectives between Caucasus and Stalingrad in 1942, and forbidding withdrawals to shorten the front.[18]

There is a lack of realism in these arguments. Even the more moderate generals of Imperial Germany in World War I had created puppet states in the humilitating treaty of Brest-Litovsk on Russia in March 1918. How could the brutal fascists, who viewed Slavs as *unterrmenschen* and Jews and gypsies as fit only for the massive concentration camps already created by 1941, possibly have instituted a liberal, "humane" occupation policy? For Germany's major policies in the east—colonization, economic exploitation, and extermination—flowed inexorably from Nazi ideology. As Alexander Dallin argued in his superb study of Russia under German rule, there existed

> the long nurtured preconceptions and irrational stereotypes of Russia and Bolshevism, which led the Nazi leaders to create a false image of the Soviet Union. In harmony with the basic racism, messianism and immorality of National Socialism, the executors of the Fuhrer's will relegated the 'Easterner,' the Slav, and particularly the Russian, to a position of predestined, inescapable inferiority. . . . In essence, the objectives of the invasion were the liquidation of Bolshevism; the destruction of the U.S.S.R. as a state; and the acquisition of a vast new area for colonial exploitation and settlement.[19]

Furthermore, however revolting, German occupation policies in

World War II cannot be alloted more than a minor role in the ultimate Soviet victory. This unpalatable truth arises from three factors. First, as Charles Tilly has demonstrated, harsh repression generally cows a population, rather than leading it to revolt, at least in the short-run.[20] This was certainly true in the one-third of the Soviet population that came under German rule in 1941 and 1942. Repression, combined with anti-Soviet attitudes, kept the partisans a weak and scattered force until 1943. Secondly, the rise of the partisan movements occurred in a number of other countries, including some that had not experienced the mass repression and genocide practiced by the Germans in Russia. The strength of the French Resistance under the (comparatively) far milder Vichy regime indicates that many other factors contributed to its successes. These included imminent expectation of external military deliverance from the Nazis, Allied propaganda, and Allied aid in strengthening the resistance movement.

Despite the many heroic deeds of the partisans, it is important not to exaggerate their importance and be attracted by the romantic "myth of the guerrilla." Even in Maoist thinking, victory can only be achieved by transformation of such units into regular, mainline army units. In 1943 and 1944 several hundred thousand Soviet guerrillas could harrass German units and disrupt supply lines. But, operating in scattered units without planes, tanks, or heavy artillery on the fringes of the battle zone, the partisans could not be a serious force compared to the vastly larger Red Army. Nor could they drive regular German troops out of any significant outpost during the war. Thus, while German occupation policies did in the long run contribute to Soviet victory by swelling partisan ranks and stiffening the resolve of the Red Army to fight, they cannot be given a decisive role, and especially not in 1941 and 1942.

If we turn to the more elusive subject of military errors, a similar pattern presents itself. Given the inevitable limitations on the military decision-making process, serious errors almost invariably are made by armies at war. And, in retrospect, the German army in World War II made its share of errors—the diversion of forces to the south in 1941, the attack at Stalingrad in 1942, and the insistence on rigid defense lines in the latter stages of the war. But in order to be a significant factor accounting for Russian failures in World War I and Russian successes in World War II, it would be necessary to demonstrate that German errors in World War II were of far greater scope than in World War I. For Germany made a series of errors in World War I—from weakening the right arm of the Schlieffen Plan in

1914 to failure to utilize tanks in 1917—that easily equalled its errors of World War II.

One can easily argue the reverse position, that the military performance of the German army was *better,* not worse, in World War II than World War I. In World War II Germany decisively defeated most major European powers, including France, while in World War I it could not even capture Paris. In World War II the German army pioneered the blitzkrieg, while in World War I it failed to use such new inventions as the tank. Furthermore, German victories on the eastern front in 1941 and 1942 were far more spectacular than in 1915 and 1916. Military execution was far better in World War II since all major commanders were sent to the eastern front, while in World War I most German commanders never did a tour of duty on this secondary front.

A final reason commonly adduced is that of Russian nationalism. Adam Ulam, for one, has alluded to this as an important factor in the final Soviet victory.[21] And there is no doubt that Russian nationalism played a role in strengthening support for the regime. However, resurrected traditional Russian nationalism could not have provided the basis for victory in World War II, for it could not provide the basis for victory even in World War I with that arch-Russian chauvinist, Tsar Nicholas II, in power. Compare these two Western analyses of the state of Russian patriotism in the two wars:

World War I
[There was an] absence of real self-sacrificing patriotism in the masses of the population. . . . The bulk of them went willingly to war in the first instance chiefly because they had little idea what was meant. They lacked intelligent knowledge of objects they were fighting for. . . .

World War II
The thought that this was their war was, in the main, as strong among civilians as among soldiers. . . . the spirit of genuine patriotic devotion and self-sacrifice shown by the Russian people during those four years has few parallels in human history, and the story of the siege of Leningrad is altogether unique.[22]

Indeed traditional Russian chauvinism had ultimately a limited appeal, for the tsar by 1914 had alienated the majority of society from his regime. All attempts at popular support were ruthlessly suppressed. Great Russian nationalism, with its attempts at forcible Russification of almost half the population, strongly alienated Ukrainians, Belorussians, Poles, Transcaucasians, Asians, Jews, and other repressed minorities. Even the Russian half of the population was not easily mobilized under this banner. The peasant majority, legally and socially segregated from the ruling educated minority and frustrated in land hunger, was alienated from society. The working class, toiling long hours in oppressive factory conditions for little pay and denied the legal right to organize unions, was deeply estranged from the regime. Much of the intelligentsia was alienated from the oppressive Tsarist regime and traumatized by the gulf between the two Russias. Material poverty, grave fissures in the social structure, lack of sense of citizenship and political community, desire for self-determination, and minimal political consciousness undermined the capacity of traditional Russian nationalism to mobilize the population.[23]

If in World War I traditional Russian nationalism could not propel Russia to victory, then in World War II it was equally unlikely to do so. Russian nationalism could be effective only to the extent that workers, peasants, and intelligentsia elements had come to identify with the new Soviet regime. In this sense the October Revolution and Stalinist social transformation of the 1930s effectively infused traditional nationalism with a new content.

Traditional Russian nationalism alienated the non-Russian half of the population whose support was so vital to the war effort. This was especially true given the support shown by Ukrainians for the Nazi occupiers in 1941 and the massive population losses early in the war that enhanced the importance of Asians and Transcaucasians in the war effort. By June 1942, Asians and Transcaucasians, normally 8.9 percent of the population, formed 22 percent of the Red Army in general and perhaps 40 percent of the units near Stalingrad.[24] Thus, to win the war the Soviet government had to promote a broad Soviet patriotism that would motivate non-Russians as well as Russians.

ALTERNATIVE EXPLANATION

All of these traditional variables, taken singly or together, had some impact but not a decisive one on the Russian army. If these traditional explanatory variables cannot fundamentally explain the sharp differences in performance between the Tsarist army and Red Army in the two world wars, then what factors can explain these changes? I suggest that the fundamental explanation lies in the nature of the Russian Revolution. This revolution unfolded in stages, first in the February and October Revolutions of 1917 and then in Stalin's "third revolution" of the 1930s. The revolution from below of 1917 and the ensuing civil war (1918-1920) did ensconce the Bolsheviks in power and rout Russia's foreign and domestic enemies. But by 1921 the Bolshevik control on power was tenuous, and Lenin called for a retreat from the radical policies of war communism to the concessions of the New Economic Program. Robert Tucker has well analyzed the situation during the 1920s.

> The NEP Russia that emerged from the Bolshevik Revolution of 1917-21 could be described as a society with two uneasily coexisting cultures. There was an officially dominant Soviet culture comprising the Revolution's myriad innovations in ideology, government structure, political procedures, economic organization, legal order, education, the intellectual pursuits, values, art, daily life, and ritual. Side by side with it was a scarcely sovietized Russian culture that lived on from the pre-1917 past as well as in the small-scale rural and urban private enterprise that flourished under the NEP. It was a Russia of churches, the village mir, the patriarchal peasant family, old values, old pastimes, old outlooks along with widespread illiteracy, muddy roads and all that.[25]

During the 1930s Stalin's "revolution from above" smashed the second Russia while transforming urban Russia. Through massive programs of industrialization, modernization, urbanization, and collectivization, Stalin launched a vast developmental and political revolution. In only a decade Russia was transformed from a relatively backward, rural, and semiliterate state lagging far behind Europe to a significantly literate, modernized, and industrial state ranking among Europe's major economic powers. And in this process the "revolution from above" enjoyed strong mass support from large elements of the population, who applauded the revolutionary attempt to liberate the social, economic, and military capacities of Russia to utilize its vast human and natural resources.

This is not to ignore the very high human and economic costs entailed in the Stalinist method of social transformation. Forced collectivization of agriculture, labor camps, and the Great Purges claimed a large number of innocent victims in the dubious cause of social engineering. The incredible pace of Stalinist industrialization undoubtedly engendered significant waste of economic resources. During the 1930s Stalinism unquestionably displayed significant, sharply negative dysfunctional elements. Overall, though, in a world in which social and economic transformation is exceedingly rare and alternative strategies of development have also not been without major costs (as nineteenth-century English industrialization), the truly impressive elements are the major accomplishments of Stalinism in the 1930s.

Like other revolutionary processes the Stalinist "revolution from above" occurred in stages, incorporated traditional elements, and ended in a relatively conservative order. The 1930s in Russia can be considered to have three phases: the initial social upheaval (1929-1933), the interregnum (1934-1935), and the Great Purges (1936-1939). Over time many conservative elements, including nationalism, statism, traditional social and educational norms, cult of personality and inegalitarianism, became integrated into the new order. And this revolutionary attempt to remold Soviet society ended in the petrification of the system in the postwar era.

The next several chapters will focus on the impact and achievements of the revolutionary decade of the 1930s.

CHAPTER 6

Two Armies at War

In order to illustrate the connection of revolution and enhanced military capability proposed in Chapter 5, a systematic comparison must be made of the capabilities of Soviet Russia in World War II with Tsarist Russia in World War I, using Germany as a reference point. I will comparatively examine the military industrial base, capabilities of the army and government leadership, national infrastructure, degree of mobilized popular support, and the overall mobilization capacity of the society. By stressing the economic aspects of war and the capabilities of the army leadership, the superiority of the Soviet system in every phase can be clearly demonstrated, even taking the passage of time into account.

LEVEL OF ECONOMIC DEVELOPMENT

In modern warfare the economic potential of a country, especially its industrial base, is critical for protracted struggles such as the two world wars. Given Russia's geographical isolation in the two wars, a strong economic base was essential for war. During the quarter century before 1914, Russia, prompted especially by Count Sergei Witte, embarked on rapid state-guided industrialization. However, despite significant progress and a larger population, Russia failed to come close to the levels of development of the advanced industrial powers. Although Russian GNP grew at 2.5 percent per year from 1860 to 1913, German GNP grew at 2.9 percent from 1870 to 1913, the United States GNP at 4.3 percent from 1870 to 1913, and Japanese GNP at 4.8 percent from 1878 to 1913. As a result by 1914,

Russia accounted for a meager 2.6 percent of world industrial production—compared to 6.6 percent for France, 12.1 percent for
England, 15.3 percent for Germany, and 38.2 percent for the United
States. And matters were even worse on a per capita basis in 1913,
when the U.S. and Germany exceeded Russia in GNP per capita by
a phenomenal 7.5 to 8 to 1.[1]

Table 4 shows just how far Tsarist Russia still lagged behind
Imperial Germany, despite the presence of vast natural resources and
a population far more than twice its principal enemy. The numbers
made grim reading for Tsarist military planners. In such sinews of
war as iron, steel, and iron ore, Germany outproduced Russia in
1913 by 3 to 3.6 to 1, and in coal the proportion reached 7.7 to 1
(alleviated only by great Russian superiority in oil production).
And in perhaps the most important figure for war production—
total industrial machinery value—Germany exceeded Russia by the
awesome ratio of 5.9 to 1.

Weakness pervaded the Russian economy in every area. Not only
was industrial capacity limited, but in 1912, 57 percent of Russian

TABLE 4:   Economic Production in Germany and Russia in 1913

Product	Germany	Russia	German Advantage
	(in millions of tons)		
Coal	277.0	36.0	7.7:1
Machinery	1,296.0[a]	220.0	5.9:1
Iron	16.8	4.6	3.6:1
Steel	15.7	4.9	3.2:1
Iron Ore	28.6	9.2	3.2:1
Oil	.1	9.2	1:92.0

SOURCES: Istoriya pervoi mirovoi voiny (Moscow: Nauka, 1975), vol. 2,
pp. 33, 61; D. V. Verzhkhovski and V. F. Lyakhov, Pervaya mirovaya voina
(Moscow: Voenizdat, 1964), p. 18.

[a]Value of machinery in millions of gold rubles.

TABLE 5:   Economic Production in Germany and Russia in 1939

Product	Germany	Russia	German Advantage
	(in millions of tons)		
Coal	423.6	146.2	2.9:1
Steel	22.3	17.6	1.4:1
Electricity[a]	61.4	43.2	1.4:1
Iron	18.3	14.5	1.3:1
Oil	1.1	31.1	1:28.3

SOURCES: Istoriya vtoroi mirovoi voiny 1939-1945 (Moscow: Voenizdat, 1982), vol. 12, pp. 184, 296, v. 12, p. 161; Istoriya velikoi otechestvennoi voiny Sovetskogo Soyuza 1941-1945 (Moscow: Voenizdat, 1960), vol. 6, p. 43.

[a]Value of electricity in billion of kilowatts.

industrial machinery was imported. The railroad network was so limited that in 1914 Germany had 12 times more railroad track per capita than Russia in European Russia and Poland. Agriculture was so backward that Germany used 8 times more mechanical power per farm (and the United States 17 times more) than Russia. Literacy was so limited that the 1910 census found that only 31.7 percent of all males and a miniscule 8.6 percent of all females were literate. Alec Nove has observed:

> Russia was thus the least developed European power but a European power nonetheless. She was capable of overwhelming and competing economically with partly developed European states such as Austria-Hungary. But her development was exceedingly uneven both industrially and geographically.[2]

By contrast, after a decade of massive programs of modernization and industrialization in the 1930s, the Soviet Union had greatly closed the economic gap that had yawned between Russia and Germany in 1913. By the end of the 1930s, Russia was second in the world in tractor and oil production, third in aluminum and steel production, and fourth in coal and cement production.[3] Table 5 shows the extent to which Russia had caught up with Germany by 1939.

While Germany had marginally improved its production in key areas, the Soviet Union had made major strides since 1913. It had more than tripled its steel, iron, and oil production and quadrupled its coal production. Electricity production went up over 20 times. Overall, industrial production more than quintupled, and railroad freight traffic had greatly expanded. By 1940 literacy was almost universal; the number of university graduates had quintupled. Between 1928 and 1937 Russian GNP almost doubled.[4]

A second interesting comparison is the state of military preparedness of Russia in 1914 and 1941. Tsarist Russia treated war preparation with remarkable casualness. General Yuli Danilov has written:

> Following the war of 1904-1905 Russia had to start to create her armed forces almost anew. The work progressed slowly, not only because it was so vast, but also because appropriations for the army in the years following the war were entirely inadequate . . . from 1905 to 1910 or perhaps even a longer period . . . there was a complete lack of money wherewith to meet our military needs.[5]

The reforms following the smashing defeat by the Japanese in the 1904-1905 war soon petered out, and the lessons of the war were ignored. Most striking was the lack of stress on close integration with Russia's allies. In 1913 the Russian War Office actually argued over whether to place a large order with the French Creusot factory or German Krupp works. Before 1914 Russia had trained 25 percent of its available manpower for war, compared to 52 percent in Germany and 80 percent in France. No wonder General Vasili Gourko could write that "there can be no comparison with the Central Powers and the Allies, and especially between Germany and Russia" with regard to prewar planning and production.[6]

At the start of the war there were serious deficiencies in production of rifles and machine guns. In 1913 and 1914 three Russian arms factories produced 60,000 to 65,000 rifles per year, compared to a wartime need of several million rifles a year. And these were cumbersome 1891 Mosin-Nagan rifles weighing over 10 pounds. In August 1914 the army had a shortage of 300 million rifle bullets, equal to six months production of its factories. In 1914 Russia had 60 batteries of heavy guns, compared to 381 for Germany. Furthermore, Russian artillery was provided with 800 shells per gun, compared to a German standard of 2,000 to 3,000. The air force in 1914, lacking any dirigibles and possessing only 320 planes and two engine factories, would not be able to even challenge German command of the skies until July 1917. Russian transport, relying primarily on horses, was extremely primitive. Tsarist military industry was a neglected area, and overall quality of most weapons was low. Perhaps, even more importantly, Russian factories were not prepared to shift to war production. As one author put it, "the crime of the economy in Russia was greater owing to the small output of Russian factories, which could not be depended on in an emergency to provide large quantities of shells rapidly."[7]

By sharp contrast, the Red Army in 1941 was well equipped qualitatively and quantitatively, and Soviet industry was well prepared to switch to a war base. As late as 1929 Russia was ill prepared for war, with no native tank or ship production, inadequate quantities of artillery and ammunition, and most key weapons of prerevolutionary and foreign origins. However, the massive five-year plans of industrialization and modernization changed all this. Russia responded to Stalin's call of 1931.

> Do you want our Socialist fatherland to be beaten and lose its independence? If you do not want this, you must put an end to its backwardness in the shortest possible time and develop genuine Bolshevik tempo in building up its Socialist system of economy. There is no other way. That is why Lenin said during the October Revolution: 'Either perish, or overtake and outstrip advanced capitalist countries.' We are fifty or hundred years behind advanced countries. We must make good this distance in ten years. Either we do it or they crush us.[8]

By 1938 to 1940 Russia was annually producing 8,800 planes, 2,670 tanks, 15,000 artillery pieces, 1.4 million rifles, and 113,700 machine guns. This represented a tenfold increase in planes, eightfold increase in artillery pieces, and almost fourfold increase in tanks over 1930-31. Quality was competitive with the war materiel of likely enemies, as seen by the production of T-34 and KV-1 tanks at 20 factories and numerous airplanes by 30 design bureaus led by men such as Ilyushin, Yakovlev, Mikoyan, and Gurevich. The Soviet military developed the highly effective Katyusha rocket. The result was that "by 1940 the Soviet Union had a strong defence industry and military-technical base, and had gone a long way towards attaining the goal of strategic self-sufficiency."[9] The Soviet Union spent a decade carefully preparing for war, while Tsarist Russia casually misused the time before World War I.[10]

WAR PRODUCTION

Now let us turn to an analysis of Russian war production in the two world wars. Not surprisingly, the Soviet war economy had made enormous strides over the Tsarist war economy and closed the great gap that existed in World War I between Russia and Germany.

The appalling state of the Tsarist war economy, despite maximal effort, is apparent in table 6. Germany produced more than twice as many rifles, over five times as many cannons, ten times as many machine guns, and over thirteen times as many planes as Russia in World War I. It was especially ominous for Russia that the more sophisticated the weapon, the greater the gap between German and Russian production.

The first year of World War I was especially disastrous for Tsarist Russia for it proceeded with little conscious planning. G. I. Shigalin has observed:

> The military reconstruction of civilian industry in Russia began signifi-
> cantly later than in Germany or France. Until spring 1915 the Tsarist
> government did not take serious measures to attract private industry to
> production of war materials. . . . Almost the entire first year of the war

TABLE 6:   War Production in Germany and Russia in World War I (1914-1917)

Weapons	Germany	Russia	German Advantage
	(in thousands)		
Airplanes	47.3	3.5	13.5:1
Machine Guns	280.0	28.0	10.0:1
Artillery Pieces	64.0	11.7	5.5:1
Artillery Shells	306.0	67.0	4.6:1
Rifles	8,547.0	3,300.0	2.6:1
Tanks	.1	0.0	
Bullets	8.2	13.5	1:1.7

SOURCES: Sovetskaya voennaya entsiklopediya (Moscow: Voenizdat, 1978), vol. 6, p. 275.

TABLE 7:   Military Needs and Production in Russian in January 1915
           (monthly)

Weapon	Needed	Produced
Rifles	200,000	30,000-32,000
Machine Guns	2,000	216
Artillery Pieces	400	115-120
Artillery Shells	1,500,000	403,000
Bullets	200,000,000	50,000,000

SOURCE: Istoriya pervoi mirovoi voiny (Moscow: Nauka, 1975), vol. 2,
p. 9.

> could be characterized as a period of partial, isolated and in general
> tardy utilization of industry for war production. . . . The military
> reconstruction of Russian industry was carried out without any plan,
> comparatively slowly and required colossal expenditure of means, fre-
> quently not corresponding to results.[11]

No general plan for supply of the army existed within the government. The majority of skilled workmen were taken into the army,
disrupting industrial production.

Military production was quite inadequate. Rifle production was
so poor that in 1915 only part of the army was armed, with others
waiting for casualties to get arms. Early in 1915 the whole active
Russian army had 650,000 rifles. In January 1915 the crisis reached
its height as seen in table 7. Overall, only 15 to 30 percent of military needs were met, with a serious impact on military operations.
The ammunition shortages were so bad that the tsar wrote to the
tsarina on July 7, 1915, "Again that cursed question of artillery and
rifle ammunition—it stands in the way of energetic advance."[12]
The shell crisis was so bad that in September 1914 the grand duke
reported it held up operations, and the problem continued until
1916. In August 1914 Russia produced 35,000 shells a month but
expended 45,000 shells a day.[13]

During 1915 and 1916 Tsarist Russia made a mammoth concerted effort to overcome these difficulties. In three years of war
the government spent 167 percent of the national income on the
war, more than England (130 percent) or France (105 percent). By
1917, 76 percent of all industrial workers were working for military
industry, compared to 58 percent in Germany and 46 percent in

England. As a result, by 1917 Russian output of war goods was now more satisfactory.[14]

However improved Russian war industry, it still lagged far behind need and German capabilities. Even in 1917, 35 percent of rifles needed and a staggering 88 percent of machine guns needed were not supplied the army. Artillery, the proverbial "god" of the Russian army, was still so short that in 1917 Germany had 6,819 heavy pieces to 1,430 for Russia. At the same time, Russia had 700 (largely imported) planes, Germany 2,730. Similarly, the army's General Headquarters in 1917 wanted 1,052 antiaircraft guns and got less than 50, wanted 4,476 heavy artillery pieces and received less than 300.[15]

Under the enormous strain of the war, government and industry simply disintegrated. Russian GNP declined twice as fast as other countries, and its currency depreciated 40 percent from 1913 to 1918. So bad were matters that by February 1917, factories had but one to two days of raw material and fuel on hand.[16] Under the strain the government collapsed in the February Revolution to the nearly universal joy of the Russian people.

Table 8 shows that the Soviet war economy, unlike the Tsarist war economy, was able to compete with the major Western powers and surpass them in vital areas of military production, even in the most advanced technological areas. This was especially impressive

TABLE 8:   War Production in Germany and Russia in World War II, July 1941–April 1945

Weapons	Germany	Russia	Russian Advantage
	(thousands)		
Mortars	68.9	350.3	5.1:1
Tanks	41.5	92.6	2.2:1
Rifles	7,845.7	11,820.5	1.6:1
Machine Guns	1,048.5	1,437.9	1.4:1
Airplanes	76.2	102.6	1.4:1

SOURCE: Istoriya vtoroi mirovoi voiny 1939–1945 (Moscow: Voenizdat, 1982), vol. 12, p. 168.

given the German occupation of Belorussia, the Ukraine, the Baltics, and Western Russia from June 1941 until 1943, the subsequent loss of 30 percent of Russian GNP, the loss of 80 million citizens and the ultimate death of 20 million Russians. Table 8 shows a clear superiority for Soviet arms production in every category. Russia produced more than five times as many mortars, over twice as many tanks, and 40 to 60 percent more rifles, machine guns, cannons, and airplanes than Germany during their long struggle. This was a monumental accomplishment, especially given the great gap that had existed between the two countries only 30 years earlier.

Nor was quantity achieved at the expense of quality. Soviet artillery and mortars were quite good, and Soviet airplanes were greatly improved during the war. The KV-1 and KV-2 and T-34 tanks were clearly equal, if not superior, to German models, including the Mark and Tiger tanks. German Marshal Heinz Guderian acknowledged "the vast superiority of the Russian T-34 to our tanks."[17] Alec Nove has commented:

> It is true that the USSR produced the bulk of what was used. Furthermore, to the great credit of the designers and everyone responsible for manufacturing, the quality of a great deal of Soviet equipment was very good, the tanks being especially effective. True, the Red Army was somewhat backward in signalling equipment and the air force was under-supplied with bombers. But it is quite beyond dispute that the vast majority of the best aircraft, tanks and guns were of Soviet manufacture.[18]

The result of this high rate of quality production (not matched by a tardy Germany until 1943) was that, despite very heavy losses to the more capable German army, Russia was able to eventually achieve decisive numerical superiority in key battlefield weapons. German Field Marshal Erich von Manstein, for example, has noted that from July 1943 to January 1944 on the southern front the German army received 872 tanks, the Red Army 2,700.[19] Once the second front was launched in June 1944, the end of the war would rapidly ensue in less than a year.

Table 9 shows the impact of Soviet arms production in the field. These figures demonstrate that from slight German superiority or equality in 1941 and 1942, the Soviet Union achieved a decisive superiority in all sectors by June 1944, at the time of the Allied invasion of France. By then Russia had over four times more planes, nearly twice as many cannons and mortars, and 50 percent more tanks than Germany.

However, this production was achieved only with the greatest

TABLE 9:   Russian and German Weapons on the Eastern Front 1941–1945
(in thousands)

Weapons	Country	12/41	11/42	6/43	1/44	6/44	1/45
Tanks and Self-Propelled Artillery	Russia	2.0	6.9	9.9	5.4	7.8	12.0
	Germany	2.0	6.6	5.9	5.4	5.2	4.0
Cannons and Mortars	Russia	22.6	77.7	103.1	92.6	92.6	108.0
	Germany	27.0?	70.0	56.3	54.6	48.6	28.5
Airplanes	Russia	2.2	3.2	8.4	8.5	13.4	15.5
	Germany	2.7	3.5	3.0	3.0	2.8	2.0

SOURCES: Istoriya velikoi otechestvennoi voiny (Moscow: Voenizdat, 1965),
vol. 6, p. 185; Istoriya vtoroi mirovoi voiny 1939–1945 (Moscow: Voenizdat,
1982), vol. 12, p. 283.

difficulty in the wake of the massive German advance in the first 18
months of the war. German forces blockaded Leningrad, threatened
Stalingrad, seized the Baltics, Belorussia, and the Ukraine. This massive failure of the Red Army—relieved only by success in defending
the vital centers of Moscow, Leningrad, and Stalingrad—put an enormous burden on the Soviet war economy, which needed to be largely
transported eastward and reconstructed. By December 1941, industrial production was but 50 percent of the level of June 1941, and
vital steel production only 33 percent of the level of six months
earlier. An acute fuel shortage developed with the loss of the Don-
bass, which had produced 60 percent of the nation's coal. A vital
shortage of raw materials was created with the loss of key high-
grade steel, molybdenum, and manganese. Ball bearing and nonfer-
rous metal production hit zero in December. Rail transport was
disrupted, and the labor call-up and transfer of 40–50 percent of
industrial workers eastward greatly disrupted work.[20]

    The year 1942 was exceptionally grim. Agricultural production
was 38 percent of the 1940 level, capital investment 53 percent,
national income 66 percent and industrial production 77 percent.

Coal production was only 45.4 percent of the 1940 level and steel, at a meager 8.1 million tons, was but 44.2 percent of the hard-won level of 1940.[21]

The Soviet economic and political system showed its mettle under these extraordinarily difficult conditions. At the start of the war an all powerful State Committee of Defense (with Stalin as chairman) was created to function as supreme authority. All resources were centrally allocated, and members and plenipotentiaries were repeatedly sent to key sectors to impose order and establish priorities. Special attention was given to the Urals and Western Siberia. Very detailed yearly, quarterly, and monthly plans were created, and a special emergency war plan stressing eastern development was created for the period from August 1941 to December 1942. By 1942 a remarkable 55 percent of national income was being devoted to the war effort, twice the level in Germany.[22] With thorough war mobilization, the Soviet economy staged a remarkable turnabout. By the second half of 1942, a solid economic recovery was under way, even in the face of continued military defeats in the south. By 1944, as the Red Army drove the last German invaders from Soviet soil, Soviet national income reached 88 percent of the 1940 level, capital investment 72 percent, and industrial production a remarkable 104 percent.[23] These efforts allowed Russia to sustain the massive war effort that overcame Nazi Germany.

ARMY LEADERSHIP AND CAPABILITIES

A comparison of the leadership of the Russian army in the two world wars yields some interesting results. In both wars the top leadership showed mediocre qualities at the beginning of the war. While the Tsarist leadership actually deteriorated during the war and helped cause the ultimate defeat, the Soviet leadership markedly improved and made a significant contribution to victory.

The deep problems of the Tsarist army were manifested well in the character and capabilities of its two wartime commanders in chief—the Grand Duke Nicholas (August 1914–August 1915) and Tsar Nicholas II (August 1915–March 1917). Neither man was fit for command and neither demonstrated the slightest comprehension of modern military affairs. The 58-year-old Grand Duke Nicholas was a tall, handsome, and erect man, liked by his soldiers who respected him and his military experience. Future Defense Minister Aleksei Polivanov wrote about the grand duke:

He appeared to be a man entirely unequipped for the task and, in accordance with his statement, on receipt of the Imperial order he spent much of his time crying because he did not know how to approach his new duties.[24]

To make things even worse, Grand Duke Nicholas was not allowed to choose his own assistants or to make changes in a war plan that went against his own wishes.

Not only did Grand Duke Nicholas preside over crushing defeats in 1914 and 1915, but his sudden replacement by the tsar himself made matters even worse. All but two of the tsar's ministers fruitlessly tried to dissuade him from this rash step. The tsar was even less suited to the post than the grand duke for he lacked any serious military experience or inclination to learn. Indeed, Defense Minister Polivanov wrote, "The organization of the army and strategical considerations were foreign to him. He had done little work in this field and was poorly informed."[25] As a result he was little involved in the daily military work of the Stavka. His assumption of command left a serious vacuum at the top.

So little absorbed in his work was the tsar that, when there were no meetings to attend or visitors to entertain, he would spend his time reading third-rate English and American novels and writing letters to the tsarina about them. This at a time when millions of Russian soldiers were dying at the front! And, in return from his wife came frequent messages from the illiterate Rasputin on military affairs. The tenor of the tsarina's letters to the tsar borders on the incredible. On November 28, 1915 she writes, "Now before I forget I must give you a message from Our Friend prompted by what he saw in the night. He begs you to order that one should advance near Riga." On November 18, 1916 she writes, "A man who is so terribly against our Friend as poor Alekseyev is—cannot have blessed work." A conversation between the new Chief of Staff Alekseyev and a journalist in December 1916 highlights the problem.

Q. Have you said anything to the Tsar about it (supply problems)?

A. I have . . . but it does no good.

Q. Why?

A. While you talk to him, he pays attention, gets worked up, is eager to do something . . . but as soon as he leaves you he forgets about it. All kinds of pressure are brought to bear upon him; he is not a free man.[26]

Similar problems manifested themselves with the two chiefs of staff, and especially the first one, General Nicholas Yanushkevich. Appointed chief of staff in March, 1914, Yanushkevich had spent the previous decade in military administration where he was well versed in organization, logistics, and accounting. Incredibly he had no field experience at all (even in 1904 against Japan) and had never commanded anything higher than a company. He had attracted the attention of the tsar while a captain of the palace guard and gained his promotions as a courtier rather than a professional soldier. Yanushkevich, as commandant of the Russian staff college, in 1913 had fired five of the academy's best professors for teaching the theory of firepower in modern warfare. He favored the thoroughly outdated Suvorov creed of the bayonet. His successor in August 1915, Michael Alekseyev, was one of the few capable, experienced leaders, but he alone could not stem the tide.[27]

Similarly, of the four defense ministers during the war, only one was qualified—and he (Aleksei Polivanov) was allowed to serve nine months. The first, Defense Minister Vladimir Sukhomlinov, served from March 1909 until June 1915. Already 66 years old by 1914, he was a hidebound reactionary in military matters who, like Yanushkevich, believed in the triumph of spirit and bayonets over all. Sukhomlinov had spent his whole career in the cavalry. He boasted of his ignorance, saying that he had not read a military manual in 20 years since warfare had not changed since 1877. His administrative incompetence and negligence, combined with his indiscreet personal life involving association with embezzlers and high living and debts, ultimately led to his removal in June 1915, trial for treason and sentence of life imprisonment at hard labor in 1916 (and freedom in 1918 by Lenin). Critics have labeled him an "Olympian misfit" and the "General from defeat." His superficiality and strong reactionary views however, did please the tsar and the Court, which Sukhomlinov assiduously cultivated. Major General Alfred Knox has observed that his "influence over the Emperor was ascribed to his fund of excellent stories."[28]

His successor, Aleksei Polivanov, compiled a good record as war minister, especially in military production. The same cannot be said of his two successors. The 62-year-old Dimitri Shuvaev (March 1916–January 1917) had devoted the previous four years to the army commissariat. General Vasilil Gourko related that Shuvaev was a man of limited horizons who invariably turned every question to a discussion of boots. And Major General Alfred Knox has given the following picturesque description of Shuvaev.

A nice old man quite straight and honest. He had no knowledge of his work, but his devotion to the Emperor was such that if . . . His Majesty were to . . . ask him to throw himself out of a window he would do so at once.[29]

The final general to come through the revolving door of the defense ministry was General Michael Belayev. A good desk worker, he lacked independence or any authority among the troops. He had almost no major fighting experience. When Belayev in December 1916 asked for a field commission, he thought he would be given a corps command (Gourko felt a division would be enough). Instead, this "harmless" person was made defense minister, a soldier described as "an extremely weak man who always gives way in everything and works slowly."[30]

Other key military figures were cast in the same mold. Assistant War Minister General Vernander was an aging 70-year-old figurehead. The head of the Artillery Department was the Grand Duke Sergei, whose incompetence was certain and who was possibly corrupt. The head of the Army Medical Service was the elderly 70-year-old Prince Alexander Oldenburg, whose memory was failing.[31]

Furthermore, the army in 1914 was sharply divided within itself. The officer corps was sharply split between a patrician wing under Grand Duke Nicholas and a praetorian wing under Sukhomlinov. Traditionalists fought reformers, and supporters of concentration against Germany fought those who wanted to concentrate against Austro-Hungary. The result was the absence of a clear plan and creation of two separate fronts that fought virtually separate wars. And the makeshift Stavka did not even exercise real control over these separate fronts.

The overall quality of Russia's generals and staff officers was quite poor, especially compared to those of Germany. Chief of Staff Mikhail Alekseyev in March 1917 derided "our extreme poverty in outstanding generals," while Count Witte caustically observed, "The majority of our officers of the general staff know everything, except what they should really know: the art of waging war."[32]

Why did Tsarist generals, in the words of that dedicated conservative Alexander Solzhenitsyn, give a picture "of such unrelieved blackness" that "a Russian general's badges of rank came to be seen as symbols of incompetence," in a country with a rich military tradition?[33] Four reasons endemic to the regime were of primary importance. First, the tsar, without any real military capabilities, repeatedly intervened to promote incompetent Court favorites, such as Yanushkevich and the Grand Duke Nicholas, to positions for which they were not qualified. Influence at the Court or Defense Ministry was the key to success. Second, seniority was the key to promotion. As a Duma Military and Naval Committee reported to the tsar in August 1915:

> It is therefore neither gallantry, nor genius, nor knowledge, nor experience as proved in action that determines promotions but external considerations. Under these conditions really able men, gifted military leaders capable of leading us to victory seldom have reached the higher commands. They have usually been reserved for officers less able but senior in service.[34]

Third, strong preference was given to incompetent generals who had been especially zealous in suppressing all revolutionary manifestations. Finally, military talent was predominantly chosen from the very thin stratum of talent in the aristocracy, with minimal representation from over 130 million peasants, workers, and bourgeoisie or nationality minority groups. One statistic says it all: in 1912, 87.5 percent of all generals came from the aristocracy while 2.7 percent came from peasant or civil service background. And non-Russians were barely represented, as over 86 percent of all officers were Russians. Thus, favoritism, seniority, and Russian upper-class preference combined to restrict severely the talent pool for top commanders.[35]

Several characteristics helped promote the lethargy and incompetence of the top commanders. Russian generals tended to be old and often in poor health, even by European standards, reflecting the rigorous seniority system and distrust of young blood. At the beginning of the war in August 1914, the commanders of the northern, northwest, and southwest fronts (Nikolai Ruzski, Jacob Zhilinsky, and Nicholas Ivanov) were 60, 61, and 63 years old, respectively. The leading generals in the invasion of East Prussia, Pavel Rennenkampf and Alexander Samsonov, were 60 and 55 years old. Nor did matters improve during the war, as might be expected. If anything, they sometimes got worse. In the northern front, the ailing General Ruzski went on sick leave in the winter of 1915/1916, to be replaced by an equally sick 66-year-old General Plehve. By February 1916 General Wenzel von Plehve had to be removed as he was failing both mentally and physically, and he soon died. His replacement, General Alexis Kuropatkin, was a mere 67 years old. His mental health was poor, and he had been retired since 1905, due to the disastrous defeats suffered by the Manchurian army in the

1904-1905 war with Japan. Not surprisingly "this appointment astonished a great many," especially as Kuropatkin was considered an antiquated failure.[36]

Secondly, a surprising number of generals, emulating Chief of Staff Nikolai Yanushkevich and Defense Ministers Sukhomlinov and Shuvaev, lacked significant command experience before World War I. In the East Prussian invasion of August 1914, only one of four corps commanders (General Nikolai Martos) had serious military experience and competence. One corps commander, General Blagoveshchensky, having been in charge of military communications before 1914, had never even commanded a company, let alone a corps, in war before World War I. Another corps commander, General Klyuev, had never seen military action in nearly 40 years in the army. And while General Rennenkampf at least had extensive military experience, General Samsonov had not been in an operational post for seven years and had never commanded even a corps in action.[37]

Finally, most of the generals were woefully ignorant of, and unprepared for, modern warfare and lacked the flexibility and intelligence necessary to adapt. Again the East Prussian invasion that led to the disaster at Tannenberg was instructive. The three major generals directing the invasion—Zhilinsky, Samsonov, and Rennenkampf—had all made their careers in the cavalry, and the latter two had been commanders of Cossack units. None of the three had particularly distinguished themselves in the past. Not interested in modern development, they preferred to live in their cavalry past.

These general problems pervaded the officer corps as a whole. In 1912 a striking 69.8 percent of all officers (50.4 percent in the lower ranks) came from the aristocracy. Seniority, favoritism, and class background were still decisive factors in blocking promotion of talented commanders. The pay was very low, and initiative was positively discouraged. The training of officers was incredibly outmoded in its emulation of the Prussian system of the 1870s. In whitewashed barracks decorated with icons and pictures of the tsar, officers (even called "junkers") learned to march, slash with sabers, ride horses, and attend history lessons. But nowhere was instruction or training given in the use of firepower. Demonstrating a "total lack of imagination," and uninterested in military science, officers unsurprisingly

as a whole were apathetic, lazy and unenterprising towards their profession. They cared little for the well-being of their troops or the enforcement of discipline, substituting for studiousness and serious devotion to duty a wild bravado which caused them to scorn all regard for personal safety in battle. Their reckless behavior continued despite appeals from everyone in authority up to the tsar, in consequence of which they were killed in droves, further reducing their number.[38]

The Tsarist army suffered from a serious shortage of officers both before and during the war. The low pay, stultifying seniority system and bureaucracy, and the failure in the 1904–1905 war against Japan left the army in 1910 with a deficiency of 5,000 officers, which was not remedied by 1914. By August 1915 after enormous war losses, only 10 to 20 percent of the army commanders consisted of regular officers (who originally numbered 40,000), and by September 1916 the prewar cadres were largely gone.[39] Warrant officers, soldiers, and draftees were sent to hastily established training schools to become officers.

The conservative, monarchist officer corps had been trained to disdain the "savagery" of the masses of soldiers, mostly peasants, and to look down on them and discipline them harshly. There were serious problems with the soldiers. Roughly half of them were illiterate or semiliterate, and many of the rest had only an elementary education. Physical abuse and rigid social barriers between officers and men lessened any enthusiasm for the war. Senior, titled officers, for example, had to be called "Your Highest Eminence." The non-Russians, who had often felt the whip of forcible Russification under Nicholas II, soon lost their desire for an avowedly Russian imperialist war. The Russian workers, who had been striking against the oppressive regime before August 1914, found little grounds to continue fighting for tsarism. And the Russian peasants, backward, legally segregated, and eager for repartition of the land, lost any enthusiasm for war against distant foes when millions of peasant soldiers became war casualties. Yet they formed 75 percent of the army. Thus, problems of education, nationality, and class weakened the capacity of the regime to mobilize the bulk of the population for the war effort.

Perhaps the last word appropriately belongs to the Commander in Chief of the Tsarist army, Tsar Nicholas II. In March 1916 he wrote to the tsarina that "many generals are making serious blunders. The worst of it is that we have so few good generals." By June 1916, Tsar Nicholas II was complaining to the tsarina that "many of our commanding generals are silly idiots who, even after two years of warfare, have not been able to learn the first and simplest ABC of the military art."[40]

During the entire Russo-German war, Joseph Stalin functioned as Red Army supreme commander in chief. In the first year of the war he made serious mistakes. He kept his antiquated civil war cronies, such as Voroshilov, Timoshenko, and Budenny, in key command positions where their incompetence cost the Red Army dearly. His repeated intrusions into military operations and ill-fated insistence on a policy of rigid defense played into the hands of the Germans and helped cause millions of Red Army soldiers to be taken prisoner. And his mania for details no matter how small overcentralized the command structure. Over time, his leadership improved markedly. Seweryn Bialer has perhaps best analyzed the overall impact of Stalin's military leadership.

> Thus, what was crucial to the Soviet survival and eventual victory was Stalin's ability to mobilize Soviet manpower and economic resources over a sustained period, his ability to assure the political stability of his armed forces and the population at large despite disastrous initial defeats, and his ability to recognize and reward superior miltiary talent at all levels under his command. . . . It was in just the area of Russia's greatest need the Stalin showed his greatest strength. A systematic, pedantic, indefatigable worker, he found greatest satisfaction in organizational matters. He was above all an administrator better suited to directing the gigantic military and civilian bureaucracy than to initiating and formulating military plans.[41]

By the fall of 1942, only Timoshenko of Stalin's civil war cronies remained, soon to be replaced. In place of the discredited civil war commanders, a new group of professional commanders emerged by the fall of 1941. Marshals G. Zhukov, B.M. Shaposhnikov, A.M. Vasilevsky, A.I. Antonov, and N.N. Voronov became the center of the Red Army command. These men were young (four of the five were between 42 and 46 years old in 1941), dynamic, and talented. Western sources have lauded their great ability and professionalism, with Zhukov being especially praised. Indeed Basil Liddell-Hart has spoken of that "brilliant" triumvirate of Zhukov, Vasilevsky, and Voronov.[42] Colonel Albert Seaton has gone as far as to say that "yet in spite of these [early] mistakes, the war direction of the GKO and Stavka was in many ways superior to that of the German OKW and OKH," a great compliment indeed.[43]

Further, the field generals and commanders were quite good, especially in the second half of the war. These dynamic generals demonstrated genuine talent and honed their skills throughout the war. Promoted solely by virtue of their talent and proven ability, men such as Generals I. S. Konev, K. K. Rokossovsky, F. I. Tolbukhin, R. Ya. Malinovsky, L. A. Govorov, A. I. Yeremenko, K. A. Meretskov and I. Khn. Bagramyan, were comparable with the best generals in any army. Basil Liddell-Hart singled out Konev and Rokossovsky as "outstanding offensive leaders" for their role in the January 1945 winter offensive. Seweryn Bialer has provided a fitting summary of the field commanders.

> The quality of field command in large operational units improved radically over the course of the war. According to both German and Western sources, it was excellent for the most part during the second half of the war . . . the achievements of their rank they owed to success in demonstrating their ability as soldiers in the ultimate test of combat.[44]

These top Red Army commanders shared a number of traits common to leading officers in other revolutionary armies. They were generally 15 to 20 years younger than their counterparts in the German army in World War II and the Tsarist army in World War I. A survey of 45 top commanders shows that over one-half were less than 46 years old in 1943. An overwhelming 80 percent came from worker and peasant origins. And they were experienced—nearly all had fought in the civil war two decades earlier. Even more interesting is the extent of their professionalism. Fully one-half had fought in the Tsarist army in World War I, most as noncommissioned officers and some as junior officers. Their political commitment was strong, as half joined the Party during the civil war.[45]

The officer corps underwent regeneration in the war. By 1945 it bore little resemblance to the officer corps of 1941. During the war a staggering two million officers were commissioned through training programs lasting from three months to one year. The general command evolved successful strategies first to thwart the blitzkrieg and then to go on the offensive itself. By 1942 armor was being handled more effectively, and the Red Army largely managed to avoid encirclement. And in the 1943–1945 period the Red Army successfully made the difficult transition from defense to offense and evolved strategies to keep the Germans on the defensive. Given the scope of the early disasters, these were great accomplishments for the Red Army.

The improvements of the Red Army over the Tsarist army reflected the fundamental changes in Russia over 30 years. Promotion in the Red Army was solely based on talent, not seniority and court favoritism as in the Tsarist army. As a consequence, by the end of the war almost half of all commanders of rifle divisions had been only colonels at the beginning of the war.[46] Youth was an asset in the Red Army, a liability in the Tsarist army. Red Army commanders were largely recruited from the workers and peasants, who formed over 80 percent of the population; Tsarist army commanders were drawn primarily from the thin layer of aristocracy that represented but 1 percent of the population. Red Army commanders and commissars tried to mobilize the newly literate peasant soldiers for action, while Tsarist army officers were disdainful of the "primitive" peasant soldiers. And, finally, Red Army officers were frequently recruited from minority nationalities (especially Ukrainians), while Tsarist army officers were almost exclusively Russian.

Especially after the early disasters, many interests held by the soldiers were effectively galvanized to fight for the regime. The workers, Communists, and Komsomolites fought heroically for a socialist regime with which they identified. Russians fought for the motherland, while religious soldiers supported a regime that was reconciled with the church. Nationality minorities such as Ukranians and Jews were motivated by German atrocities committed to their brethren and the need to destroy facism. Overall, officers and especially commissars were increasingly effective in mobilizing the soldiers for battle as the war proceeded. Thus, an admixture of revolutionary and traditional factors motivated the army during the war. The very nature of the Russian army changed between the two wars.

CHAPTER 7

Wartime Government

Moving away from the battlefield, let us consider key government functioning in such vital areas as manpower mobilization, evacuation, foreign policy, intelligence, government leaders, and political mobilization.

MANPOWER MOBILIZATION

One of the key indicators of a government's efficiency is its capacity to mobilize its manpower for military service in wartime. As the tables in this chapter make clear, the Soviet Union had a markedly higher mobilization capacity than Tsarist Russia in wartime. The comparison is facilitated by the fact that both wars saw Russia with a relatively similar population, averaging 150 to 160 million people, with a slight edge to Tsarist Russia (mainly from Russian Poland).[1] Table 10 shows the greater Soviet army mobilization effort.

The two armies started the war with virtually identical sizes (5.3 million men in 1914, 5.4 million men in 1941). By the end of the war the Soviet Union had mobilized 42 percent more men into the army (22.4 million) than Tsarist Russia (15.8 million), despite a population pool that was slightly smaller. In spite of higher battle casualties, by the end of the war the Soviet army in 1945 (11.4 million men) was significantly larger than the Tsarist army in 1917 (8.6 million men). This was especially important because of Germany's impressive mobilization figures despite her inferior size of 67.5 million people in 1914 and 78 million people in 1941. In World War I Russia mobilized only 1.8 million more men than Ger-

TABLE 10:   Russian Military Manpower in the Two World Wars

War	Beginning of War	End of War	Russian Army (in millions)	Percentage of Population
			Mobilized	
World War I	5.3	8.6	15.8	9.9
World War II	5.4	11.4	22.4[a]	14.6

SOURCES: Nicholas Golovine, The Russian Army in the World War (New Haven: Yale University Press, 1931), p. 112; M. M. Kiryan, Voenna-tekhnicheskii progress i vooruzhennye sily (Moscow: Voenizdat, 1978), p. 273; Istoriya velikoi otechestvennoi voiny Sovetskogo soyuza 1941-1945 (Moscow: Voenizdat, 1960), v. 6, p. 123.

[a]This number represents an educated guess, derived from manpower and casualty figures.

many's 14.0 million men, while in World War II Russia mobilized 4.5 million more men than Germany's 17.9 million men.[2]

The really dramatic evidence of the Red Army's greater effectiveness came in the area of number of combatants in its active army. Table 11 shows that the Red Army was able to supply and keep in the field an active army twice or more the size of the active army of Tsarist Russia. In the 1944 campaign in Belorussia (2.4 million men) and 1945 battle for Berlin (2.5 million men), the Red Army raised forces equal to 70 percent of the entire active Tsarist army at its peak in 1916.[3]

These capabilities allowed the Red Army to utilize Russia's two to one manpower advantage over Germany in an opportunistic way that was wasted by the Tsarist army. Except in August 1914, when Russia fielded more divisions than Germany on all fronts (108 to 94), Germany actually had more divisions in the field on both fronts during the entire rest of World War I than Russia. In December 1914 the German advantage was 117 to 108, in May 1915, 149 to 112, in August 1916, 169 to 142, and in October 1917, 234 to 202. But in World War II the situation dramatically changed although Germany's population had increased 15 percent while Russia's population had decreased. In June 1941 Russia enjoyed a slight advantage in divisions of 211 to 199. But unlike in World War I this advantage greatly increased throughout the war until by January 1945 there were 473 Russian divisions and only 276 German divisions (split on two fronts) in the field.[4]

FORCED EVACUATION

When the German army threw much of its weight eastward in 1915 and 1941, the Russians were forced to evacuate significant western borderlands in which tens of millions of people lived and important industries were located. In 1914 and 1915 the Germans occupied Russian territory with 25 million people and 20 percent of industrial production, while in 1941 and 1942 they occupied territory with 80 million people and 50 percent of industrial production. The reaction of the two Russian governments to these dire circumstances told a great deal about their natures and capabilities.

The Tsarist government carried out its industrial evacuation of threatened areas amidst "great confusion," "without any plan, without preparation in the rear of a base for housing the equipment and living space for workers."[5] Only after most of the work had been done on an ad hoc basis were three evacuation commissions established in Pskov, Minsk, and Berdichev in November 1915. Much valuable equipment was lost; 427 evacuated enterprises were scattered amidst 33 provinces, and significant equipment was not evacuated. By January 1915 no less than 4,500 train cars of freight were listed

TABLE 11:   Size of Russia's Active Army in the Two World Wars
            (in millions)

Date (Month/Year)	World War I	Date (Month/Year)	World War II
12/14	1.5	6/41	2.9
11/16	3.5		
9/17	3.0	6/45	6.7

SOURCES: Nicolas Golovine, The Russian Army in the World War (New Haven: Yale University Press, 1931), p. 112; and Istoriya vtoroi mirovoi voiny 1939-1945 (Moscow: Voenizdat, 1982), vol. 12, p. 217.

as damaged in transit. And, most strikingly, fully a year after evacuation began, in February 1916, only 17 percent of the evacuated enterprises (70 out of 427) were working smoothly in their new locations. Major General Alfred Knox described the evacuation from Riga in 1915:

> All important factories removed their plants to the east, and owing to a shortage of suitable accommodations elsewhere and defective organization, many of them were unable to re-start work satisfactorily during the war. . . . Unfortunately the mere threat to Riga deprived the great manufacturing town of all usefulness for national defence.[6]

Manpower evacuation was handled far worse. In 1915 General Yanushkevich ordered the mass "evacuation" of 700,000 Jews from Galicia and other frontier areas. Accused of espionage, they were given 24 hours to move under penalty of death, were forcibly uprooted, and driven deep into Russia. In an analogy with the 1812 campaign against Napoleon, the army ordered the complete destruction of equipment and evacuation of the population. Without serious planning, the result was chaos, the loss of valuable equipment not shipped eastward, and the irrational flight of the Russian labor force into the interior of the country without any destination. Notes from a Council of Ministers' meeting on August 12, 1915 and a follow-up meeting on August 17, 1915 reveal the military mismanagement of evacuation.

> Headquarters has lost its head . . . [the refugee] is torn from his native home, given a few hours to collect his worldly possessions and told to move on, no one knows where. What he cannot take along is burned right in front of its eyes . . . All this embittered mass of humanity spreads like a flood in all directions. They die by the hundreds from hunger, thirst and disease . . . they accentuate the difficulties of wartime conditions, they bring on food crises, high cost of living and excite an already aroused population . . . their trail is like that of a flight of locusts or bands of Tamerlane on the warpath.

And along the way of their retreat this mass of humanity was "passed by trains piled full of furniture from officers' clubs, including canary bird cages."[7]

By contrast, under sharply more difficult and fast-moving conditions of the 1941 German blitzkrieg, the Soviet Union carried out a massive movement of men and material eastward. The key was centralized planning, efficient administration, and hard work. Three days after the German invasion, on June 24, 1941, a Soviet for

Evacuation was created under N.M. Shvernik, with talented organiz-
ers Aleksei Kosygin and Mikhail Pervukhin as deputy chairmen. In
September a separate Soviet for Population Evacuation was created.
The decisions of the Soviets were binding on all party, government,
and economic organs; its plenipotentiaries became deputy people's
commissars of all central bureaucracies, and evacuation committees
were established in all threatened republics and oblasts. By July a
plan existed as well for routing and restructuring industries to the
east. Nearly 3,000 plenipotentiaries helped direct over 32,000 youth
groups in this vast enterprise. By October 1941, Politburo member
Nikolai Voznesensky was permanently entrusted with work in the
east.[8]

The results were impressive. Between June and December 1941,
the Soviet Union evacuated 1,360 large industrial enterprises and
1,230 smaller ones eastward, utilizing almost 1.5 million railroad cars
and 870,000 tons of cargo ships. Over 10 million people were evacuated by plan, including 30 to 40 percent of workers, technicians, and
engineers of the factories sent eastward. Along with them went large
quantities of fuel, equipment, grain, and cattle.[9]

By early 1942 eastern plants were producing in significant quantities, and at the end of 1942 the economy was on a full war footing.
Despite enormous problems of fuel, resources, and transportation, in
1942 military production in the Urals was over 5 times greater than
in 1940, in the Volga area 9 times greater, and in Western Siberia 27
times greater. Perhaps the ultimate testimony to Soviet evacuation
procedures to the east was given by none other than Adolf Hitler;
Basil Liddell-Hart has written that in the winter of 1941/42:

> [the offensive] instinct made him [Hitler] insensitive to uncomfortable
> facts. For example, the German Intelligence Service had information
> that 600–700 tanks a month were being produced by the Russian fac-
> tories in the Urals and elsewhere. But when Halder gave him the evi-
> dence he slammed the table and declared that any such rate of produc-
> tion was impossible. He would not believe what he did not want to
> believe.[10]

FOREIGN POLICIES

By making a comparative analysis of the policies of the Russian government in the two world wars, the superiority of the Soviet government by a large margin is again quite evident.

The foreign policy of the Tsarist government on the eve of and
during World War I left much to be desired. Tsarist foreign policy

had been marked by dangerous adventurism as far back as 1903. Although Japan in August 1903 had proposed to discuss all points of contention in the Far East with Russia, the Russians did not even reply to this proposal until October 1903. And even then Russia, led by Plehve, continued to intrigue against Japan in the hope of provoking a "small war," which would distract attention from domestic problems. Given Japan's thorough military preparations, quantitative and qualitative superiority over Russian forces in Manchuria, and Russia's tenuous connection to the Far East, this was the rankest adventurism. Japan soon annihilated Russia's army at Port Arthur and Mukden and smashed the Russian fleet at Tsushima in 1905. In 1903 and 1904 Russian adventurism was a prescription for disaster, which ignited the 1905 Revolution.

Similarly, in 1914 Russia's lack of caution or awareness of the weakness of its position led to policies that helped ignite the war. On July 28, Austria declared war on Serbia, thereby throwing down the gauntlet to Russia, Serbia's protector. Within a day, after hearing erroneous reports of Austrian general mobilization, Russia declared a general mobilization, which meant war. Hugh Seton-Watson has lucidly analyzed the situation:

> The war was not something which suddenly happened to Russia. It was a result of the policy of Russia and her two German neighbors. Certainly, it is not fair to throw the whole blame for the war on Russian "Panslavist imperialism." But it is hard to see how Russian and Austrian aims—or if Austria had dissolved, Russian and German aims—could have been reconciled.[11]

During the war Russian foreign policy was often not in line with Russian capabilities and interests. In August 1914 the Russian army invaded East Prussia on the fifteenth day of the war, even though it would not be ready until the thirty-sixth day, to help save France from the invading German army. The result was the disaster at Tannenberg. During the 1915 occupation of Galicia, heavy-handed Russian policies alienated the local population. During 1915 and 1916 the Russian government ordered massive and bloody, futile attacks to help the Western allies, although there were few corresponding moves to help the Russians. As the Russian position deteriorated, its war aims nonetheless expanded. By 1916 Russia was demanding control of the Dardanelles and a series of Russian satellite states in Eastern Europe, including an enlarged Poland. Russian dependence on France grew throughout the war. Even when it became evident that the only hope for a bloodied and defeated Russia was to search

for the best possible peace terms, Tsarist Russia adamantly sought
to continue the war with expanded war aims.

Soviet foreign policy before and during World War II followed a
very different course. Eminently aware of the weakness of Russia
and ferverishly preparing for war, Stalin sought to stay out of war as
long as possible. Ever the realist, Stalin first sought a defensive alliance with England and France, then thought to be the most powerful
sea and land powers in the world. When they failed to conclude an
alliance with him, he rapidly signed a Non-Aggression Pact with
Germany in August 1939. By this pact he diverted German forces
westward and ultimately gained the Baltic states, western Ukraine,
western Belorussia and Bessarabia, and a respite of 22 months from
the war.[12] In April 1941 Stalin signed a Non-Aggression Pact with
Japan, which averted a possible two-front war. During the war Stalin
assiduously cultivated the Allies when he thought he needed them—
urging a second front, pleading for more war supplies, and even sug-
gesting in the fall of 1941 that 25 to 30 Allied divisions should land
in Russia to help the war effort. Even then, at his maximum weakness, Stalin continued to emphasize the need for recognition of the
expanded 1940 borders.

As the tide of battle turned in Stalin's favor after Stalingrad, he
skillfully utilized all of Russia's assets to achieve a favorable postwar
settlement. Especially after the liberation of all Soviet territory from
German control, Stalin tailored Red Army moves to his political
goals. In 1944 and early 1945, large Soviet forces were sent to occupy
Rumania, Bulgaria, Hungary, and Czechoslovakia. Over one million
Soviet soldiers lost their lives in this bloody but rapid decimation of
the Third Reich, which culminated in the extremely violent battle
for Berlin.

On the political front Stalin pursued a number of options simul-
taneously. During the war the Russians prepared foreign Communists
who had survived the Great Purges for leadership roles in Eastern
Europe. Especially in Poland, Stalin worked relentlessly to destroy
the political base of the London Poles, including standing aside while
the Home Army launched a premature uprising against the Germans
in August 1944. At the same time strong European Communist parties, as those in France, Italy, and Yugoslavia, were urged to cooper-
ate with the Allies and not to attempt to seize power at the end of
the war. John Erickson has described Stalin's consummate realism
on the eve of victory in the summer of 1944:

> He was, in short, prepared to bargain. . . . He was fully deployed to
> negotiate, with Rumanians, with Finns, even with Germans . . . to ease

and speed the Red Army's advance to the west and south, Stalin was obviously prepared to strike almost any bargain—with Britain, even though he mistrusted them deeply; with the petty dictators of south-eastern Europe, with the Germans through his special 'Free Germany' committees . . . the Communists were urged to 'compromise' and the nationalists pressed to be realistic.[13]

On the diplomatic front, the Soviet Union was remarkably adept, especially for a newcomer to Great Power politics, at attaining what it wanted from its new allies and former enemies, the United States and Great Britain. It was especially skilled at exploiting differences among the Anglo-American allies and making military and political moves to benefit its diplomatic position. Russia was able to reap significant gains and translate military victories into political achievements at the major diplomatic conferences. At the November 1943 Tehran Conference, Stalin gained Allied agreement for a second front in France in 1944, as well as expansion of Russian borders westward into Poland and Polish borders westward into Germany. At the February 1945 Yalta Conference, Stalin gained recognition of Russia's 1940 borders, a relatively free hand in Poland, and an American promise to withdraw her troops in two years. At the July 1945 Potsdam Conference, Russia gained control of East Germany, the right to take reparations from the war zone, and final agreement on the new Polish borders.

Of course, Russia did not get everything it sought. There was to be no American help to rebuild a shattered economy, no control of the Dardanelles, and no Soviet role either in occupied West Germany or in Japan. But the overall balance sheet on Soviet foreign policy had to be extremely positive for the war years. Russia had regained its maximal western boundaries, created an assured buffer zone in Eastern Europe, and emerged as a recognized world superpower by 1945.

GOVERNMENT LEADERS AND CAPABILITIES

A similar difference emerges in a comparative analysis of Tsarist and Soviet leaders and government capabilities. Tsarist Russia had the great misfortune, not uncommon among hereditary monarchies who rely on the accident of birth to determine leadership, to be ruled by Tsar Nicholas II, a man uncommonly ill suited to be a twentieth-century monarch. Weak and indecisive and an isolated, genial mystic, Nicholas II was an ultrareactionary, self-proclaimed autocrat and honorary member of the anti-Semitic Union of the Russian People. He looked backwards to medieval Muscovy for his inspiration. The tsar fervently believed in the antiquated trinity of orthodoxy, autocracy, and nationality. Nicholas thought police repression and his political credo could still the revolutionary tide and that economic problems of the various classes were irrelevant. He found politics dull, tedious, and of little interest. Donald Treadgold has made this point extremely well.

> Industrialism was beyond his understanding, revolutionaries were to him simply manifestations of evil to be crushed at any cost, good government not an ideal to be sought but an irrelevance compared to the fulfillment of the commands of his ancestors and maintenance of loyalty of the Russian people to his own person. Politically he was completely at sea. In his public utterances he never thought it necessary to define his policy or to allow that there might be such a thing as his 'policy.'[14]

His massive incompetence was seen dramatically in his August 1915 decision to leave Petrograd and move to army headquarters as the new commander in chief. This represented a virtual abdication of governmental responsibility at a time of heightened demands on the government. Into the vacuum came the malicious figures of the tsarina and Rasputin.

A fervently religious mystic, the tsarina found the Duma and all institutions of public support repulsive. She considered leaders of the Duma, zemstvo, and semiofficial war organizations to be virtually criminals. In a December 1916 letter to the tsar she lauded the reactionary Black Hundreds as "healthy, right thinking, devoted subjects ... their voice is Russia's and not society's or the Duma's."[15] Despite her abysmal lack of knowledge and sheer ignorance, she dealt with major issues of public interest. Bernard Pares has commented, her letters to the tsar showed that "she is dealing with a whole number of subjects of which she has no idea: food supply, transport, fuel, medical service at the front ... even naval appointments."[16] Increasingly bitter and isolated, she came under the influence of the noxious Rasputin.

The Rasputin scandal undermined Tsarist authority and cost the regime whatever legitimacy it still had. With his hold over the hemophiliac Tsarevich Alexis and his bizarre mysticism, the illiterate Siberian wonder monk soon came in 1915 and 1916 to exercise a powerful influence on Tsarist policies. Soon there was the stupefying spectacle of the militarily and politically illiterate Rasputin and tsarina discussing military policy, praying over it, and sending advice to the tsar![17] Even worse, the two conspired to rid the Cabinet of its few remaining honest and efficient ministers and replace them with ultrareactionary careerists of the lowest quality. Rasputin's reign came to an end only in December 1916 when Prince Yusupov and his associates murdered him. But it was too late to save the monarchy. Rasputin's ascendancy had symbolized the utter decadence and black pit into which the monarchy had fallen.

Under these conditions it was hardly surprising that Tsar Nicholas II's War Cabinet, with some notable exceptions, was composed of reactionary, aging, and incompetent men, incapable of discharging properly their vital wartime functions. The tsar himself took little interest in his cabinet, finding the whole notion of ministers distasteful to his concept of absolute monarchy. He innately distrusted capable, creative, and enlightened men, preferring to surround himself with servile incompetents. He frequently and capriciously changed his ministers, having not less than 41 ministers in 12 positions during the war, a tenure of only nine months for each minister. From August 1914 to February 1917 he had no less than four prime ministers and six ministers of the interior. The chaos caused by these constant changes was clear, but the grounds for these actions were obscure.

His choices to serve as prime minister during the war were exceedingly strange and dysfunctional to the war effort. Ivan Goremykin, who served as prime minister from January 1914 to January 1916, was a feeble, servile, and incompetent 75-year-old bureaucrat, whose chief reputation was as a "butler" to the tsar. A leading Russian noble called him "the worst product of the Russian bureaucracy." His views were incredibly antediluvian. In 1915 he dismissed the patriotic Fourth Duma, echoing his 1906 speech to the First Duma in which he called most Duma demands "inadmissible," and he submitted but two insulting bills (creation of a hothouse and laundry at Derpt University) as his program. His health was so bad that he spoke cynically of candles that were only waiting for his coffin. Yet Goremykin, who often offered to resign, served in the most important governmental post for the first 17 months of the war at a time of national emergency.[18]

His replacement for 10 months, Boris Sturmer, was, if possible, worse. While Goremykin at least had honesty and integrity on his side, Sturmer was an unprincipled adventurer. A creature of Rasputin and the tsarina, Sturmer was an ungifted, aging 68-year-old reactionary politician. His undistinguished career included six years of service as the dishonest Governor of Yaroslavl Province, and as former master of ceremonies at the Court. As director of the Interior Ministry's Department of General Affairs, he had made his reputation for having illegally disbanded the liberal Tver provincial *zemstvo* assembly. While Rodzianko in his memoirs called him a "non-entity" of whom "those who had known Sturmer formerly had no respect for him," N. N. Pokrovsky, later the foreign minister, derided him as a "notorious" "man of extremely limited mental gifts, of one who was suffering from an acute state of sclerosis due to advanced age."[19]

In November 1916 Sturmer was replaced by Alexander Trepov, a strong, independent conservative, who naturally barely lasted a month. His successor, Prince Nikolai Golitsyn, was to serve less than four months as the last Tsarist prime minister. Golitsyn was a comparatively unknown leader whose sole qualifications lay in his honesty, past governorships of Archangel and Tver provinces before 1905, and chairmanship of a war committee for relief of Russian POWs (through which he had met the tsarina). Lacking recent political or administrative experience, even he was distressed by the appointment, not to speak of the public. Yet worse, he was an aging gentleman (66 years old), in poor health, showing signs of senility. He was, in short, the ultimate epitome of the complete decay of vitality in Tsarist Russia.

A brief analysis of the five ministers of the interior (one served twice) during the war shows a similar pattern. Nikolai Maklakov, minister of the interior from January 1913 until June 1915, was an openly ultrareactionary member of the anti-Semitic Union of the Russian People. A champion of absolutism, he opposed even the concessions of 1905 and wanted to dissolve the Duma permanently. In October 1913 he had called on the tsar to stage a coup d'etat and abolish the Duma. An erratic politician, Maklakov saw enemies everywhere except on the extreme right. Although his successor, Prince Nikolai Shcherbatov, represented a distinct improvement, he lasted but four months. During the next nine months, the post was twice occupied by Aleksei Khvostov, an unprincipled adventurer with no visible qualifications for office, and by the notorious Boris Sturmer. Finally, in September 1916, Alexander Protopopov, a Rasputin follower, became the last Tsarist interior minister. A timid, impoverished aristocrat, he never got to know anything about the ministry and was ridiculed by the Duma. Several observers stressed that he was mentally unbalanced and well on the road to going insane. Bernard Pares declared that "at the best his appointment could only be regarded as a very bad joke."[20]

The political disintegration of the Tsarist government increased with the prolonging of the war, reaching its height in 1916 and early

1917. In 1916 alone there were four prime ministers, four ministers of internal affairs, three ministers of foreign affairs, and two ministers of war. Even the conservative Kadets attacked the "dark forces" of government in 1916, while the reactionary Purishkevich coined the term "ministerial leapfrog" for the rapid succession of ministers. Attacking the "chaos prevailing among our rulers," and characterizing the Cabinet as "nothing but a dozen Sleeping Beauties," Purishkevich penned the following poem in 1916 (Sturmer = Stormer).

The Stormers

The "Stormer" period still goes on;
   the pace it goes is simply mad;
Whatever else we lack, there's none
   could count the ministers we've had.
The order of our State is sage;
   It's founded on a solid plan;
Portfolios are now the rage
   And those would want to get them can.[21]

The quality of government ministers was indicative of the nature of the Tsarist bureaucracy in general. The hidebound Tsarist government recruited bureaucrats largely from the aristocracy, which constituted only 1 percent of the population, and only from its less talented part at that. The Soviet historian Zaionchkovsky has shown that in 1900, 100 percent of the governors, 85 to 100 percent of the higher-level civil servants, and 40 percent of all middle-level bureaucrats came from the nobility.[22] Advancement was largely by family connections and favoritism. Under these conditions, the overall quality of the bureaucrats was distinctly mediocre.

Corruption was so endemic that the Grand Duke Michael told the French military attache in 1915 that at least 25 percent of all goods on the railroads failed to reach their destination. Despite this, almost none of the highly placed officials suspected of corruption were brought to trial. Between military interference from without and decay from within, the bureaucracy lurched towards collapse. Merel Fainsod concluded his discussion of "the torpidity and passivity" of the bureaucracy, "At a sheer technical level the inefficiency and venality of the bureaucracy helped to contribute to the disastrous military defeats and the economic breakdown on the homefront which prepared the way for revolution."[23]

When a women's bread line turned into the February Revolution, the abdication of the tsar was met by nearly universal joy, even among monarchists. Not even the largely monarchist army high com-

mand came to the defense of the tsar. Nor during the Russian civil
war of 1918-1920 did the most conservative White generals dare
raise the banner of monarchist restoration. Rather the total bankruptcy of tsarism was seen in the relative ease with which an elemental, spontaneous uprising ended tsarism in Russia.

Overall, by contrast the Soviet bureaucracy, despite numerous
defects, had significantly greater capabilities than the Tsarist burea-
cracy. The top governmental leaders in charge of the war effort—
Joseph Stalin (overall leader), Lazar Kaganovich (railroads), Anastas
Mikoyan (fuel), Georgi Malenkov (airplanes), Vyacheslav Molotov
(tanks), Aleksei Voznesensky (military production), and Lavrentiya
Beria (security)—were all capable, hard-working bureaucrats. Their
associates, such as People's Commissar of War Industry Dmitri Usti-
nov, were equally talented. Indeed, administration was such a key
talent of the Bolsheviks that Samuel Huntington considered it to
be the major contribution of Leninism to twentieth-century politics.[24]

While retaining some talented "bourgeois specialists," the greatly
expanded Soviet bureaucracy recruited capable and energetic, technically trained workers and peasants in large numbers in the 1930s.
By 1933 the results were evident. Workers constituted 30.4 percent
of all employees, and 28.6 percent of employees were Communists.
Nearly one-fourth (200,000) of the employees of civil service had
gone to universities, an impressive achievement. While problems
clearly remained, the level of venality significantly decreased and
efficiency increased by wartime. Merle Fainsod captured this change
when he observed that

> the Soviet industrializing elite crossed its Rubicon when it managed to
> create a technical intelligentsia capable of staffing a modernizing bur-
> eaucracy and when it began to succeed in communicating the values,
> habits and the requirements of industrialization to the backward
> society which it sought to transform.[25]

MILITARY INTELLIGENCE

In the twentieth century the importance of military intelligence has
increased greatly in ensuring success in battle. Nations have needed
both to penetrate and discover vital military secrets of their enemies
and to prevent other nations from discovering their own secrets. Yet,
vital differences existed in the capabilities of the two regimes in this
critical area.

Tsarist Russia was quite weak in this area. Its penetration of foreign intelligence services did not yield significant results. When Russia invaded East Prussia in August 1914, it had almost no intelligence on the area. Still worse, the Russians did not prevent German penetration of Russian secrets. An effective German network of agents created a situation where, as Major General Alfred Knox reported, "the German system of espionage is efficient and reports all moves of the Russian forces immediately."[26] Typical of this German penetration was the arrest and hanging for treason in 1915 of Colonel Myasoyedov, former chief of the frontier railroad police and intimate friend of Defense Minister Sukhomlinov and his wife. Similarly, when the 58-year-old Defense Minister Sukhomlinov was divorcing his first wife so that he could marry his second (who was at the time 23 years old), Altschiller gave key testimony at the 1906 divorce trial. Later Altschiller was discovered to be Austria's main agent in Russia. Awareness for the need for vigilance was so low that uncoded operational radio messages in East Prussia and Galicia in 1914 were easily intercepted and read by the German High Command. Finally, with widespread official corruption the result was that "the ease with which the plans of the Russian General Staff could be bought was a standing joke among the Germans who consequently know more about the Russian army than did its allies."[27] As a result, the Germans enjoyed a major advantage over the Russians in the vital area of information in the First World War.

Yet in World War II the Russians, with some Allied assistance, greatly outpaced the Germans in military intelligence. They effectively penetrated the German High Command while carefully protecting their own secrets. In Tokyo, Soviet GRU agent Richard Sorge had by 1939 become the German embassy press attache. Having breakfast every morning with German Ambassador Eugene Ott and establishing a network led by the well-connected Japanese journalist Ozaki Hotsumi, Sorge was able to warn of the impending German attack in late June 1941. Before his arrest, he was able to inform Moscow in October 1941 that Japan would move southward and not against Russia, allowing Stalin to transfer 100,000 soldiers from the east for the battle of Moscow.[28] In Europe the "Red Orchestra," led by Leopold Trepper, in France and Belgium provided excellent information from 1940 until the end of 1942.

Perhaps most critical was the "Lucy Network," run by Alexander Rado and Rudolf Roessler, which involved 50 agents in cooperation with Swiss and English intelligence. From June 1941 until 1944, the plans and orders of the German High Command down to the brigade level were daily sent to Moscow, a total of over 5,500 messages in the course of three years. Among the sources evidently were Major General Hans Oster of the Abwehr, who was close to many generals, and probably Colonel Boetzel, head of the ciphers department of the German General Staff. Before the network was destroyed and over 100 people executed by the Nazis in 1944, it had provided extraordinary information to Moscow. As Alexander Foote, who had been Rado's deputy, has stated:

> In fact in the end Moscow largely fought the war on Lucy's messages—as indeed any high command would who had access to genuine information emanating in a steady flow from the high command of their enemies. . . . In effect, as far as the Kremlin was concerned, the possession of Lucy as a source meant that they had the equivalent of well-placed agents in the three service intelligence staffs plus the Imperial General Staff plus the War Cabinet Officers.[29]

Numerous authors have testified to the effectiveness of Soviet measures to protect Soviet plans from a well-orchestrated German penetration effort. The NKVD border guards, NKVD work among the population, a Soviet penchant for secrecy, the unfriendliness and regimentation of a population just recovering from the Great Purges, and small foreign community all combined to block German intelligence work. The Germans in 1941 knew little about even the Soviet High Command or leading Red Army officers and could not successfully penetrate the army command structure. During the war they lacked precise information about the Soviet order of battle, number of armies and divisions on the eastern front, and even the production figures for tanks and airplanes. Consistently they underestimated Soviet capabilities.[30]

The most elemental critical figures evaded German intelligence. In August 1941 General Halder wrote in his diary that "we underestimate Russia: we reckoned with 200 divisions but now we have already identified 360."[31] German maps were so inadequate that German soldiers often found it easier to ask local inhabitants for directions.

POLITICAL MOBILIZATION

In the two world wars, which involved total mobilization of human and material resources, the political capacity of the government to mobilize and direct its citizens to participate wholeheartedly in the war effort was vital to ultimate success. But, the Tsarist government, fearful of the revolutionary impulses of the masses and jealous of middle class elements did everything it could to *prevent* political mobilization of the population. The government bureaucracy in 1915 refused the help of any public organization except for the Red Cross and blocked all public meetings of patriotic groups. The Duma was treated with undisguised hostility. Thomas Riha aptly analyzed the situation.

> The monarchy . . . did everything to discredit itself in the public eye. Instead of cooperating with his nation, which had unexpectedly offered its hand to the monarchy for the last time, the Emperor drew farther than ever away from Russian realities. Neither the Duma, nor *zemstvo*, nor the union of Russian cities, nor committees of individual leaders, all of whom did essential work on behalf of the war effort, were deemed worthy of trust or support. The bureaucracy, taking its cue from the Emperor, displayed more arrogance than ever and did its best to stifle public initiative whenever it could. The most moderate Russians began to lose all hope.[32]

By contrast, the Soviet leadership launched a massive program of political mobilization to engage nearly all segments of the population, except for some small nationality groups.[33] Rather than invoking a narrow socialist appeal, the regime fought the war in defense of the motherland, a universal appeal redolent of 1812. Socialist appeals were targeted only for the youth, workers, Communists, and Komsomolites inculcated with Marxist-Leninist ideology. A rapprochement with the Russian Orthodox Church led to church appeals to the religious faithful to support the regime. Heavy stress on Russian nationalism, with the invocation of the memory of great Russian tsars and creation of Guards units, rallied the population against the German invaders. And nationality minorities were not ignored, with the formation of groups such as the Jewish Anti-Fascist Committee. All possible instruments of mobilization were utilized, including emphasis on Allied aid and support and Nazi brutality, the spreading of rumors that life would be better after victory, and the firing of artillery salvos to mark victories.

The Soviet leaders had a vital mechanism for political mobilization lacking to Tsarist leaders—the Communist party. The Communists provided the vital glue holding together the economy, society, and army, especially during the disasters of 1941 and 1942. During the war Communists were 6 percent of the adult population. They rallied and directed the partisans and served as political workers in the army. During the war, 81.8 percent of all Communists served in the armed forces or war industry. No less than 1.6 million Communists and 3.5 million Komsomolites were sent to the army during the war. A further 4.1 million soldiers joined the Party as candidate members, and 2.7 million soldiers actually joined the Party during the war. Fully 3 million Communists were killed in the war. By 1944, 23 percent of all soldiers and officers were Communists. In January 1945, 1.1 million Communists were at the fronts. The party served as the critical mass in the army and the nation during the war. They were indeed that "band of samurai" that Trotsky had already called them in an earlier war, the Russian civil war.[34]

Frederick Barghoorn has testified to the effectiveness of the Soviet system:

> However the Soviet system, both Stalinist and post-Stalinist, possesses strengths which we who are committed to the civic political culture can easily overlook. These consist, very briefly, of a high sense of relevancy about matters of significance for survival and power of the nation, clarity in relating public policy to centrally determined community goals, and the sense of purpose and confidence in ultimate success conferred by dedication to an ideology of worldwide revolutionary social transformation. At least a considerable proportion of the population derive from these practices and perspectives sufficient satisfaction to generate enthusiastic support for the total Soviet system.[35]

*   *   *

Protracted war is the ultimate test of the soundness and capabilities of any social system. While the disintegration of the Tsarist government in February 1917 and army by February 1918 showed how badly tsarism had failed this test, the triumphal march of the Red Army into Berlin, Prague, and Vienna at the end of the war demonstrated the fundamental soundness of the Soviet system. The major role played by the Soviet Union in the Allied victory was well appreciated at the time by Russia's World War II allies. In January 1943 Prime Minister Winston Churchill wrote that "all our military operations are realized on a very insignificant scale in comparison with the enormous resources of England and the United States, even more in comparison with the gigantic efforts of Russia."[36]

Essentially it was the Russian Revolution, with all its strengths and weaknesses, that helped turn Russia into a modern industrial state capable of defeating a powerful Germany. Stalinism, as the heir to the desire to lead a third revolution in Russia, manifested both great strengths and debilitating weaknesses. To its credit, it liberated the potential of tens of millions of peasants and workers, both Rus-

sian and non-Russian in a massive cultural leap forward. It centralized and drove Russia from a backward, semideveloped country with
huge untapped potential to a modern, developed state. No longer, as
Stalin emphasized in 1931, would Russia be beaten as so many times
in the past. And yet the costs were quite high as well—the Great
Purges, coercion, and regimentation. Isaac Deutscher best captured
the dual process at work here:

> Stalin undertook, to quote a famous saying, to drive barbarism out of
> Russia by barbarous means. Because of the nature of the means he
> employed, much of the barbarism thrown out of Russian life has crept
> back into it. The nation has, nevertheless, advanced far in most fields of
> its existence. Its material apparatus of production, which about 1930
> was still inferior to that of any medium-sized European nation, has so
> greatly and rapidly expanded that Russia is now the first industrial
> power in Europe and the second in the world. . . . The whole nation has
> been sent to school.[37]

Thus, it was the revolution and its heirs that destroyed the old forms
and created more modern, powerful institutions.

PART 3

The Chinese Revolution

CHAPTER 8

China and Two Major Wars

Our analysis of the impact of revolution on societies and their militaries becomes even more compelling when we move eastward from Russia to China. For Tsarist Russia, even in the last decades of its existence, had remained a significant actor in European politics. From the defeat of Napoleon to the Crimean War, Tsarist Russia had assumed the role of the feared gendarme who maintained the European status quo that had been so carefully crafted by the Congress of Vienna. Even as Tsarist Russia tottered and disintegrated under the impact of the Russo-Japanese War and World War I, many Europeans awaited or dreaded the appearance of the "Russian steamroller," which never arrived.

In the east even the illusion of power had eluded China, which once had known the glories of its great dynasties and the Middle Kingdom. In the hundred years before the Sino-Japanese War and World War II, China had become "the sick man of Asia." Ever since the Opium War of 1839-1842 in which the British had seized Hong Kong and opened six treaty ports to the West, China had been repeatedly humiliated and defeated by Western powers and Japan alike. In the Second Opium War of 1860 the British and French forces smashed Chinese forces, occupied Peking, and forced the legalization of the sale of opium, creation of foreign courts, and opening of ten more treaty ports. In 1885 the French took over Tonkin and Annam, and the British seized North Burma. Even worse, in 1894 the Japanese, having destroyed Chinese forces in South Manchuria, occupied Korea, Formosa, and the Ryukyus and forced China to pay a large indemnity. In 1899-1900 Western forces crushed the Boxer Uprising, occupied Peking, and forced payment of a huge indemnity and accession of the right to garrison troops in Tientsin and Peking. World War I continued to show the impotence of China and the extent of ongoing violations of its sovereignty. Although China had aligned with the victorious powers, it was forced at Versailles to transfer German rights in Shantung to Japan. The ridiculous ease with which Japan invaded and occupied the valuable provinces of Manchuria in 1931 and 1932 showed that even the rise to power of the Kuomintang after the Northern Expedition of 1926 had not fundamentally altered China's impotence in international politics. In light of these repeated defeats and humiliation of the Chinese armies, it is hardly surprising that "most foreigners were convinced that an understrength battalion of Western troops could have disposed of a Chinese warlord division before breakfast."[1]

Against this background of venality, warlordism, disintegration and generalized weakness of China, we turn to an examination of the two major wars fought by China against foreign powers in this century—the Sino-Japanese War (1937-1945) and the Korean War (1950-1953).

SIMILARITIES

There are a number of similarities between the Sino-Japanese War and Korean War that validate a comparison of Chinese performance in these two wars. In these two wars China faced the armed forces of two of the world's most powerful and rising countries—Imperial Japan and the United States. And it faced these enemies relatively alone. Although fighting was intense in the beginning of both wars, slacked off in the middle, and resumed towards the end, the level of fighting was at times very high. In the Korean War, for example, more shells were fired than in all of World War II. In both wars the numerically superior Chinese army faced a technologically superior foe with complete air and sea dominance. The result was a catastrophic casualty rate for the Chinese armies. In the Sino-Japanese War over eight years the Chinese army suffered 3.2 million casualties, in the Korean War over three years the People's Liberation Army (PLA) suffered 600,000 to 900,000 casualties. Equally revealing is the fact that while in the Sino-Japanese war there were 3.3 Chinese casualties for every Japanese casualty, in the Korean War the rate was 3.2 to 4.1 Communist casualties for every Allied casualty. In both wars the enemy escalated troop levels to somewhat reduce the inevitable manpower edge of a China with its 450 million people compared to 155 million Americans and 70 million Japanese. The

Japanese commitment to China rose from 300,000 men in the summer of 1937 to 1,050,000 men in August 1945, while the American and Allied commitment to Korea rose from 230,000 men in October 1950 to 932,000 men in June 1953. And, as important, such top American commanders in Korea as Douglas MacArthur, Maxwell Taylor, James Van Fleet, and Matthew Ridgway had equally fine Japanese counterparts in the Sino-Japanese War.[2]

In both wars against technically advanced enemies, the Chinese, lacking a major industrial base, faced serious problems. These problems were aggravated by the loss of its primary industrial base in Manchuria. By 1937 Japan had fully occupied Manchuria, and by 1950 the impact of Japanese occupation (1937–1945), Russian looting (1946), and Chinese civil war (1946–1949) had sharply reduced Manchurian output. With limited foreign help, the Chinese armies in these two wars remained quite primitive infantry armies without significant tank, air, or naval forces deployed in combat (in later stages of the Korean War the Chinese Air Force remained in a defensive role). In both wars the Chinese armies began the war (in 1937 and 1950) with two to three million men and gradually increased in size during the war. The foot soldiers remained overwhelmingly poorly educated peasants deployed in large numbers with commanders ill prepared for fighting on a modern battlefield. In the Korean War 50 to 70 percent of all PLA soldiers in October 1950 had previously fought for the Kuomintang armies in the civil war or Sino-Japanese War.[3]

However, of great importance to China was the fact that its enemies eschewed total war with China and deployed only a fraction of their capabilities, opting in each case for a limited war. Throughout the Sino-Japanese War the principal dreaded enemies of Japan were Russia in the north and the United States in the south, not China to the west. In December 1941 the Japanese army kept 22 divisions in China, while 23 divisions were deployed in Manchuria, the Pacific, and Southeast Asia, and 6 divisions were held back in Japan, Korea, and Formosa. By the end of the war a mere 15 percent of the 7,200,000 men in the Japanese army, or 26 of 169 Japanese infantry divisions, were located in China. Only 25 percent of all Japanese war deaths from 1931 to 1945 occurred in the Chinese theater. Similarly, the United States viewed the Korean War as a sideshow, albeit an important one, to the main confrontation in Europe. By December 1950 the seven American divisions in Korea represented 10 percent of total American military manpower. By the summer of 1953 the 250,000 American troops in Korea still represented a small fraction of American capabilities.[4]

Both Great Powers entered war with China overconfident and underprepared for the conflict. Japan, having scored such easy triumphs in Manchuria in 1931, "was misguided by her victory and looked down upon China." At Wake Island in October 1950 no one disagreed with General MacArthur that the Chinese would risk "utter destruction" if they intervened.[5]

Nevertheless, these two Great Powers, even fighting with only part of their capabilities, posed an overwhelming military threat to backward, underdeveloped China. The Imperial Japanese Army represented a formidable fighting force. Given the short distance separating it from China, Japan could deploy its modern navy, the third largest and most powerful in the world, with devastating effectiveness against a small and antiquated Chinese army. The highly skilled Japanese air force could gain total and unchallenged supremacy in the sky against Chiang Kai-shek's pitiful air force. On the ground the traditional Chinese army would have grave difficulties standing up to a more modern Japanese army in which each division had four times more firepower than a Chinese division.[6]

The same was true for the United States. No less than 1.4 million Americans were mobilized to serve in Korea, where the United States spent 18 billion dollars, exclusive of soldiers' pay. President Truman in December 1950 announced a state of national emergency, created an Office of Defense Mobilization, nearly doubled the defense budget, and announced plans for a one-million-man increase in the size of the armed forces. The American air force, with over 1,000 planes, put on an awesome display of firepower in the Korean War. A major American naval effort played a key role in bottling up the Communist navies, bombarding important targets, and leading amphibious assaults, as at Inchon. Overall, as in the latter Vietnam era, the American military possessed and utilized its massive technological capabilities against the enemy.

The American and Japanese armies were considered to be among the best armies of the world when they confronted China. Since the Meiji Restoration of 1868, the Japanese army had been ever-victorious. In 1894–1895, the Japanese army had easily defeated the Chinese army in Manchuria; in 1904–1905 it had crushed the Russian army at Port Arthur and scattered the Russian navy in the straits of Tsushima and in 1931–1932 easily conquered the Chinese armies in Manchuria. Too, in 1941 and 1942 the Japanese military would destroy the American fleet at Pearl Harbor and conquer a vast colonial territory of 1.7 million square miles with a population of 150 million people. Even in defeat in the latter years of World War II, Japan would fight with notable courage and determination.

Similarly, the American military had earned a very high reputation as a fighting force. In 1898 the Americans had easily routed the Spanish in the Caribbean and Philippines. In both world wars the Americans had entered late (1917 and 1941) but had provided a decisive impetus to ultimate Allied victory. In 1945 the United States, having played a major role in smashing Nazi Germany and almost single-handedly defeating Imperial Japan, emerged as a nascent superpower. Thus, in 1937 and 1950 China found itself face to face with two of the world's most feared—and in the previous one hundred years, unbeaten—military powers.

COMMUNIST DISADVANTAGES IN THE KOREAN WAR

Nature of the Enemy

Beyond these numerous similarities between the two wars, there were a number of factors that made the Korean War considerably more difficult for the Chinese army than the Sino-Japanese War. The greatest single obstacle for China in 1950, which was lacking in 1937, was the powerful nature of its enemy. For, simply put, the United States was a far more powerful country, both industrially and militarily, than Japan. In the direct confrontation between these two powers in World War II, the United States had crushed and occupied Japan, suffering perhaps 130,000 American battle deaths in the Pacific to over 1,000,000 Japanese battle deaths. This occured at a time when, as Admiral Ernest King observed at the Casablanca Conference, the Allies were devoting only 15 percent of their total resources against Japan in the Pacific and Asia.[7]

Similarly, encounters with the world's other emerging superpower, the Soviet Union, had also ended disastrously for Japan. In July and August 1938 at Lake Hassan on the Korean-Soviet-Chinese border a powerful Soviet force inflicted over 10,000 casualties on a Japanese division and seized a strategic hill. In August 1939 at Khalkin-gol on the Manchurian-Outer Mongolian border, Soviet General Zhukov's Red Army troops routed 60,000 Japanese troops, inflicting nearly 50,000 casualties. In August 1945 in a period of several weeks the Red Army smashed the vaunted Japanese Kwangtung Army, occupied the bulk of Manchuria, and inflicted 677,000 casualties (including 84,000 deaths) on the Japanese army.[8]

The Japanese army was not in the same class as the American

or Soviet army. The essential problem was that in 1937, unlike today, Japan lagged far behind the world's leading economic powers, and most notably the United States, in its industrial base and military production capacity. Table 12 quite dramatically makes this point as it demonstrates just how much American production of key economic resources exceeded Japanese production during World War II. In electricity and grain, American superiority over Japan was of an order of between 7 and 8 to one and in steel and coal between 10 and 11 to 1. And in oil the United States produced more in a day than Japan did in a year.

Table 13 shows the great advantage enjoyed by the United States in all areas of war production. Especially telling is the fact that while the United States produced 98,600 tanks and self-propelled artillery pieces from January 1942 until August 1945, Japan produced but 2,600 such vehicles. In all other key areas—from rifles and cannons to ships and planes—the United States outproduced Japan by margins ranging from 3.6 to 1 up to 6.8 to 1.[9]

These vast differences in economic production made the United States a considerably more dangerous foe for China than Japan. The Americans made far greater use of their air and naval superiority

TABLE 12:   American and Japanese Economic Production During World War II, 1939-1945

Resource	United States	Japan	United States:Japan Ratio
Oil	1,392.6	1.7	819.2:1
Steel	511.7	43.1	11.9:1
Coal	3,754.6	365.0	10.3:1
Grain	837.0	242.9	8.4:1
Electricity	1,678.3	242.9	6.9:1

SOURCE: Istoriya vtoroi mirovoi voiny 1939-1945, vol. 12 (Moscow: Voenizdat, 1983), pp. 176, 193.

Note: All figures refer to millions of tons, except for electricity, which is calculated in billions of kilowatts.

TABLE 13:   American and Japanese War Production (January 1942–August 1945)

Weapon	United States	Japan	United States:Japan Ratio
Tanks and Self-Propelled Artillery	98,600	2,600	37.9:1
Machine Guns	2,594,100	380,000	6.8:1
Rifles and Carbines	12,292,100	2,328,000	5.3:1
Military Planes	190,600	49,000	3.7:1
Cannons	545,500	148,700	3.7:1
Large Fighting Ships	733	205	3.6:1

SOURCES: Istoriya vtoroi mirovoi voina 1939–1945, vol. 12 (Moscow: Voenizdat, 1983), pp. 181, 202.

than did the Japanese. With an air force in Korea of 960 planes in July 1951 and 1,710 planes in April 1953 (of which 775 were jet fighters), the Americans, averaging over 10,000 sorties a month by early 1952, wreaked such havoc on enemy installations, supplies, and supply lines that close to 500,000 men had to be mobilized to repair the damage and fortify Communist positions. In a typical January 1951 interdiction campaign, thousands of miles of roads and tracks and hundreds of bridges were destroyed, while traffic choke points were attacked almost daily. The use of no less than three naval task forces replete with four major battleships and five carriers provided massive firepower, which repeatedly raked Communist positions along the coast and inland. As the Joint Chiefs of Staff observed in a November 17, 1952 memo to Secretary of Defense Robert Lovett:

The principal factor favorable to the UNC (United Nations Command) in the present military situation in Korea is the air superiority which the UNC air forces hold over North Korea. This air superiority has enabled the UNC to defeat, in large measure, attempts by Communists to rebuild and restore airfields, railroads, bridges and other communication facilities. This action combined with the naval blockade of North Korea ... constitutes the most potent means, at present available to the UNC, of maintaining the degree of military pressure which might impel the Communists to agree, finally, to acceptable armistice terms.[10]

By contrast, the Japanese armed forces, possessing a far lower level of technical capabilities and viewing China only as a secondary theater of action, deployed much less air and naval power in the vast expanses of China than the United States deployed in the far smaller confines of the Korean peninsula. Japanese air power in China grew slowly from 450 planes in 1937 to 800 planes in 1945, representing only 29 percent of the Japanese air force in 1937 and declining to 11 percent in 1943 and 7 percent in 1945. By 1944 the Japanese had even lost air superiority over much of China. At the end of 1944 in West China the United States deployed 653 fighters and bombers to only 94 for Japan. Similarly, the bulk of Japan's considerable naval power was deflected to the south against the American navy. By 1945 there were a mere 64,000 naval personnel among the over one million Japanese troops in China.[11]

There was also a great disparity between American and Japanese firepower on the ground. So massive was American artillery capability that in less than a week of fierce fighting in October 1952 the Eighth Army sent 533,000 howitzer shells at the Communists. From October to December 1952 the UN fired 6.1 million artillery shells at the Communists receiving 1.1 million shells in return. Combined with tank, air and naval power, the result was that "even atomic bombing could hardly have pulverized man and his property more thoroughly than this ultimate of conventional warfare."[12] By contrast, the Japanese army, stockpiling its limited supply of artillery shells for possible use against the Russians in the north and Americans in the south, expended minimal firepower on the ground. While Japanese troops at Shanghai in September 1937 were rationed to two to three shells per cannon per day, in 1938 Field Marshal Hata Shunroki suffered from "grievous shortages" of artillery shells for his offensive to Hankow. With Japan deploying only 300 to 500 tanks and limited quantities of artillery and artillery shells, Alvin Coox has correctly stressed that, "essentially the Japanese were still relying on infantry, cold steel, 'human bullets' and the so-called 'Yamato Spirit'."[13]

The United States represented a more dangerous threat than Japan in other key areas as well. While Japan had no nuclear weapons, the United States not only had them, but both Presidents Truman and Eisenhower expressed a willingness to use them. At a press conference of President Truman on November 30, 1950, shortly after Chinese intervention in the Korean War, there ensued the following exchange:

> *President Truman:* We will take whatever steps are necessary to meet the military situation, just as we always have.
>
> *Question:* Will that include the atomic bomb?
>
> *President Truman:* That includes every weapon that we have.
>
> *Question:* Mr. President, you said 'every weapon that we have.' Does that mean there is active consideration of the use of the atomic bomb?
>
> *President Truman:* There has always been active consideration of its use. I don't want to see it used. It is a terrible weapon.[14]

Similarly, having become president in January 1953, General Eisenhower actively considered using nuclear weapons to break the stalemate in Korea. Notes taken at a February 11, 1953 National Security Council meeting reveal that "the president ... then expressed the view that we should consider the use of tactical A-bombs on the Kaesong area, which provided a good target for this type of weapon."[15] At a National Security Council meeting on March 31, 1953, President Eisenhower suggested that "it would be worth the cost if, through the use of atomic weapons, we could (1) achieve a substantial victory over the Communist forces and (2) get to a line at the waist of Korea." Indeed, notes of the meeting show that "the President and Secretary Dulles were in complete agreement that somehow or other the tabu which surrounds the use of atomic weapons would have to be destroyed."[16]

Furthermore, the United States was at peace in 1950 and able to mobilize its full resources against China. By contrast, Japan was at war with the United States and its European allies from December 1941 onward and fearful of Russia during the entire Sino-Japanese War. By 1942, with 1.1 million Japanese troops held immobile in Manchuria, there were more Japanese troops committed to a cold war against Russia in the north than actually fighting a hot war against China in the west. As the American charge in England, Johnson, wrote to the secretary of state in October, 1937:

> Some observers believe, in fact, that the best of the Japanese troops are

not being employed against the Chinese, but only the younger and
older troops, while the best of the younger and physically fit reserves
are being held for later possible use against the Russians. This is difficult to confirm but it is fairly certain that the army in 'Manchoukou'
and Korea is being kept at full strength and at peak efficiency to meet
all possible eventualities.[17]

Of considerable importance here too was that South Korea ultimately proved to be of far more value as an American ally in the war
than North Korea was to its Chinese ally. This might seem surprising
since the North Korean army had almost obliterated the South
Korean army in the summer of 1950. But the American counterattack in September 1950 soon led to the seizure of Pyongyang, surrender of 135,000 North Korean troops, and virtual disintegration of
the North Korean army. By the end of October 1950 there were only
20,000 North Korean troops in combat. Having been installed by
the Red Army rather than through a revolution, the Kim Il-sung
government proved unable to mobilize the population to effective
resistance. The North Korean army, shattered after Inchon, never
regained its strength. In 1953 it was estimated to number only about
50,000 men. By contrast, the South Korean army, which had largely
disintegrated under the impact of the North Korean invasion in the
summer of 1950 and performed poorly for the next year, staged a
remarkable comeback. By the summer of 1953 the South Korean
army had expanded to over 550,000 men, providing the bulk of
allied manpower.[18] Thus, while allies were largely irrelevant in the
Sino-Japanese War, in the Korean War the Chinese army got little
help from a shattered North Korean army while the American
army received major help from a reconstituted South Korean army.

Japanese and American Policies

In a number of other vital areas, the United States was to prove to be
a far more difficult enemy than Japan. While Japan had become
China's historic enemy by wresting vital territory from it by force in
1894-1895 (Taiwan and Korea) and 1931-1932 (Manchuria), the
United States had been its erstwhile ally, providing significant assistance during the Sino-Japanese War. In 1950 many Chinese had a
positive view of the United States, which had destroyed and occupied their enemy, Japan, while in 1937 few Chinese had a positive
view of Japan, which had just completed the rape and plunder of
Manchuria. In addition, popular mobilization against the United
States was further hindered by the fact that the American military,

despite General MacArthur's wishes, scrupulously avoided any air attacks against or ground incursions into Chinese territory during the Korean War. The Japanese from 1937 to 1945 not only occupied large areas of Chinese territory but raped, pillaged, and plundered their way across China in a grotesque manner, exceeded in their brutality only by the conduct of Nazi Germany in occupied Europe during World War II.

A brief catalogue of Japanese war crimes in China shows why Chalmers Johnson considered Japanese misconduct to be the best vehicle for Chinese popular mobilization against Japan during wartime—albeit by the Chinese Communist party and not the Kuomintang. The Japanese pursued a multifaceted program aimed at the political, economic, and military subjugation of China. At the political level, almost no Japanese concessions were made to even attempt to maintain the charade of national independence under the puppet leaders such as Wang Ching-wei. The puppets weren't allowed to even have their own flag; Japanese troops were in evidence everywhere, and Japanese "advisers" ran the civil service. Streets were renamed for Japanese generals; Chinese clocks were set to Tokyo time, and giant rallies were staged to celebrate the capitulation of Chinese cities to the Japanese army.[19]

Economically, Japan tried to turn China into its own colonial servant. No less than 700,000 Japanese civilians flooded into China to assist in this process. China became a monopolistic market for Japanese manufactured goods. The Japanese expropriated all Chinese government-run enterprises, mainly comprising railroads, utilities, coal mines and iron works, while repudiating all local and foreign debts. They took over almost all significant private enterprises in areas ranging from cement factories and coal mines to chemical plants and cotton mills. They confiscated or purchased at low prices existing stocks of raw materials and created monopolies in vital areas. As a result of these varying forms of economic exploitation, George Taylor found that in North China "almost nothing in which any profit could be made was left to the Chinese. Chinese were not only ousted from the main lines of economic enterprise but also were driven out of governmental, municipal and educational positions."[20] The lower classes suffered equally at the hands of the new Japanese rulers. In Shanghai in 1938 over one million Chinese were unemployed, while those who could find work were more nakedly exploited than ever. In rural areas, all pretense at reforms were abandoned in favor of Japanese exploitation.

The most striking aspect of Japan's "New Order" in China was the systematic and massive terrorization of China's civilian population in order to subjugate them and ensure their passive acceptance of Japanese rule. The atrocities began shortly after the initiation of hostilities in July 1937. The Japanese conquest of Paoting in September 1937 led to "a week's drunken frenzy of rape, murder, burning and looting" in which much of the city was destroyed, and 25,800 Chinese died by Japanese estimation. In the infamous "rape of Nanking" at the end of 1937, Japanese troops burned over one-third of the city to the ground, raped countless thousands of women, and wantonly slaughtered 200,000 to 300,000 helpless victims. Elsewhere the Japanese repeatedly bombed villages, often on market days, killing many innocent civilians.[21]

The worst was yet to come. Frustrated by continuing Chinese resistance in the face of numerous Japanese victories, the Japanese commanders in North China, led by General Okamura Neiji, in 1940 devised the infamous "three-all" policy—"kill all, burn all, destroy all"—to try to obliterate civilian opposition. After General Doolittle's flyers were rescued in Chekiang after a raid on Japan, for example, 100,000 Japanese troops ravaged Chekiang and Kiangsi provinces from June to August of 1942, killing perhaps 250,000 Chinese civilians. American Ambassador to China Gauss related to the U.S. secretary of state that when the Japanese retreated from West Hupeh in May, 1943

> they burned villages and killed people on a vast scale. . . . Large towns and small villages in the battle area were reduced to ashes and most of the people were killed or taken away by the enemy, who also carried off or destroyed all movable property, broke dikes and burned boats in the area affected. The population was greatly reduced and the destruction effected by the enemy will require twenty to thirty years to repair.[22]

The ferocious brutality of the Japanese occupiers inevitably mobilized the population. Chinese fury at Japanese brutality led to the killing of perhaps 80,000 Japanese civilians (from a total of 330,000) in Northern Manchuria after the surrender of Japan in 1945.[23]

Internal Problems

The People's Liberation Army in the Korean War faced a series of difficult internal problems not faced by the Kuomintang Army in the Sino-Japanese War. The PLA went into Korea only a few months after the conclusion of a bloody three-year civil war, which itself had started only a year after the conclusion of the eight-year-long Sino-Japanese War. The lack of any respite in fighting for over a decade meant there had been no time to tackle vital tasks. Over one million captured Kuomintang soldiers and their equipment still had to be integrated in the PLA, which needed a new and more modern standardized training system. Major foreign operations, such as the occupation of Tibet and Formosa, were high military priorities. Even more important was the suppression of over two million scattered "bandits" and Kuomintang soldiers, especially in central and southern China. And while all these tasks remained for the People's Liberation Army, it suddenly and unexpectedly found itself plunged into war against the world's leading superpower.[24]

The Chinese government in 1950 faced huge tasks in achieving political unity and economic reconstruction and growth. The achievement of political unity in a war-shattered country—and especially the integration of newly conquered South China—was a high priority. The mobilization for war of a people extremely war-weary after 13 years of internal and external war would be particularly difficult. For as a British embassy memo to the American State Department on September 28, 1950 argued about China, "Her people overwhelmingly want peace, not war. . . . the difficulty particularly in the case of Korea might well be to whip up any indignation at all."[25] On the economic front the devastation from years of bloody warfare had been intensified by a series of natural disasters, including floods, famine, diseases, and drought, in 1949 and 1950. In 1949 grain production was 74 percent of the 1936 level, coal production 50 percent, and iron and steel production a meager 20 percent. Inflation was still rampant in the cities where millions had fled to escape the war.[26]

And all these problems would be exacerbated by entry into the Korean War. Attempts to gain control of the economy, and carry out large-scale social and economic reforms would be hindered by the diversion of efforts to a major war. A war would accelerate inflationary pressures by increasing defense spending, delaying demobilization, and siphoning off needed talented manpower from the civilian economy. An unpopular foreign war would hinder the creation of much needed popular unity. As a CIA memo of October 12, 1950 asserted about China, "Their domestic problems are of such magnitude that the regime's entire domestic program and economy would be jeopardized by the strains and material damage which would be sustained in a war with the United States . . . the regime's very existence would be endangered."[27]

By contrast, the Kuomintang went into the Sino-Japanese War in 1937 much better prepared. After the 1926 Northern Expedition, the Kuomintang had a decade in power (the "Nanking Decade")

before the war began in 1937. Despite recurrent sallies against warlords and Communists, the central government was able to build up
its army and power in this relatively peaceful decade. Internal tasks
were the main task of this time. Furthermore, the war with Japan,
far from being unexpected, had been long awaited ever since the
Japanese occupation of Manchuria. Thus, although there was inter-
mittent warfare and difficult tasks of national integration performed
in the "Nanking Decade," this era nevertheless gave the Kuomintang
far more time in power and a quieter period of construction before
the Sino-Japanese War than the Communists possessed before the
Korean War.

External Problems

There were several crucial external problems that existed for the
People's Liberation Army in Korea but not for the Kuomintang army
in the Sino-Japanese War. Most importantly, while the Chinese army
could fight the Japanese army in the vast expanses of China with
unlimited space for maneuvering and mobility, in Korea the Chinese
army found itself forced to fight in the narrow space of the mountainous Korean peninsula, only 90 to 200 miles wide and 525 to 600
miles long. Under these conditions, the lack of Chinese firepower on
the battlefield and concomitant air and naval power, certainly a
serious problem on the endless territory of China, became an overwhelming deficiency in the narrow confines of the Korean peninsula.

Beyond this, the Kuomintang army had the enormous advantage
of fighting at home among a supportive population mobilized by
Japanese brutality. In this favorable environment the Communists
developed the highly successful "people's war" strategy of guerrillas
operating with a strong popular base. By contrast, the PLA faced
tremendous difficulties in operating on alien Korean territory uncon-
genial for its preferred strategy of people's war. Despite attempts to
build support among the local population, the Chinese found the
North Koreans "generally cold" and South Koreans "actively hostile." This forced the Chinese to adopt more traditional professional
tactics, replete with a more conventional system of logistics and
intelligence. Living off the countryside was far more difficult a
proposition in Korea than China.[28]

THE PROBLEM

The preceding analysis brings us to the fundamental question of this
chapter—if the Sino-Japanese War and Korean War are broadly com-

parable and if the Chinese Communists in 1950–1953 faced a series of additional political, economic, and military obstacles not faced by the Chinese Nationalists from 1937 to 1945, then why did the Chinese army perform so much better in the Korean War than in the Sino-Japanese War? In all three phases of the two wars, the Chinese army performed at a far higher level in the Korean War than in the Sino-Japanese War.

The contrast is especially vivid if we compare the initial phase of the two wars, July 1937–December 1938 in the Sino-Japanese War and November 1950–June 1951 in the Korean War. The first 18 months of the Sino-Japanese War can be considered a period of unmitigated disaster for the Chinese army as the Japanese army seized all major coastal cities of East China. Although Chiang Kai-shek's troops possessed great numerical superiority (between two and four to one), external aid, and the inestimable advantage of fighting on native territory, disaster piled on disaster.

In July 1937, only three weeks after the Marco Polo Bridge incident, the Japanese army encircled and occupied Peking as the Chinese army withdrew in disarray. Other key provincial capitals, as Paoting and Tientsin, soon fell. In the heavy fighting at Shanghai that lasted three months, Japanese troops occupied the city in November 1937, having inflicted over 300,000 casualties on the Chinese army compared to 40,000 Japanese casualties. In December 1937 the Japanese army stormed and seized Nanking in less than a week, routing a Chinese army of over 100,000 men. In 1938 the Japanese advance continued, seizing such important cities as Wuhan, Canton, Hsuchow, Amoy, and Foochow. Thus, by October 1938 the five most populous cities in China—Peking, Nanking, Shanghai, Canton, and Wuhan—were in Japanese hands; the government of Chiang Kai-shek had been driven far away to the southwestern stronghold of Chungking, and his best armies had been smashed on the battlefield. By October 1938 Kuomintang China was largely isolated with Japanese occupation of all main seaports and 1.5 million square kilometers of territory with a population of 170 million people.[29]

Compared to this record of disastrous Kuomintang defeats, the PLA's performance in Korea from November 1950 to June 1951 was simply outstanding. In October and early November 1950, 300,000 Chinese troops moved rapidly, undetected into North Korea. After a brief but decisive destruction of a South Korean division at Ohjong, they withdrew and then dealt the American army nearing the Yalu a massive surprise blow on November 25, 1950. By December 5 the PLA occupied Pyongyang; by December 25 all of North Korea was totally under Chinese control; and on January 4, 1951, the PLA marched into Seoul. In the process, the U.S. Eighth Army's 275 mile retreat would go down as "the longest retreat in American military history," necessitated by the fact that as David Rees has reported, "At the front throughout December the moral collapse of the Eighth Army was complete, as bug-out fever raged everywhere and even GHQ succumbed to what the naval historian M.C. Cagle calls 'panic and inertia'."[30] By January 1951, the Central Intelligence Agency's National Intelligence Estimate no. 10 would conclude that

> under present circumstances the Chinese Communists probably have the military capability of concurrently carrying on their operations in Korea, intervening effectively in Indochina and Tibet, attacking Burma, and capturing Hong Kong, while continuing to contain opposition groups within China.[31]

During the first six months of 1951, there ensued a series of offensives on both sides without decisive results. In the middle of March the American army had retaken Seoul and by the end of the month reached the Thirty-eighth Parallel where the war had originally begun in June 1950. Then in April 1951 a major offensive by 21 Chinese divisions and 9 North Korean divisions mauled some South Korean units and pushed the Eighth Army back 35 miles to within 5 miles north of Seoul. In May 1951 a major Chinese attack failed, permitting an American advance in June 1951 to Line Kansas, 8 to 10 miles north of the Thirty-eighth Parallel. Despite these defeats, China still retained more than enough military power to maintain and impose a lengthy stalemate during the negotiations that ensued at this time. On July 26, 1951 General Matthew Ridgway would report in Walter Hermes' words to General J. Lawton Collins that despite good UN morale, "the picture was not all rosy. The enemy was increasing his strength steadily and could launch a full-scale offensive at any time."[32] Thus, by the end of the first phase of the two wars, the Kuomintang army in October 1938 was a defeated, disheartened, even passive force, while the Communist army in July 1951, having experienced victories and defeats, had become a strong and capable force.

These same pattens continued during the middle, relatively passive phases of the two wars. From the end of 1938 until the summer of 1944 the Japanese army, distracted by preparation for and war against American and British forces in the south and fear of war against Russian forces in the north, conducted only a sporadic war in China. The Kuomintang armies continued to stay on the defensive and withdraw even though they significantly outnumbered the Japanese troops. China under Chiang Kai-shek awaited its deliverance from without rather than relying on its own considerable internal resources. This is not to say that there were no victories scored by Chinese troops. In May 1939 a Japanese attack failed to take Sian. In all three battles for Changsha (1939, 1941, 1942) the Chinese army successfully protected the city from determined Japanese attack. And in 1943 and 1944 Chinese divisions spearheaded the successful Allied invasion of Burma.

Overall, though, the record was dismal. The Japanese army, whenever it was willing to divert resources from the other fronts, could move most of the time almost at will against a prostrate China—and there was not a single successful Chinese offensive in this period. In March 1939 the Japanese army, outnumbered three to one, easily stormed and seized Nanchang. By late 1939 all major north-south rail lines were in or near Japanese positions. A rare winter offensive, employing 50 percent of all Chinese military manpower, turned into a "debacle," showing that "Chinese generals would not and could not fight."[33] In June 1940 the Japanese army administered a "sound drubbing" to the Chinese army and seized Ichang, only 240 miles from Chungking. In the fall and winter of 1940 a Japanese offensive in four key provinces destroyed no less than 24 Chinese divisions. A May 1941 offensive in Shansi scattered the organized Chinese units north of the Yellow River into ineffective guerrilla forces. In May 1942 the Japanese destroyed an Anglo-Chinese force to take over Burma.[34]

Compared to the Kuomintang armies which floundered, the Communist armies in 1952 in Korea continued to improve their capabilities and performance. During the summer and fall of 1952 there ensued a savage fight over a series of strategic hills in the Iron Triangle complex. Despite the massive application of American air and artillery support in a six-week campaign of hard fighting in October and November of 1952, the United Nations made only limited gains at very high costs.

The American military command in private was quick to acknowledge the power of the PLA late in 1951 and throughout 1952. In December 1951, National Intelligence Estimate no. 55 said that "the growing power of Chinese Communist forces . . . will enable them to deal severe damage to the UN forces and may make it impossible for the United Nations to conduct general offensive operations except at prohibitive cost."[35] In late September 1952, General Mark Clark, UN commander in Korea, reported to the Joint Chiefs of Staff:

> Our problem is, of course, difficult. We confront undemoralized enemy forces, far superior in strength, who occupy excellent, extremely well organized defensive positions in depth and who continue to provide themselves with sufficient logistics support. Under these conditions, it appears evident that positive aggressive action, designed to obtain military victory and achieve an armistice on our terms, is not feasible by this command with current forces operating under current restrictions.[36]

And the November 1952 National Intelligence Estimate no. 64 concluded that "communist ground forces have a high offensive potential and are capable of launching a major attack with little warning."[37]

Especially impressive was the growth in the defensive capabilities of an army known primarily for its zest for the offensive. The PLA in this period of static warfare built a massive system of deep underground fortifications across the waist of Korea to a depth of between 15 and 25 miles. Dug on the reverse slopes of hills, these formidable fortifications equalled Japanese efforts in World War II. During the intense fighting on Sniper Ridge and Pyramid Hill in November 1952 it took 50 rounds of accurate artillery fire to destroy one PLA artillery piece because of the Communists' skillful use of protection. Similarly, the PLA developed such effective countermeasures to American air attacks on rail lines that Operation STRANGLE early in 1952 had to be abandoned when naval pilots reported rail lines were fully repaired within 12 hours of air strikes![38]

Perhaps the last phase of the two wars showed most strikingly the differences between the two armies. Everywhere in 1944 the Japanese forces were in headlong retreat as the American forces island-hopped their way towards Japan. In November 1944 armadas of B-29s based in the Marianas were attacking Tokyo, and by December American forces had broken through Japanese defense lines in the Philippines. Only in China was the Japanese army, with yet most of its air power, naval transport, experienced troops, and supply stockpiles transferred to other more pressing fronts, able to score smashing victories over the disintegrating Chinese armies.

Outnumbered three to one by Chinese troops and poorly supplied, the 500,000 Japanese troops in Operation ICHIGO, which lasted from April until December 1944, pushed aside and humiliated the Kuomintang army. In eight months the Japanese army occupied Chinese territory in eight provinces with a population of 60 million people, greater than that of France. And it accomplished all its operational goals. By late May 1944 the Japanese had cleared the Peking-

Hankow line and seized Chengchow and Loyang. In June they finally occupied Changsha and in August Hengyang. By November they had destroyed all American air bases in East China, with the occupation of Kweilin and Liuchow. In December a Japanese column from Indochina linked up with a Japanese column from Kwangsi at Lungchow, opening a continental land corridor from Manchuria to Indochina. With a December advance to Tushan, less than 200 miles from the Kuomintang capital, the Japanese seemed to threaten the existence of the Nationalist government.[39]

By June in two telegrams to the secretary of state, American Ambassador in China Gauss could write from Chungking that "Chinese forces have put up practically no resistance," and "it is too readily accepted as a fact by most of Chinese officialdom that the Chinese armies cannot put up effective resistance."[40] Perhaps the official American White Paper on China most trenchantly analyzed the situation at the end of 1944, which it called a "disaster":

> The entire East China front had collapsed and there was little reason to believe that the Japanese if they so elected would not have the capability of attacking Chungking. . . . Increasingly it had become apparent that the Chinese war effort had largely ceased to be an effective factor in China and that to a disturbing extent the Chinese will to fight had vanished.[41]

What a difference a decade made in Chinese military capabilities as seen in the last major fighting in Korea in 1953. After a winter lull, the PLA in fierce fighting overran a series of key UN outposts, including Reno, Vegas, and Old Baldy Hills, in March 1953. In June 1953 a major Chinese assault pushed five South Korean divisions back several miles in the center of the UN line and was halted only by 2.7 million rounds of UN artillery. This assault by the PLA "showed they could smash ROK units on the Main Line of Resistance at will."[42] Early in July after bloody and intense fighting the Chinese army finally wrested Pork Chop Hill from the American army. A major Chinese drive on July thirteenth penetrated six miles on the central front, mauled four South Korean divisions, and required nine American and South Korean divisions to contain the thrust.[43] After a brief counterattack by the United Nations, the Korean War finally came to a close.

While the Kuomintang army had deteriorated during the Sino-Japanese War, the Communist army showed marked improvement during the Korean War. Samuel Griffith has observed that in Korea "under conditions of rigorous and testing combat, the PLA vaulted into the twentieth century, and as it did so, it destroyed the long-cherished Western myth that the Chinese was an inferior fighting man."[44] The revolution had thereby created a whole new Chinese army.

CHAPTER 9

Explanations

In the previous chapter we have seen how the Chinese army performed poorly in the Sino-Japanese War and nearly disintegrated by 1944, while it performed very well throughout the Korean War and markedly improved by the end of the war. With barely five years between the two wars and the greater problems faced by the Chinese army in the Korean War than in the Sino-Japanese War, the salient question is simply: How could this happen? As with traditional explanations of Russian successes in World War II, explanations of Chinese successes in the Korean War have one thing in common: they all seek to find some external or transient factors to explain these achievements (which are often themselves denigrated) while studiously ignoring the profound impact of the Chinese Revolution on Chinese military capabilities.

TRADITIONAL EXPLANATIONS

There are seven traditional explanations of Chinese successes—four of which focus on China (numerical superiority, "human wave" tactics, militarism, and foreign aid) and three of which focus on the United States (unpreparedness for war, restrictions, climate, and geography). Let us begin by looking at Western explanations that analyze Chinese variables.

The most common explanation for Chinese accomplishments is to emphasize the vast numerical superiority of Chinese forces on the battlefield. Analysts and authors have conjured up visions of China, with its seemingly inexhaustible human resources of 450 million people, pouring vast "Asiatic hordes" on the field of battle against the hapless Americans. General Douglas MacArthur, the first UN commander in Korea, expressed this sentiment at a 1951 Congressional hearing.

> The number of troops I had was limited, and those conditions indicated the disposition of the troops I had. As a matter of fact, the disposition of these troops, in my opinion, could not have been improved upon, had I known the Chinese were going to attack. The difficulty that arose was not the disposition of the troops but the overwhelming number of enemy forces.[1]

Unfortunately for this argument, a number of scholars, including Allen Whiting and Alexander George, have concluded that in late November 1950, at the time of the PLA offensive, there were no more than 300,000 Chinese troops confronting 440,000 UN troops in North Korea.[2] Indeed, Reginald Thompson has asserted:

> Up forward there was no talk of 'Chinese hordes' and there weren't any.... It is an undisputed fact that the total enemy forces did not outnumber the United Nations, and if air, artillery and the great naval power deployed around the coast with many vital targets, well within range of its heavy guns, is taken into account, there could be no comparison in fighting strength.[3]

Rather it was Chinese skill at secret and camouflaged movement, superb infantry tactics, and the division of the UN forces that created disparity at the point of attack.

Furthermore, by analyzing numbers for the entire Korean War, it becomes evident that the Chinese army in Korea actually enjoyed overall *far less* numerical superiority than its counterparts had enjoyed in the Sino-Japanese War. Table 14 shows that in the Sino-Japanese War the Chinese army enjoyed a vast numerical superiority ranging from a low ratio of four to one in 1937 to a high ratio of seven to one in 1944. On the battlefield at Shanghai in 1937 the Japanese General Matsui found his 300,000 troops opposed by no less than 700,000 Chinese troops. At Wuhan in 1938 the 380,000 Japanese troops were dwarfed by the presence of roughly 800,000 Chinese troops.[4]

Table 15 shows that China and its North Korean partner enjoyed far smaller numerical superiority on the Korean battlefield. The table shows a relative equality of manpower on the two sides until July 1951 when the truce talks began. During the last years of the war,

Communist (predominantly Chinese) manpower exceeded UN manpower in Korea generally by margins of between 1.3 and 1.6 to 1.0.
While obviously significant, these ratios were far below the between
4 and 7 to 1 numerical superiority enjoyed by the Chinese army in
the Sino-Japanese War. An examination of the number of troops
deployed on both sides shows that numbers could hardly have been

TABLE 14: Chinese and Japanese Troop Levels in China During the Sino-
Japanese War (1937-1945)

Year	China	Japan	China:Japan Ratio
		Number of Troops	
1937	2,000,000	500,000	4.0:1
1939	3,000,000	550,000	5.4:1
1941	3,800,000	600,000	6.3:1
1943	4,200,000	620,000	6.8:1
1944	5,700,000	820,000	7.0:1
1945	5,300,000	1,050,000	5.0:1

SOURCES: For China the sources respectively are Hsu Long-Hsuen and Chang
Ming-kai, History of the Sino-Japanese War (1937-1945) (Taipei, Taiwan: Chung
Wu Publishing Company, 1971), p. 172; Sovetskaya voennaya entsiklopediya
(Moscow: Voenizdat, 1978), p. 541; Foreign Relations of the United States
1941 (Washington, D.C.: Government Printing Office, 1956), vol. 4, p. 87;
Istoriya vtoroi mirovoi voiny 1939-1945 (Moscow: Voenizdat, 1976), vol. 7,
p. 439; China Handbook 1937-1945 (New York: Macmillan, 1947), p. 286; and
Foreign Relations of the United States 1945 (Washington, D.C.: Government
Printing Office, 1969), v. 7, p. 1074.
    For Japan the sources respectively are Hsi Sheng-Ch'i, Nationalist China
at War (Ann Arbor, Michigan: University of Michigan Press, 1982), p. 47;
F. F. Liu, A Military History of Modern China, 1924-1949 (Princeton, New
Jersey: Princeton University Press, 1956), p. 205; Foreign Relations of the
United States 1942, China, p. 73; Takushiro Hattori, Yaponiya v voine 1941-
1945, abridged translation (Moscow: Voenizdat, 1973), p. 433, 597; and John
Toland, The Rising Sun (New York: Random House, 1970), p. 622.

Note: The figures for China are only rough approximation. The figures for
Japan exclude troops in Manchuria and Formosa.

TABLE 15:   Troop Levels in Korea During the Korean War, 1950-1953

| Date | Number of Troops | | Communist:UN Ratio |
	Communists	United Nations	
11/50	300,000	440,000	1.0:1.4
7/51	459,000	550,000	1.0:1.2
11/51	604,000	579,600	1.0:1.0
5/52	908,100	698,000	1.3:1.0
1/53	1,200,000	768,000	1.6:1.0
7/53	1,200,000	932,500	1.3:1.0

SOURCES: For sources see James Schnabel, United States Army in the Korean War--Policy and Direction: The First Year (Washington, D.C.: Government Printing Office, 1972), p. 405; Walter Hermes, Truce Tent and Fighting Front (Washington, D.C.: Government Printing Office, 1966), pp. 199, 283, 512; David Rees, Korea: The Limited War (Baltimore, Maryland: Penguin Books, 1964), p. 406; and Alexander George, The Chinese Communist Army in Action, p. 6.

Note: The Chinese army predominated among Communist troops. In January 1953 over 83 percent of all Communist troops were Chinese troops.

decisive, especially when one considers the early PLA victories gained at a time of numerical inferiority.

A second argument closely related to this one is that, utilizing their vast manpower in a callous way, the Chinese simply overran American and South Korean positions by "human wave" tactics. The thrust of the argument is undercut by the fact that the Chinese army in Korea lacked overwhelming numerical superiority over the forces of the United Nations. Too, these writers have misinterpreted the Chinese penchant for gaining a highly localized three to one superiority by crawling swiftly and silently towards the enemy's flanks and rear at night with mass assaults. The United States Marine Corps history of Korea has stated:

> Press correspondents were fond of referring to 'the human sea tactics of the Asiatic hordes.' Nothing could be further from the truth. In reality Chinese soldiers seldom attacked in units larger than a regiment. Even

these efforts were usually reduced to a seemingly endless succession of
platoon infiltrations. It was not mass but deception and success which
made the Chinese Reds formidable.[5]

Third, there has been a tendency to ascribe Chinese success to a
Maoist militarism that created a new Sparta. George Paloczi-Horvath
has called Mao the "emperor of the blue arts," a "warlord" who
created a new "police-state."[6] However, the argument runs into a
series of problems. Most importantly, while the military played a
prominent role in running China's six large administrative regions
from 1950 to 1952, it always acknowledged the supremacy of the
Party. After the dissolution of these regions, the influence of the
military declined sharply for more than a decade until the start of
the Cultural Revolution. Given the fused civil/military elite that ran
the Chinese Communist party for more than two decades before the
assumption of power in 1949, there never developed the dangerous
militarism so prominent in many countries in the world today.
Rather, as we shall see later in this volume, the Chinese leaders under
Mao carried out one of the most thoroughgoing social, economic,
and political revolutions in modern history. Indeed, ironically, if any
leader was militaristic it was Chiang Kai-shek, who subordinated all
programs of social and economic reform to the needs of his army.
And yet, despite—or perhaps because of—this militarism, the Kuomintang army under his leadership gradually disintegrated during
the Sino-Japanese War.

A final explanation focusing on China stresses the important role
of Soviet aid in determining Chinese capabilities. The National
Security Council Staff Study no. 166 of October 16, 1953, made the
following argument.

> But the Korean hostilities are also instructive as to the present limits of
> Chinese Communist military capabilities. All of the aircraft, and per-
> haps some 90 per cent of the ground force equipment and ammunitions
> of the Chinese Communist forces appear to have been supplied by the
> USSR. Chinese Communist military capabilities are thus in large degree
> derivative rather than primary.[7]

In addition to major Soviet arms shipments to China during the
Korean War, the rise of the cold war and emergence of the Sino-
Soviet alliance strengthened the Western conviction that the rise of
the Chinese People's Liberation Army depended primarily on Russian help.

There is no question that Soviet military deliveries, especially of planes and tanks, played a significant role in helping China in the Korean War. Yet several key points are in order. First, Soviet military deliveries were severely limited in the first year of the war, with none to the PLA before its offensive in November 1950. During the first six months of the Korean War only 5 to 6 percent of all Chinese arms were of Soviet origin. As John Gittings has observed:

> Yet Soviet military aid to China was noticeably deficient in the first year of the war; only after the military stalemate began in the summer of 1951 was the Chinese Volunteers' artillery, heavy equipment and air strength built up on a scale comparable with that of the 'UN' force. Moscow pursued a policy of an arms limitation which denied China the opportunity to exploit its early successes to the point of victory (which might have led to an unacceptable escalation of the war) while ensuring after the ceasefire that Chinese and North Korean forces established an impregnable defence against any American counter-offensive (which would be equally unacceptable).[8]

Too, the most powerful Soviet military material—including heavy tanks, howitzers and artillery, and new antitank weapons—were not provided to the PLA. Most of the arms were "obsolescent," often as much as a decade old, and "were inferior to the American weapons which they faced." With no Soviet military advisers to the PLA in Korea (as opposed to 10,000 advisers in Manchuria) and total Soviet aid probably totalling less than a billion dollars, there were clear limits to the impact of Soviet aid on Chinese performance.[9]

The Kuomintang army had received greater foreign aid during the Sino-Japanese War. While the PLA had no foreign advisers before the Korean War, the Kuomintang army had greatly benefited from the German military mission from 1928 to 1938. This mission, led by General von Seeckt and his successor Baron von Falkenhausen with 30 to 100 officers, planned and supervised the training of 30 selected Chinese divisions. After the German withdrawal, their place during the war was taken by the Soviet Union and United States, each of which provided substantial assistance. From 1937 to 1940 no less than 2,000 Soviet pilots (of whom 200 were killed in action) and 500 military advisers helped Chiang Kai-shek's army utilize over 700 Soviet planes and bombers and 40,000 tons of other military hardware, worth roughly 500 million dollars. After the Nazi invasion ended Soviet aid, the United States stepped up its aid to China. From 1937 until August 1945 the United States provided China with 846 million dollars in military aid and 670 million dollars in economic aid. During the war, the American air force in China lost 500 American planes in action and destroyed 2,600 Japanese planes. Over

650,000 tons of material were airlifted to China, much of it to support an American presence that by August 1945 numbered 60,400 men. Ultimately, 1,000 American advisers provided training and American arms for 39 selected Chinese divisions. General Stilwell even served as one of Chiang Kai-shek's two top assistants, while General Gilbert Cheeves served as Chief of Supply for the Chinese army. Clearly, the American and Soviet roles in the Chinese Army from 1937 to 1945 exceeded the Soviet role in the Chinese army from 1950 to 1953.[10]

Thus, none of the traditional explanations focusing on China are especially persuasive, particularly if viewed in a comparative context. The Kuomintang army in the Sino-Japanese War had a greater numerical superiority over the enemy, a more militarist spirit, a domestic front on which to fight, and deeper and more extensive foreign military assistance than the Communist army in the Korean War—and still performed abominably. Now let us turn to three explanatory factors that focus on American disabilities that contributed to Chinese successes—lack of preparedness, restrictions on military deployment, geography, and climate.

One especially popular argument is that the United States was unprepared for the Korean War and hence unable to fight it properly. Indeed in June 1950 the active American army had only 10 combat divisions and 591,000 men, of which 108,500 men were in the Far East Command. While General Douglas MacArthur felt America was "unprepared for war," an official United States Army history of the Korean War asserted:

> That these forces were understrength, inadequately trained and sketchily provisioned concerned mainly their commanders. These commanders, within the limits of their resources, sought to overcome inertia, imposed by years of occupation and prevailing, if uneasy, peace. But on the eve of the storm the command was soft, still hampered by an infectious lassitude, unready to respond swiftly and decisively to a full-scale military emergency.[11]

Yet, although it is clearly true that demobilization had inevitably greatly weakened the American army, even in its "decrepitude" the American military in 1950 was still quite a powerful force. It deployed three thousand tanks, several thousand planes, large flotillas of ships, and nuclear weapons. This seemingly depleted force in the summer of 1950 was able to stem the North Korean offensive at Pusan, in September launch a brilliant landing at Inchon, and by November smash the North Korean army and advance to the Yalu.

The United States had a remarkable ability to vastly expand its military capabilities in a relatively short period of time. And this was especially the case with regard to massive expenditures of firepower—by ships, planes, and artillery pieces—which could compensate for manpower shortages.

A comparative analysis also shows the limitations of the unpreparedness argument. If the United States was caught off guard in 1950, so too had been China, which thought it could stay out of the war. Even more important, China's enemy in 1937, Japan, was no better prepared for war than its enemy in 1950, the United States.

In some ways Japan was even less prepared for war than the United States, even though it took the offensive in 1937. In July 1937 the War Minister Sugiyama Hajima told the lord keeper of the privy seal that "we'll send large forces, smash them in a hurry and get the whole thing over with quickly" and one leading general thought five divisions would be enough to subdue the Chinese.[12] As a result, there was no real mobilization of munitions or training of soldiers and reserves in preparation for war. Thus, Japan entered its war in 1937 quite unprepared for the protracted conflict that lay ahead.

A second common argument is that the United States could have decimated the Chinese forces had it not been for restrictions placed on American military actions by political considerations. American forces were banned from air attacks on Chinese territory, a blockade of the Chinese coast, use of the atomic bomb, or a large increase in the number of American troops. Furthermore, none of Chiang Kai-shek's troops could be used in Korea. In December 1950 General Douglas MacArthur called these restrictions "an enormous handicap, without precedent in military history."[13]

While this argument has some surface plausibility, and there is no doubt that UN troops operated in Korea under far more restraints than Japanese troops in China, a detailed examination shows its limited validity. In all these cases the restrictions made military sense as well as political sense. The troops of Chiang Kai-shek were not used because they had just been overwhelmingly defeated in the civil war by these same Communist troops and because "it was highly possible that a few reverses for Chiang's ground forces would bring wholesale defections, such as had occurred the last time Chiang's troops had met the Communists head-on."[14] In addition, use of these troops might have provoked the wider war with China, which Washington wanted to avoid.

As to atomic weapons, there were strong military reasons against their use. As Paul Nitze, then director of the Policy Planning Staff of the State Department, argued in a November 1950 memo:

> If the bomb were used in Korea it would be for tactical purposes against troop concentrations and artillery support positions. Against such targets it should prove effective. However, such targets would probably not come about normally; they would have to be created by the tactical maneuvers of UN forces. Very few atomic bombs could be used as few targets could be created. . . . It does not appear that in present circumstances the atomic bomb would be militarily decisive in Korea.[15]

Beyond the lack of targets and elusive nature of Chinese troops, there was also the danger that use of atomic weapons could lead to a wider war with China or the Soviet Union.

Nor would large increases in American combat troops have been likely to make a significant difference. As it was, by the end of the war the United Nations was deploying 932,000 troops. Any further increase in the ground forces of the United Nations could be easily matched by the larger Communist forces, drawing on the reserves of the People's Liberation Army. To successfully smash the elaborate defense system effected by the PLA in Korea after June 1951 would have taken a far larger American force than any contemplated by American commanders—and with far higher American casualties. More importantly, if only a fraction of American ground forces were deployed in Korea, a much higher percentage of American air power and naval power was actively engaged in the conflict. Thus, a further enlargement of the war would have been of little value to the United States.

Finally, while the prohibition against American air attacks on Chinese territory or naval blockade of the Chinese coast may have seemed irksome to some commanders, it actually worked to the military advantage of the United States. For while the Chinese gained an important sancturary in Manchuria, the United States gained an even more important sanctuary in South Korea and Japan, free from any enemy air attacks. The American forces were more vulnerable to air attack than the Chinese forces, given the far higher degree of mechanization and smaller staging areas available to the Americans. At a White House meeting of the National Security Council on November 28, 1950, Air Force Secretary Thomas Finletter conceded that "a Chinese air attack would be very serious," and General Omar Bradley warned,

> There are some 300 aircraft back in Manchuria, including 200 two-

engine bombers. They could strike a severe blow. The JCS do not think
we should violate the border pending developments. Our airfields, both
in Korea and Japan, are crowded and we are depending heavily on an
airlift. Our fields are therefore very vulnerable. So too are our road con-
voys. One enemy plane dropped a few bombs on one field and damaged
six of our planes.[16]

By April 1951 Secretary of State Dean Acheson cautioned in a top
secret telegram that "We are vulnerable to heavy air attacks. . . . Our
ports are generally unprotected . . . the enemy could do us considerable damage."[17]

A final, and familiar argument is that the American forces
were hampered by the harsh climate and difficult geography. It is
undoubtedly true that the extremely cold winters, hot summers, and
rugged mountainous terrain hampered American mechanized activity
and air and sea activities. However, to a lesser extent they also hampered the vaunted mobility of Chinese troops. And, equally important, the ideal geography for modern war—such as the plains of
Central Europe and Sinai desert—is found only in a relatively few
locations in the world. Thus, the difficulties inherent in war in Korea
are typical, rather than exceptional.

ALTERNATIVE EXPLANATIONS

Again we have seen the failures of traditional interpretations to
explain the sharp differences in performance between the Chinese
army in the Korean War and the Sino-Japanese War. As in the previous cases, I suggest that the basic explanation lies in the nature of
the revolution that created a new social system that liberated the
social, economic, and military capacities of China to utilize its vast
human and natural resources. Unlike in Russia, there was no massive
program of industrialization, either by 1953 or 1985, to transform
the level of economic development. Unlike the Russian Revolution,
the Chinese Revolution was a mass rural, peasant-based movement.
But while it lacked the capacity to economically transform China,
its mass appeal allowed it the power to transform China politically
and socially. And it did so in a far shorter time than Russia, where
the fundamental transformation of the 1930s occurred more than
a decade after the October Revolution.

CHAPTER 10

The Two Armies at War

By making a detailed analysis of the actual functioning of the Chinese army in the two major wars in this century and by examining in detail the war economy, officer corps, and soldiers in the two armies, we can create an integrated view of the nature of the performance of the Chinese army in the Sino-Japanese War and Korean War.

WAR ECONOMY

Although China in the period between its two major wars scarcely had time to undergo the kind of industrial transformation wrought in Russia between the two world wars, nevertheless there were significant differences between the war economies during the two conflicts. These changes were particularly impressive since the period between the two wars, 1945–1950, was dominated by a bloody and destructive civil war (1946–1949) and a series of natural disasters (1949–1950).

Although military industrial production was unimpressive in China throughout this period, the Communists made far better use of limited resources than the Nationalists. As table 16 shows, the Communists were producing two to three times more rifles and rounds of ammunition and nearly five times more hand grenades than the Nationalists. The Communists made full use of their limited resources in an organized manner. Kuomintang China, on the other hand, did not even have a War Production Board until late 1944 when one was organized under American pressure. Donald Nelson, on a Presidential mission to China in September 1944, found that

TABLE 16:   Military Production in China During the Sino-Japanese War
(1937-1945) and the Korean War (1950-1953)

Weapon	Production (Monthly Average) 1951	March 1941–June 1945
Rifles	15,000	5,100
Hand Grenades	150,000	32,000
Rounds of Ammunition	30,000,000	12,000,000

SOURCES: Declassified Documents Series, 1979, No. 267 B, p. 4 and Charles
Romanus and Riley Sunderland, Stilwell's Command Problems (Washington,
D.C.: Government Printing Office, 1956), p. 413.

China's war economy "had steadily disintegrated and production
declined" to a point where China's arsenals were operating at only 55
percent of capacity. Deriding China's "feeble war production effort,"
Nelson wrote to President Roosevelt that

> the economic effort of the nation was poorly planned and entirely
> uncoordinated. Chinese ordinance procurement officers made little use
> of plants owned by other agencies of governments and by private
> sources. Government departments had no mechanism for cooperation
> with each other or with private industry in the war effort. Procure-
> ment was piecemeal. Statements of requirements by government
> departments were non-existent or completely unrealistic. No system of
> priorities existed nor any mechanism to subsidize the high cost of pro-
> duction of essential materials such as iron and steel.[1]

Perhaps one statistic tells it all: in 1944 the vital steel industry was
operating at less than 20 percent of capacity![2]

Let us now turn to a comparison of the rates of economic growth
in China during the Sino-Japanese War and the Korean War. Both
regimes faced serious problems at the beginning of their wars, in
1937-1938 and 1950. In Kuomintang China, the rapid Japanese conquest of the populous coastal cities deprived China of its small
modern sector and key salt, customs, and industrial tax bases. By
the end of 1938 the Chiang Kai-shek government was confined to
only 14 provinces with 230 million people. The Communist leader-

ship in October 1949, on the eve of the Korean War, faced different, serious problems. While it had unified the country, natural disasters in the form of pests, droughts, and floods in 1949 affected 40 million people. The cumulative devastation of the Sino-Japanese War followed by the civil war left China in 1949 with agricultural output down 40 percent from prewar 1936 levels, coal production down 50 percent, and steel production down a striking 82 percent. The situation in some areas was quite catastrophic and had contributed to the downfall of the Kuomintang regime.[3]

The two regimes dealt quite differently with hardships during the war years. The Kuomintang government did not successfully foster economic development, even with American aid. Even in 1945, agricultural production was a mere 2.6 percent higher than in 1936, while industrial production in the peak year of 1943 was but 12 percent of the 1936 level. Arthur Young, an economic adviser to Chiang Kai-shek, has recalled that "the wartime economy was tragically weak and the structure of government far from ready for the strain of total war."[4]

The Communist government effectively and energetically promoted economic development. While China's real gross national product was the same in 1950 ($60.6 billion) as in 1933 ($60.8 billion) (in itself a damning testimonial to Kuomintang economic mismanagement), it grew a remarkable 27 percent from 1950 to 1953. Coal and cotton production more than doubled; oil production quadrupled, and steel production soared more than ten times. A chronic trade deficit turned into a trade surplus.[5]

One of the most telling indicators of economic policy was inflation. In Kuomintang China the war led to a galloping inflation that by 1945 had raised prices to a level of 2,167 times higher than in 1937. The inflation rate accelerated during the war from a mere 14 percent from August to December 1937 to 250 percent from January to August 1944. Although the government repeatedly, as in December 1942, tried to curb inflation, it lacked the will, information, planning, and institutional levers to do so.[6]

The impact of runaway inflation on Chinese society was devastating. The salaried classes suffered enormously as the real wage of teachers and civil servants at the end of 1943 at Chungking was only 20 percent and 10 percent respectively of the 1937 level. Many lost their life savings; others took several jobs, while yet others resorted to graft and corruption. The integrity of the civil service was destroyed, while millions of workers and small businessmen suffered. Inflation had a disastrous impact on production since it stimulated the more profitable enterprises to engage in hoarding and speculation. It encouraged trade with the enemy in which devalued, essential Chinese goods were exchanged for more valuable, nonessential Japanese goods.[7] The impact of hyperinflation on societal morale was very great.

By sharp contrast, the new Communist government through a series of radical measures brought inflation under control. While prices rose close to 100 percent in 1950, they increased only 10 percent in 1951, actually declined in 1952, and remained stable in 1953. A. Doak Barnett, noting that "currency and prices were in a shambles" when the Communists took over in 1949, has observed that "it is remarkable, however, that the Communists have been able to stop currency inflation and to maintain stable prices for basic daily necessities."[8] While the Kuomintang government covered 69 to 79 percent of all spending through printing money and instituting ineffectual measures to curb inflation, the Communist government balanced the budget, sharply raised the amount of taxes collected, controlled money and credit, and temporarily created exchange in kind for employers.

A comparative look at the wartime budgets of China during the two conflicts dramatically demonstrates the impact of revolution. Table 17 indicates the enormous differences in the mobilization capabilities of the two governments. Kuomintang China was able to marshal only 2 to 3 percent of its GNP for the support of governmental activities during the war. And even this minimal capacity declined during the war. In 1945 the Kuomintang government spent in real terms only $1.2 billion, a sharp 44 percent decline from 1937. Its revenue-generating capabilities were so paltry that fully 67 percent of this small amount had to be generated by deficit financing with only 33 percent coming from taxes. This amount represented a 70 percent decline from 1937. By contrast, the Communist government dramatically expanded the government budget from $3 billion in 1950 to $10 billion in 1954, a level more than eight times greater than the Kuomintang budget of 1945. And the revenue picture was even brighter, with an 11 percent budget deficit of 1953 shrinking to nearly zero by 1954. This meant that at the end of the two wars the Communists were able to mobilize a phenomenal 25 times more tax revenues ($10 billion) than the Nationalists ($400 million). Little wonder that Alexander Eckstein called this enhanced fiscal capacity "the outstanding achievement of the regime."[9]

How did these remarkable differences come to pass? Chiang Kai-shek's government lacked any serious budgetary process. Spending, as we can see from table 17, was vastly out of line with revenues. A huge army was allowed to expand from two million men in 1937 to

TABLE 17:   Government Budgets in China During the Sino-Japanese War
(1937-1945) and Korean War (1950-1953)

| Year | Budget (in billions of U.S. dollars) | | |
	Expenditures	Revenues	Deficits
1937	2.1	1.4	37%
1945	1.2	.4	67%
1950	3.0	2.6	11%
1954[a]	10.0	10.0	0%

SOURCES: Arthur Young, China's Wartime Finance and Inflation, 1937-1945
(Cambridge: Harvard University Press, 1965), pp. 30-33; Harold Quigley,
Far Eastern War 1937-1941 (Boston: World Peace, Foundation, 1942), p. 96;
Alexander Eckstein, China's Economic Development (Ann Arbor, Michigan:
University of Michigan Press, 1975), p. 203; and A. Doak Barnett, Communist
China: The Early Years, 1949-55 (New York: Praeger, 1966), p. 212.

[a]Data for 1953 were unavailable.

over five million men in 1945 when General Stilwell thought one-third the number would do. A large government bureaucracy of several million men was maintained, yet no control was exerted over provincial and local governments, which issued their own bank notes and had budgets far larger than the central government by 1945. Allocations were often made on personal and functional grounds without any system of priorities. Accounting systems were ineffective and even outright corrupt. While Lauchlin Currie could report to President Roosevelt after a February 1941 trip to China of his impressions of the "completely chaotic condition of the budget," Arthur Young could write of his years in China during the war:

> Budgetary procedures were faulty. The various branches of government put in requests which, as customary elsewhere, were well-padded. There was no system of priorities for expenditures, nor was there an adequate procedure for comparison with past appropriations, for examining requests and requiring justification in detail by asking the organizations, or for determining the real merits under war conditions. . . . The budgets were more a matter of negotiations than of financial planning . . . the pressures for spending all too often too strong to be withstood.[10]

Tax collection, marked by ineptitude, evasion, and outright corruption, was so bad that only 1 to 2 percent of the GNP was raised even in the best of years. Lauchlin Currie in his 1941 report to President Roosevelt, found tax revenues "negligible," "little hope" of selling more than a "negligible" amont of bonds to the public, and "much land (that) escapes any taxation."[11] With a government unwilling to levy any significant taxes on its wealthier supporters among the urban businessmen and rural landlords and unable to subordinate provincial and local governments to its will, the outcome was preordained. Most spending was financed by printing money. By 1945 the major source of revenue became sales of gold and six-month gold deposits. Even here there was corruption and scandal for the government in 1945 was selling gold at $32,000 CN an ounce when the black market price was $101,500 CN—thereby ensuring an immediate profit of 190 percent for the privileged buyers. Tax collection was so inept and corrupt that only one-third of all revenues collected ever reached the government.[12]

Against these reckless and inept policies and procedures of Chiang Kai-shek's government, Mao Tse-tung's government would seem the paragon of fiscal virtue. The Communists created a far more disciplined and centralized system of fiscal management with rigorous subordination of provincial and local governments to the will of the center. The budget process was now regularized and unified. The very nature of the budget changed from an inept instrument to finance government operations to an economic budget to control the contours of the whole economy. Spending became a mechanism of public policy rather than a medium for negotiating demands of rival bureaucracies. While the overall level of spending by 1953 ($10 billion) was five to nine times greater than in the Kuomintang era, the major increases went to support the enlarged army and government bureaucracies, and economic development projects. In 1952 almost 45 percent of all government spending went into investment projects, compared to a paltry 8 to 12 percent in the Kuomintang era. By 1953 the Communists were spending more on economic development projects than the Chinese government was spending in all areas in 1945. The Communists were relentless in expanding the taxing capabilities of the state. They regularized, simplified, and rationalized the tax system while clamping down vigorously on prevalent tax evasion. These mobilization techniques, as demonstrated in the 1950 "Victory Bond" campaign, 1951 "Arms Donation" campaign, and 1952 *Wufan* campaign, collected over a billion dollars. In addition to voluntary and involuntary campaigns, the government instituted new taxes, withheld a significant portion of wages, and confiscated land-lord and foreign property.[13]

MILITARY LEADERSHIP

Next we turn to a detailed comparative analysis of the capabilities of the top leaders, generals, and soldiers of the two armies during the Sino-Japanese War and Korean War. The comparison between Mao Tse-tung and Chiang Kai-shek as top leaders and Lin Piao and Peng Teh-huai and Ho Ying-chin as professional commanders, is especially compelling.

Chiang Kai-shek seemingly possessed excellent qualifications to direct his nation's war effort yet fared quite poorly in practice. He attended Paoting Military College and graduated in 1909 from a Japanese military college. Surprisingly he had little experience in battle or as a junior field commander. His military philosophy, with its belief in the value of stationary defense and spirit, was thoroughly outdated. He preferred the illusion of strength as measured by titles and divisions to improving the harsh reality of weakness. He grandi-loquently promised to remain and die in Nanking and then Hankow, only to flee when the Japanese army came near.

Chiang's performance as military commander was hardly over-whelming. General Li Tsung-jen could contemptuously write, "Speaking from a purely military standpoint, Chiang could command neither generals nor soldiers. He routinely put personal political con-siderations above military efficiency."[14] Chiang constantly meddled and interfered in military operations, even when he was 500 to 1,000 miles away from the battle. By 1944 President Roosevelt was so upset by his poor military leadership that he even urged that General Stilwell replace Chiang as head of the Chinese army!

By contrast, Mao Tse-tung justly earned an international reputa-tion for his military abilities. Although he never pursued a formal military education, he developed the successful theory of "people's war." From the five encirclement campaigns of the early 1930s to the civil war of the late 1940s, Mao repeatedly bested and defeated Chiang's forces—even though Chiang's army inevitably started the conflict with between two and four to one numerical superiority and an overwhelming technological edge. Rather than interfering with operations, Mao issued broad directives to commanders, who were given significant operational autonomy. Mao was a hard-nosed political realist who candidly discussed Communist weaknesses and emphasized military capabilities in his commanders. Overall, Mao was demonstrably a far superior military commander than Chiang.[15]

A similar striking dichotomy emerged between Ho Ying-chin on the one hand and Peng Teh-huai and Lin Piao on the other. Few kind words have ever been penned about War Minister and Chief of Staff Ho Ying-chin, whose main virtue was unswerving loyalty to Chiang Kai-shek, whom he had served since they were fellow students at a Japanese military academy before 1911. Lacking combat experience, he was mainly a skilled bureaucrat. General "Vinegar Joe" Stilwell was especially scathing on the subject of Ho. In his diary he wrote about Ho, "Military education and ability a joke, and so, very susceptible to clever suggestion. . . . He makes inaction a virtue by providing conclusively the impossibility of action."[16]

The PLA commanders in Korea, Lin Piao (October 1950–March 1951), and Peng Teh-huai (March 1951+), were highly experienced military leaders. Lin Piao expertly guided the PLA forces in their rout of American forces in November 1950. After the failure of the Chinese offensives early in 1951, he was replaced by Peng Teh-huai who created a new defensive strategy. General Mark Clark called Peng "an expert tactician," "a foe of high merit," and one of a core of "solid" leaders.[17]

OFFICER CORPS

A broader comparison of the leading officers in the two armies shows the same wide disparities in their capabilities. The command structure of the Kuomintang army was a model of inefficiency. Chiang Kai-shek maintained his own large and loyal personal staff, which duplicated and interfered in the work of the general staff. The Chinese chain of command was complex, cumbersome and incredibly overstaffed. Captain Frank Dorn in a letter to Colonel Stilwell in September 1937 expressed his contempt for the quality of Chinese military staff work he had witnessed.

> But, flabby inertia, almost stupid incompetence and complete lack of staff work of any kind—one division headquarter did not even have a map of its area—I have lost my former glimmer of optimism . . . I could not help but smile at your request for information on operations, maps, orders, staff work, etc. I saw one operations map at 10th Division Headquarters at Shinkiachuang, but it was several days out of date and full of lines indicating great offensives which have never even started. If you graded their staff work with a grade of 100.00 for percent, I would

give them a mark of about .0001. There must have been a little or they could not have got on the trains.[18]

The very structure of the sprawling army was a major source of its weakness. Although both General Stilwell and General Wedemeyer called for massive reductions in the number of divisions from 200 to 300 to 30 to 60, the number of soldiers under arms more than doubled from 1937 to 1945. The central command did not exercise effective control over the army. Chiang Kai-shek could count on the loyalty of only 25 to 40 percent of his divisions, those mainly led by officers from his Whampoa faction. As for the rest, he frequently had to cede them considerable autonomy and include them in battle plans only after protracted negotiations. Many of the divisions not directly under Chiang's control were quite hostile to central orders, a hostility reinforced by the tendency of Chungking to give marked preference in supplies, replacements, and uniforms to central units. The result was a totally fragmented army with many semi-independent regional satraps.[19]

In this environment of discord and suspicion, treason and blatant cowardice was quite common among senior officers. In the battle for Peking in July 1937, General Song Zhe-yuan lamely handed the northern capital over to pro-Japanese civilians after only one day of fighting. In December 1937 Shantung General Han Fu-chu, despite having 70,000 troops, so blatantly yielded Tsinan and other towns to the Japanese with almost no fighting that Chiang Kai-shek had him executed. In June 1938 Japanese bribery secured the seizure of the vital Matang boom—thought impregnable by German experts—without firing a shot. In October 1938 the Chinese General Yu Han-mou, who had 55,000 soldiers, yielded the vital port of Canton without firing a shot. During the 1941–1943 period no less than 69 Kuomintang generals defected with a staggering 500,000 troops to the Japanese, who used them as puppet troops. As morale declined even farther towards the end of the war (despite Allied victories), cowardice and treachery continued as major problems. In December 1943 a plot by several hundred young officers was uncovered, and 16 generals were executed. By the end of 1944 a number of prominent provincial military leaders had agreed to remain neutral if the Japanese moved to destroy Chiang's army.[20]

Treason inevitably was coupled with a high level of corruption in the officer corps fed by low salaries and many opportunities. Divisional commanders routinely inflated the number of men in their units in order to sell the surplus grain allotted to them on the open market. They frequently gave the men less grain than they were supposed to receive. Ordering rifles from the central government and then selling some of them on the open market was another lucrative practice. Perhaps the worst corruption came in border areas where many Chinese officers, in the words of John Davies, "have settled down with their wives and families and gone into trade. They control and profit enormously from traffic across 'fighting lines.'"[21]

Probably the most noteworthy characteristic of Chinese officers was their extreme passivity, defensiveness, unwillingness to undertake any offensive action, and lack of serious planning. Regarding the crucial battle for Hankow in 1938, Frank Dorn, deriding the "vague" Chinese plans that "were full of unrealistic pomposities," has asserted:

> The whole tone of the Chinese directive was one of delay, step-by-step withdrawal, and defense in depth that presaged retreat and eventual acceptance of defeat. Like most antiquated Chinese military thinking, the operational guiding principles for the defense of Hankow were the product of a sort of dream world of correct words and resounding phrases. Not once in the long-winded document was a commander ordered to stand in place, face the enemy and fight. By instinct, a few leaders would fight anyway. Most would welcome the escape clauses and turn tail.[22]

Similarly, there was no real planning for the defense of Canton. By May 1943 the second secretary of the American embassy in China could despair that "in the occupied areas the Japanese with a few hundred troops are able to sit behind their elaborate fortifications and contain thousands, if not hundreds of thousands, of idle Chinese troops."[23] When the Japanese struck in 1944, an American air force intelligence report noted no evidence of any Chinese planning to stop Operation ICHIGO.[24] General Joseph Stilwell acerbically noted in 1944:

> It would of course have been undiplomatic to go into the nature of the military effort Chiang Kai-shek had made since 1938. It was practically zero.... The big job was to change fundamentally the defensive attitude of the Chinese to an offensive attitude.... Chiang Kai-shek had made defense his policy in the present war. He was going to trade 'space for time,' a very catchy way of saying he would never attack.[25]

There were many causes for this Chinese fatalism. When the United States entered the war in December 1941, many Chinese officers felt that, after four years of fighting the Japanese, it was now the turn of the United States to deliver China from Japan. The early successes of the Japanese army instilled such fear in the Chinese that, in a March 1942 meeting in Chungking with General Stilwell, Chiang Kai-shek said it would require at least five Chinese divisions before there was any prospect of success in attacking one Japanese division. Many of the best weapons and troops were hoarded for later use against the Communists, who were seen by most as a greater threat than the Japanese. Many commanders struck tacit nonaggression pacts with local Japanese forces, which allowed them to pursue more lucrative commercial ventures. A large number of commanders saw their divisions not as a military force but as an economic and political asset. Intact armies were a method of ensuring economic wealth and political stature. Dissipation of these forces in hopeless offensives against a powerful and determined enemy was nothing more than reckless adventurism.[26]

While there were some good Kuomintang generals (as Sun Li-jen, Li Tsung-jen, and Hsueh Yueh), they were the exception and not the rule. Talented officers were not recognized and promoted, while the mindless loyalty of incompetent officers to Chiang was rewarded. Many of the leading officers were inept and even cowardly political appointees. They were men like Liu Chih who was so inept that when he was made commander of the Fifth War Zone in 1943, the Japanese proclaimed, "We welcome the ever-defeated general to Laohok'ou." When asked about the appointment, Chiang Kai-shek stated, "It is true that Liu Chih is a bad commander in war. But where can you find a man so obedient?"[27] There were men like Yu Han-mou, a poor soldier who had endeared himself during the Kwangsi-Kwangtung rebellion of 1936 by changing sides to support Chiang. And there were men like the commander of the navy, Admiral Yang, "who never seemed to be near a ship but who never missed a party."[28]

It is little wonder then that American officers in China had such contempt for the bulk of Chinese officers. General Stilwell called for eliminating the majority of top commanders. General Albert Wedemeyer found "very few" good officers, labeling Kuomintang officers "incapable, inept, untrained, petty . . . altogether inefficient."[29] The final word should be left to the commander in chief of the Kuomintang army in those years, Chiang Kai-shek. In June 1942 Chiang scathingly deprecated his commanders in a meeting with General Stilwell, saying "I have to lie awake nights thinking of what fool things they may do. Then I write and tell them not to do these things. But they are so dumb, they will do a lot of foolishness unless you anticipate them." In a similar vein in 1948 after humiliating losses to the Communists, Chiang proclaimed that his commanders had such "miniscule abilities" that Kuomintang army and division commanders "would not be qualified to serve as regimental commanders" in foreign armies. Indeed, he exclaimed, "the brains of most of our soldiers are actually asleep."[30]

The contrast with the People's Liberation Army's officer corps is almost overwhelming. A Joint Chiefs of Staff top secret study of the PLA in March 1951 praised their "excellent leadership."[31] This sentiment was echoed by General Samuel Griffith, who described the "high quality" of the Communist officer corps. At the elite level all senior officers were devout Communists who had spent several decades fighting in the new Communist army. Corruption and treason were virtually unknown. Planning and adaptability were a trademark. While the junior officers and noncommissioned officers in general lacked real educational training or lengthy military education, they were tough, combat-hardened men who knew how to lead their men in battle. Promotion was based solely on merit proved in battle and devotion to the cause.[32]

The revolution produced an army strongly loyal to the Communist movement. All senior officers, most company commanders, and even two-thirds of the platoon leaders were Communists. The bulk of them were recruited from the peasantry. Even during the bleakest moments of the Korean War, desertion by officers was a rare event. Similarly, corruption was very rare in the officer corps. Far from being fragmented, the Communist officer corps displayed a strong revolutionary esprit de corps, forged by common experiences of revolutionary struggle and personal cooperation often dating over two decades. The Chinese army showed remarkable adaptive tactical and strategic capabilities in Korea, as well as strong offensive capabilities.

The officers deliberately used any and all opportunities to cancel the massive enemy firepower superiority. The PLA demonstrated a mobility and march capability which an official American army history observed "equalled the best examples of antiquity." In one documented case, three PLA divisions marched 286 miles from Antung in Manchuria to an assembly area in North Korea over difficult terrain in only 16 to 19 days. The Chinese troops moved only at night and with such perfect march discipline and camouflage that 300,000 men moved into North Korea in October and November of 1950 such that none were ever discovered by the U.N. Command prior to actual contact. Night movement, combined with a masterful use of terrain, deception, dispersion, surprise, and reconnaisance, enabled the Chinese soldiers to gain local battlefield superiority over enemy forces, who suddenly found themselves surrounded on all sides. Indeed the UN technological edge was even turned into a liability by the more mobile Chinese forces who were not bound by the roads for transportation and logistics. As one author has depicted the terrifying impact of a Chinese small unit attack, "Appearing to rise out of the very earth, the Chinese either struck the American positions frontally or crept and wriggled around them in infiltration attempts."[33]

The Chinese demonstrated defensive skills that were at least as formidable as their offensive capabilities. After June 1951 they spent a vast amount of time building an elaborate defense line. General Maxwell Taylor found the defense belt more formidable than the elaborate German Siegfried Line and Western Wall of World War II.[34] Too, the Chinese developed such skillful and effective methods of avoiding and repairing air damage that massive air strikes, as in the 1951 Operation STRANGLE, were eventually deemed failures by the American military and called off. Trucks and trains were kept in caves and by the roadside during the daytime and moved mainly at night. Tens of thousands of coolies moved supplies silently at night. Many straw airplanes and dummy installations, factories, camps, and barracks were set up to deflect UN attention. Good airfields and depots were camouflaged to appear inoperative.

When the UN air force did strike real targets, the Chinese set in motion a well-organized and disciplined labor-intensive system. Roads and railways were rapidly repaired by labor gangs who lived in nearby caves dispersed at intervals that were two to three miles along all rail routes. They made use of an abundant supply of tools and natural materials stored in hidden dumps.

Finally, perhaps the ultimate testimonial to PLA capabilities was its capacity to adapt to failure and develop a new and more successful strategy. This adaptability is a classic attribute of effective armies. In the spring of 1951 Peng Teh-huai, the new PLA commander in Korea, concluded that the classic Chinese civil war tactics of fluid movements based on popular support would not work against a heavily armed and tough enemy fighting on a narrow peninsula in a foreign country. Accordingly, Peng set out to modernize the primitive logistic system of the PLA and to massively upgrade its firepower. In addition, a new defensive strategy, with few roots in PLA history, emerged in the last two years of the Korean War. Overall, then, a professional, modern, and powerful Chinese army emerged from the Korean War in 1953 to replace the primitive guerrilla force that entered the war in 1950.

SOLDIERS

A comparison of the condition and treatment of soldiers in the two armies is equally revealing. First, there was the great difference in the methods of conscription. With no centralized national Kuomintang office for military recruitment in existence until November 1944, recruiting was done in disorganized, localized manner by provincial and district governments assigned quotas by Chungking. This left enormous room for abuse—by the local village chiefs and district magistrates who took bribes for not conscripting men, by the conscripting officer who received a bounty for each recruit, and by the officer who profited by squeezing on allotments for food and care of the conscripts. The great majority of wealthier and better educated men, who could have served as officers or noncommissioned officers, evaded conscription through payment of bribes and rice contributions. Only the poorer village families with no money provided children for the army. John Service in 1944 described "a pernicious and corrupt conscription system" that "works to ensure the selection and retention of the unfit—since the ablest and strongest can either evade conscription, buy their way out or desert." General Albert Wedemeyer in an August 1945 report to Chiang Kai-shek provided the most graphic description of the process of conscription.

> Conscription comes to the Chinese peasant like famine or flood, only more regularly—every year twice—and claims more victims. Famine, flood and drought compare with conscription like chicken pox with plague. . . . The virus is spread over the Chinese countryside. . . . Only office, influence and money keep conscription out of your house. There is first the press gang. For example, you are working in the field looking after your rice . . . [there come] a number of uniformed men who tie your hands behind your back and take you with them. . . . Another way of being taken is arrest. Nine will be given a chance to buy their way out. The poorest stays in jail until the conscription officer takes him over.

General Wedemeyer then proceeds to describe even more nefarious, common practices.

> Private dealers in conscription have organized a trade. They are buying able-bodied men from starved families who need rice more urgently than sons, or they buy them from the county magistrate who have surplus or they pay a man who wants to sell himself. . . . The dealer might give $30,000 CN to the man who sells himself, or to the family or to

the official. He sells the man for $50,000 CN to the county magistrate or conscription official who had just let off a peasant's son for $100,000 CN. So everyone is happy except the conscript.[35]

Yet, this was only the beginning of a tale of horrors. Many conscripts were tied together by rope and force-marched under armed guard hundreds of miles to their destination. They were provided with little food or warm clothing, minimal shelter, and almost nonexistent medical care. Conscripts were treated so much like prisoners that in 1942 in Kiangsi, Colonel David Barrett found that it was a common practice to keep conscripts in prison while on transit to the front. General Albert Wedemeyer in 1945 again provided a graphic description of conscripts on the march.

> As they march along they turn into skeletons: they develop signs of beriberi, their legs swell and their bellies protrude, their arms and thighs get thin. . . . Dysentary and typhoid are always with them. They carry cholera from place to place. Leaving behind them a wake of the sick and the dying, they are still fulfilling the most important function of a citizen of free China: to be a source of income for officials.[36]

Statistics tell an equally horrifying story of a staggering waste of manpower. In 1943 General Stilwell noted that an incredible 44 percent of all conscripts, or 750,000 men from a total of 1,670,000 conscripts, died or deserted on the way to their army units. Similarly in 1944 nearly 50 percent of all recruits were lost through sickness, death, or desertion. And, at times, the situation became even worse. A 1945 National Planning Association study of the Ninth War Area found that an astounding 78 percent of a levy of conscripts died of dysentary traceable to malnutrition.[37]

Nor were conditions any better for the conscripts who reached their army units and became soldiers. Their training in the rear was minimal, hurried, and of such poor quality that a common Chinese saying of the time was: "It is better to die under bombs at the front than to endure training in the rear." Officers often treated soldiers with a casual, even brutal, indifference. Their equipment was sparse and outdated. The pay of soldiers was meager (about US $1-$2 per month in 1937), constantly shrinking due to inflation, and often partially withheld by greedy commanders.

In combat the soldiers, usually poorly clothed, were weak from hunger and exhaustion and night-blind from diet deficiencies. Many troops were literally starving to death. The men, often without prior training in sanitation or hygiene, were devastated by epidemics of smallpox, typhus, and dysentery. Medical facilities, food supplies, and evacuation procedures for the wounded were in abominable shape and of little value. By December 1942 American Ambassador in China Gauss could report that "the mass of soldiers is sadly under-nourished and hence in no condition physically to engage in active military operations."[38] Losses due to malnutrition and disease, reaching as much as 40 percent of a unit's strength per year, could wipe out a division in two years, without any fighting. American studies in 1945 found only 30 percent of all soldiers fit to fight, with 57 percent suffering significant nutritional deficiencies from horrifying conditions under which soldiers had to live.[39]

There was no significant political training to tell the soldier, often an illiterate peasant, why he was fighting this war. His meager three weeks of basic training provided minimal political guidance. The few army political workers, with little training or financial support, devoted most of their time to intelligence work against Chiang Kai-shek's enemies. Even Kuomintang General Zhang Zhi-zong conceded that real political training "was almost non-existent, except in the Communist armies."[40]

The result was an army with low morale, low combat capacity, and a high desertion rate. By 1942 General Stilwell, arguing that the army "could not act of itself," claimed that for every soldier who died at the front, ten died of disease or deserted in the rear. And in May 1944, O. Edmund Clubb, citing a British estimate that only 30 percent of Chinese troops were good troops by British standards, asserted that the majority of troops, "by virtue of neglect, in terms of equipment, training and essential food and medical supplies, are not in a fit condition for battle service."[41]

In addition, the army repeatedly plundered the populace, earning their undying hatred. The local populace often feared the Chinese armies almost as much as they feared the Japanese. In North China, villages would be evacuated when soldiers were sighted. And civilians often took revenge on soldiers. In April and May 1944 during Operation ICHIGO, peasants attacked the retreating army of Tang En-po and reportedly disarmed and killed 50,000 Chinese troops.[42]

By contrast to this sordid record, the PLA treated its soldiers far better and reaped the benefits accordingly. This was a remarkable performance, as the PLA lacked any significant material resources to create a new army. During the civil war and Korean War the Communist army had poor medical facilities, weak transportation and communication capabilities, and limited firepower. The transformation in China, unlike in Russia, did not originate in a technological transformation of the level of economic development.

The key lay thereby in China in a full-scale mobilization of its human, rather than technical, resources. A major key lay in treating the soldiers well and shattering the traditional Chinese image of the soldier as a lonely outcast at the bottom of the social ladder. Soldiers were encouraged to volunteer for the army and fight for a revolution that improved their lives. They were well fed and cared for in training that prepared them for the army. Once in the army they encountered a system that stressed small-group ties, with limited democracy and egalitarian features. Leadership was based on performance. Officers had few formal distinctions from the men; soldiers were encouraged to participate and advise on military affairs, and soldiers had a little freedom to criticize the behavior of officers. Units were organized from the same villages and regions to promote solidarity. Soldiers underwent a two to three month program of special combat training and political indoctrination before being sent to Korea. The quality of this training could be seen in General Douglas MacArthur's December 4, 1950 message to Washington: "The Chinese troops are fresh, completely organized, splendidly trained and equipped and apparently in peak condition for actual operations."[43]

Political work was extensive and highly successful. A typical infantry division had 65 political officers and 1,200 men engaged in political work. Company political officers performed many functions from ensuring material welfare and medical care to allocating rewards and punishments and regulating relations with civilians. Through an unceasing process of propaganda, criticism meetings, and a mutual supervision system, these dedicated Communists managed to reshape the thought and behavior of soldiers. The surveillance and control system was "quite effective" in isolating potential dissidents and preventing plans of desertion. Equally important, in General Samuel Griffith's words, was the prevailing attitude "that he [the Chinese soldier] was engaged in a just war, in a wholly righteous cause, that the enemy he was about to face was vicious, cruel and predatory, the average Chinese soldier was convinced."[44]

The Communists, who had no counterpart in the Kuomintang army, were the samurai of the PLA. Communists fought courageously in Korea and almost never deserted. And they were everywhere, down to squad level. Roughly 24 percent of all soldiers were Communists, and by 1953 another 20 percent of all soldiers were members of the New Democratic Youth League.[45] Thus, they provided dynamic and honest leadership in the army.

The end result was a superb performance by the PLA in the Korean War. As American Ambassador in Korea John Muccio in December 1950 wrote to the secretary of state, "Chinese troops encountered thus far have fought hard and well though losses have been extremely heavy. They are well maintained, organized and disciplined."[46] What a contrast from the American evaluation of another Chinese army only five years earlier!

CHAPTER **11**

Wartime Government

In this chapter we turn away from the battlefield to an analysis of the functioning of the government, Party, and military bureaucracies during wartime. In these more prosaic areas we shall, as in the last chapter, find some startling differences between Kuomintang China and Communist China.

MILITARY TASKS

In modern warfare there are four key military tasks—manpower mobilization and maintenance, intelligence, unified war effort, and guerrillas. And, for a major war against a brutal and rapacious army, mobilization of manpower in Kuomintang China was positively anemic. Even though table 18 exaggerates Chinese impotence by overstating the Chinese population, which had been sharply reduced by Japanese occupation and Communist expansion, it still makes an important point. The Kuomintang government was constitutionally incapable of transforming its huge manpower resources into battle-field assets.

The Kuomintang government, unlike the Communist government, squandered the manpower resources it did manage to mobilize. Although the Kuomintang army grew from 2.0 million men in 1937 to 5.3 million men in 1945, it recruited 14.1 million men (and this figure is thought by many to be an understatement) in this period. Of these 14.1 million men, 3.2 million men were casualties and 3.3 million men were added to the army's size. Even if none of the casualties (70 percent of whom were wounded) returned to the army, what happened to the other 7.6 million men? They represented an enormous "wastage" of almost 55 percent of all men mobilized. We know that perhaps 500,000 men committed treason and went over to the Japanese, who reorganized them as puppet troops, and probably 1.0 to 3.0 million men simply deserted the army. The other 4.0 to 5.5 million men evidently just "disappeared," probably mainly through deaths via disease, malnutrition, and abuse. Since no one uninjured was demobilized during the war, it took nearly two million recruits a year to maintain an army of two to five million men in action.

By contrast, the PLA made remarkably efficient use of its manpower, with minimal wastage. During the Korean War it actually reduced the size of the army from 5.0 million men in 1950 and 1951 to 3.5 million men by 1953. The PLA demobilized 2.94 million men

TABLE 18:   Manpower Mobilization of Major Powers in World War II

Country	Population (in millions)	Number of Men Mobilized into Military	Mobilization[a] Index
Germany (9/39-5/45)	79.5	17.0	3.8
Soviet Union (7/41-9/45)	170.5	22.0	3.0
United States (7/41-9/45)	156.7	14.0	2.4
United Kingdom (9/39-9/45)	141.7	12.0	1.4
Japan (7/37-9/45)	77.0	8.0	1.3
China (7/37-9/45)	450.0	14.1	.4

SOURCES: F. F. Liu, A Military History of Modern China, 1924-1949 (Princeton: Princeton University Press, 1956), p. 136.

[a]The mobilization index is based on the average number of men mobilized per year as a percentage of the population.

and recruited 1.75 million men in 1952.[1] The PLA was able to replace all its losses in the Korean War without any net recruitment, despite maintaining almost a million men there by 1953. Indeed, the bulk of the 600,000 to 900,000 casualties were returned to the army, while only 20,000 Chinese soldiers (compared to 130,000 North Korean soldiers) were taken prisoner by UN forces. While the PLA suffered heavy casualties on the battlefield, it managed to make full use of its manpower resources.

A second vital task, military intelligence, presented an interesting picture. In neither war did China penetrate the enemy (Japan and the United States) and unearth significant material on its plans and intentions. There were significant differences in the capability of the regime to protect its own secrets. The Kuomintang government, riddled with treasonous individuals such as Wang Ching-wei, and potentially treasonous allies such as the provincial warlords, found it difficult to protect its secrets. Foreign leaders were often openly contemptuous of the "porousness" of Chungking. In June 1944 the American ambassador to the Soviet Union, Averell Harriman, related that Stalin told him that, "With respect to the Chinese Government a good part of Chiang's entourage were 'crooks,' even traitors and everything going on in Chungking became known to the Japanese the next day."[2] By contrast, the new Communist regime in Peking jealously guarded its secrets so well that the American intelligence community was stunned by the PLA offensive in November 1950. The Declassified Documents Series does not seem to indicate any significant penetration of the Chinese planning process.

Third, there is the question of achieving a unified war effort. Kuomintang China was especially weak in this crucial area. Much of the war effort was directed not against fighting the Japanese enemies but in controlling erstwhile allies, such as the provincial warlords and Communists. Chiang Kai-shek was more interested in the postwar correlation of forces than in the wartime fighting. During the battle for Peking in 1937 and Operation ICHIGO in 1944, Chinese generals not part of Chiang Kai-shek's Whampoa clique felt that they were sacrificial lambs. Much effort was futilely spent in suppressing the Communists, who were also fighting the Japanese.

The Kuomintang army took both active and passive action against its Communist "allies." A series of armed clashes between the two forces in 1939 and 1940 culminated in January 1940 with the "New Fourth Army Incident," in which the Kuomintang army of Ku Chu-tung inflicted 6,000 casualties on the Communist army. Then, from 1941 to 1945 Kuomintang General Hu Tsung-nan used 400,000 of the best trained and equipped Chinese troops to blockade the

growing Communist forces in northwest China. This situation infur-
iated American officials. In January 1945 American Ambassador in
China Patrick Hurley wrote to Washington that a unification of Kuomintang and Communist forces against Japan "would have a battle
effect, equal at least, to one fully equipped American Army."[3]

By contrast, the Communists organized a unified war effort in
Korea. By carrying through a revolution and winning the civil war,
they crushed the power of the provincial warlords and the Kuomintang. Through the revolution they created a new, unified centralized
government that could rally the masses effectively through nationalist and socialist appeals. After 1949 there were no longer multiple
centers of authority in China; there was only one.

Finally, there was the important political question of organizing
popular resistance to the enemy in the occupied areas during the war.
While China failed in this endeavor in both wars, an analysis of these
failures is particularly instructive. In Korea, the Chinese Communists
tried and failed to implement a people's war. A significant Communist guerrilla movement in South Korea in 1950 soon petered out in
1951 and 1952. This was hardly surprising. Kim Il-sung, unlike Mao
Tse-tung, had not come to power through a popular revolution but
by the friendly intervention of the Soviet Red Army in 1945. The
tenuous base of Korean Communism could be seen in the spectacular
disintegration of the North Korean army in the fall of 1950. In this
unfriendly environment the Chinese, as foreigners, could hardly build
a strong base for guerrilla operations.

But, the Kuomintang, on native grounds amidst a friendly population aroused by Japanese barbarism, should have been able to build
a strong guerrilla movement in Japanese-occupied territory. Certainly
the Chinese Communists were very successful at this, building 19
rural base areas with 95 million people by 1945. And so, too, the
Yugoslav and Russian partisans had become equally adept at guerrilla warfare behind German lines in World War II.

And yet the forces of Chiang Kai-shek were miserable at developing guerrilla warfare against the Japanese, even in the most promis-
ing circumstances. Although Chiang Kai-shek set up a guerrilla school
in 1938 and ordered hundreds of thousands of soldiers to remain
behind the lines of Japanese advance, the results were dismal. By
September 1944, in a conversation with the British journalist Gunther Stein, Chief of Staff Ho Ying-chin, denigrating guerrilla warfare
as "useless," conceded "there are virtually no guerrillas in occupied
areas." And according to a 1944 Kuomintang report, those guerrillas
that did exist on the Hupei-Honan border region had low fighting

strength and "curse and abuse the populace and even steal things, commit rape, etc."[4]

What caused this sad state of affairs? The Chinese Communists, through strong social reformist and nationalist appeals and persistent populist organizational work, were a dynamic force that rapidly absorbed many of the more idealistic Kuomintang guerrillas into their own ranks. Second, the Kuomintang guerrillas, fearing the Japanese army and its reprisals, often reached tacit nonaggression pacts with Japanese forces. And finally, the Kuomintang government, resting on the support of the privileged classes, was unwilling to make the kinds of social reforms that could have mobilized the population and made guerrilla warfare successful.

FOREIGN POLICY

Now we turn to an analysis of the foreign and domestic policies of the two regimes. A comparative foreign policy analysis shows a similar pattern of Kuomintang irresponsibility and Communist responsibility. The Chiang Kai-shek regime did not seek to maximize cooperation with its allies or to do its utmost to defeat the Japanese enemy. Rather it often alienated its allies and at times even enhanced Japanese military capabilities. It allowed domestic concerns to overwhelm foreign policy necessities.

Although the Soviet Union actively aided China in the 1937–1941 period and China needed Russian help against Japan, China remained ambivalent in its attitude towards Russia. After the 1941 Russo-Japanese Neutrality Pact, relations began to cool between the two states. In 1942 Chiang Kai-shek coaxed Sheng Shih-ts'ai, the ruler of Sinkiang province, away from Russia and Russian influence, and advisers were expelled from Sinkiang. In 1944 there was even a clash between Mongolian forces and Chinese troops on the Mongolian border. Relations with their erstwhile Russian ally continued to deteriorate during the war.

Nor did the Chinese, despite their anticommunism, treat the United States any better. In July 1942, after the United States reduced its commitments to the Chinese theater, Chiang Kai-shek presented an ultimatum—either put three American divisions in Burma, ship 500 planes to China, and transport 5,000 tons a month over the Hump or else. The "or else" was put in terms that "China cannot go on without help" and "the pro-Japanese activity is very strong," even though none of these demands could possibly be met.

In February 1943 China again hinted that without more aid China might withdraw from the war. By December 1943 President Roosevelt was so angry at Chinese conduct that he threatened to cancel Lend-Lease unless China took a more active part in the war. Chiang's demands for a billion dollar loan and 20,000 tons a month over the Hump further alienated America. As American Ambassador in China Gauss wrote the secretary of state at that time, "there is a strong disposition in the Chinese Government to exploit to the full the existing openhandedness and good will of America, with little or no thought of accepting any refusal of Chinese requests or of giving any *quid pro quo* or even of considering mutual benefits."[5] Sino-American relations reached a new low in February 1944 when Finance Minister H.H. Kung told U.S. Ambassador Gauss that a separate peace with Japan was possible since Japan had "made some very good offers."[6] Overall, Chinese tactics of bluff and blackmail, lack of open cooperation, and exorbitant demands thoroughly disgusted American officials.

Chinese foreign policy hardly waged a resolute struggle against the Japanese enemy. With his main focus on preserving his forces to fight domestic enemies, Chiang Kai-shek was reluctant to actively attack the Japanese. Numerous warlords had "understandings" with their Japanese enemies. In Shansi province from 1942 to 1945, Yen Hsi-shan had a secret pact with the Japanese that involved a nonaggression pact and even a visit (with pictures taken!) by the Japanese commander with Yen. In the south in 1944 the local commander, Yu Han-mou, agreed not to attack Canton when the Japanese moved north in a broad offensive. Chiang Kai-shek kept up strong contacts with the Japanese puppets in Nanking and Peking. Yet worse, there was a strong and flourishing trade between Chungking and the occupied territories. As early as 1940 the American Office of Strategic Services estimated this trade at $120 million. This trade, by corrupting and demoralizing the army, weakened Chinese morale. Also, by supplying Chinese raw materials and foodstuffs to Japan, the trade clearly aided the Japanese war effort.[7]

By contrast, Communist foreign policy during the Korean War demonstrated a high degree of rationality and pragmatism. The Chinese, despite misgivings about the Soviet Union and past Stalinist errors in China, consciously cultivated Soviet aid and support during the emerging cold war. Stalin had openly backed the Kuomintang regime during the civil war and provided only minimal assistance to the Communists. Although the Communist victory in China in 1949 was of incalculable value to Russia, Stalin seemed determined to treat Mao as a junior partner in the international Communist movement.

Mao had to spend over two months in Moscow to negotiate the 1950 Sino-Soviet Treaty, at a time when much remained to be done at home. The Chinese could hardly have been ecstatic over treaty provisions, which included perpetuation of Soviet interests in Sinkiang through creation of joint stock companies, recognition of the independence of Outer Mongolia, provision of special Russian rights in Port Arthur and Dairen, and extension of a meager $300 million loan, which had to be repaid. During the Korean War, Soviet weapons were provided at a slow rate and had to be paid for by the Chinese. In addition, China took heavy casualties, while Russia took none. Yet, throughout this period, China pursued its relationship with Russia for the military, economic, and diplomatic benefits that flowed from alliance with a superpower.

Furthermore, the Chinese tried to avoid involvement in the Korean War and intervened only when the threat to security and vital interest loomed large with the failure of deterrence. In June 1950 the PLA did not provide aid to the North Korean invasion force. When in August 1950 the UN forces were pinned down in the Pusan perimeter, the PLA sat idly by. Nor even after the spectacular Inchon landing in September 1950 and American moves toward the Thirty-eighth Parallel, did the PLA intervene. As a November 1950 CIA memo observed, "failure to act on those occasions appears to indicate that Peiping was unwilling to accept a serious risk of war, prior to U.S. crossing of the 38th parallel."[8]

The Chinese repeatedly sought to deter an American advance north of the Thirty-eighth Parallel. On September 25 PLA Chief of Staff Nieh Jung-chen told Indian Ambassador K.M. Pannikar that China would not "sit back with folded hands and let the Americans come to the border." On September 30, Premier Chou En-lai told a political meeting that "the Chinese people absolutely will not tolerate foreign aggression nor will they supinely tolerate their neighbors being savagely invaded by imperialists." And on October 10, the Chinese Foreign Ministry issued a statement calling the American military action "a serious menace to the security of China" and declaring that "the Chinese people cannot stand idly by with regard to such a serious situation."[9] These political warnings were accompanied by a military build up. Then on October 26, the PLA attacked South Korean forces and on November 2 American forces in North Korea. When after a pause of yet three more weeks the American response was to plunge toward the Yalu, the PLA struck in force on November 20. Clearly, as Walter Zelman has noted, "There can be little doubt that China did make a concerted effort to deter UN and US troops from crossing the 38th Parallel."[10]

Given the collapse of North Korean forces and the rapid movement of the American forces to the Yalu border with China, it can be argued that the Chinese reacted only belatedly and defensively when all else failed. With Japanese aggression in China fresh in their memories, the Chinese leaders were quite alarmed by the rapid movements of the army of a superpower, aligned with their Kuomintang enemy, to their border. This alarm was heightened by the widely circulated views of UN Commander in Chief Douglas MacArthur who wanted to bomb and blockade Chinese territory and use Kuomintang forces in Korea. Despite administration disclaimers, a CIA memo for President Truman on November 8, 1950 stated, "The Chinese Communists probably genuinely fear an invasion of Manchuria despite the clear-cut definition of UN objectives."[11] Too, many have found Chinese concerns natural for as American Ambassador to the Soviet Union Alan Kirk wrote to the secretary of state on November 7, 1950, "I cannot imagine that were Mexico in so deplorable a situation as Korea that the U.S. Government would not be considerably concerned."[12]

There were a number of other logical reasons for limited intervention. Indeed the National Intelligence Estimate no. 2 of November 8, 1950 lays the case out nicely. A UN victory in North Korea would be a serious loss of face for China. A Western-oriented regime in North Korea would be seen as a threat to China. Loss of North Korea would turn a key source of Manchurian power over to hostile hands. Militarily, North Korea seemed to possess good terrain for a Chinese offensive. And a Chinese offensive could create conditions favorable to a political solution of the Korean conflict.[13]

Furthermore, Chinese policy during the Korean War, contrary to popular misconceptions, was far from irrational or intransigent. We have already seen that China refrained from possibly devastating air attacks on crowded South Korean air fields, despite a demonstrated air capability by 1952. They accepted a limited war almost from the start. After the truce talks began in the summer of 1951, the Chinese by November 1951 had conceded the cease-fire lines should be the battle lines and by 1952 had stressed the need for a solution to the war. John Gittings has concluded that "the truth at Panmunjon still has to be unravelled in full, but the Chinese and North Koreans had at least as much reason to accuse the American side of obstruction."[14]

Overall, then, Chinese foreign policy during the Korean War was pragmatic and goal-oriented. Unlike the Kuomintang, the Communists focused all their resources on pursuing their war aims. They made their alliance with Russia, despite grievances, a high priority.

After all other alternatives had been exhausted, they finally agreed to the end of the war in 1953, having demonstrated their capabilities in a series of tough battles in 1952 and 1953.

DOMESTIC POLICIES

We now turn to a comparative look at the domestic policies of the two regimes, starting with the leaders and officials of the two governments.

Chiang Kai-shek was a brilliant factional leader, adept at strategies and intrigues that held together his shaky coalition of diverse central and regional leaders. He was a past master of artful maneuver and the game of divide and rule. For over two decades he managed during extremely turbulent times to remain the undisputed leader of Kuomintang China.

But even if staying atop the greasy pole of politics represented a major accomplishment for Chiang Kai-shek, the war with Japan and World War II demanded, as in the United States (Roosevelt), Britain (Churchill), and Russia (Stalin), a leader who could mobilize the people for a sustained war effort. This Chiang Kai-shek could not do, for he saw the people as objects to be controlled rather than subjects to be mobilized. He had a thoroughly paternalistic view of the people in whom he had little faith. In March 1941 Lauchlin Currie, after a visit with Chiang in Chungking, reported to President Roosevelt that Chiang "remarked again and again that they (the people) were uneducated and easily influenced by rumors and that they had to be more fully trained and educated before they could be trusted with any political power."[15]

As an archconservative, Chiang Kai-shek, like another leader whom we studied, Tsar Nicholas II, was deeply hostile to all modern currents of thought. He opposed all liberal and radical movements, including the May Fourth Movement, and praised the Confucian virtues of Tseng Kuo-fan who had suppressed the Taiping Rebellion. In a 1936 speech he praised traditional Chinese Legalists and neo-Confucian writers, recommending not a single modern work except those written by Sun Yat-sen and himself. In *China's Destiny* he attributed all of China's troubles to foreign domination and unequal treaties, completely ignoring the internal social and economic factors that had made China an easy target for Western imperialism. With his emphasis on the Bismarkian notion of blood and iron combined with traditional Chinese martial virtues, Chiang would do nothing to mobilize the people through much-needed social reforms. Under him, "the defense of the status quo," wrote Hsi-Sheng Ch'i, "had become the prerequisite for realizing the KMT's revolutionary mission" of eliminating foreign imperialism in China.[16]

In this atmosphere, where factional loyalty to Chiang overshadowed considerations of merit, the overall quality of Cabinet ministers in Chungking left much to be desired. There was a strong palace clique of Chiang Kai-shek's relatives, including his in-laws, the Kungs and Soongs, and his wife, Madame Chiang. Chiang's brother-in-law, H.H. Kung, served for over a decade as finance minister even though, in the words of Cyril Rogers, Bank of England representative in China, he had "the mentality of a child of 12. If I were to record his conversations with me about banking and play it back, nobody would ever take Chiang's government seriously again."[17] The long-time minister of education, Ch'en Li-fu, was a leading reactionary politician who admired European fascism and ran the party's secret police. The minister of agriculture, Shen Hung-lieh, was described by Vice-President Henry Wallace in a report to President Roosevelt after a China visit, as a man "who incidentally knows little about agriculture."[18]

In this environment of intrigues and cliques, mediocrity flourished. Capable men found their paths to advancement and power solidly blocked. In October 1938, Chiang Kai-shek himself even denounced his own officials as "wholly unworthy of their positions," although he took no steps to change them.[19] While General Stilwell in 1942 despaired of "the colossal ignorance and indifference of responsible officials," the U.S. consul general in Kunming, William Langdom, could in 1944 write to the secretary of state about "the men of second-rate minds" who "direct the building of future China."[20]

Matters were far worse in the provinces and localities where failure to consolidate power and carry out a revolution in the Nanking Decade (1927-1937) left many warlords in command. Without effective central control, each province could and often did issue its own notes and carry out its own grain collection and conscription. Mismanagement in these areas was to cost the regime dearly. The center was left without access to local resources in vast areas of the country.

At the local *hsien* (county) level, the quality of government officials reached its nadir. The bulk of the *hsien* magistrates were appointed irregularly, often by the local military commander, on the basis of power, friendship, family, or financial considerations. Frequently the local officials were highly corrupt and arrogant in their attitude toward the people. At the lowest level, a 1941–1942 government survey found the 6.6 million *paochia* chiefs to be low quality, while in 1944 Sun Fo, vice-chairman of the Executive Yuan, publicly stated:

> All these chiefs are bad elements. Not even one out of ten is any good; all of them are local rascals and oppressive gentry and were formerly opponents of our revolution but are now holding important positions in our government.[21]

The contrast with the leaders of the new Communist regime is evident. The leaders of the government bureaucracy—men like Mao Tse-tung, Chou En-lai, and Liu Shao-chi—were all highly capable men who had shown remarkable ability in creating and running flexible and adaptive government structures in the past two decades. Their very success in the face of overwhelming odds of conquering all of China during the civil war was testimony to their capabilities. Too, unlike the Kuomintang, the Communists had managed to maintain clear-cut, civilian control over their powerful military organization. The military, which in the 1950-1952 period helped rule China throughout six large administrative regions, by 1954 had withdrawn from any significant role in the new civilian government. Equally important was the fact that, despite inevitable internal political differences, the new government demonstrated an impressive unity during the Korean War. Thus, the Chinese Communists managed to create a civilian government in which merit was rewarded, factionalism was limited in scope, and the military was subordinated to civilian authority.

The biggest problem facing the Chinese Communists, as the Russian Bolsheviks in 1917, was how to build a new government bureaucracy with a dearth of educated Communists. In December 1949 only 720,000 of the 4.5 million Communists had even the minimal skills needed to be government or Party officials to carry out expanded bureaucratic functions. The discredited Kuomintang officials would be retained only as long as it took for more reliable cadres to be trained. Even worse, some new Communist recruits and poorly educated revolutionary cadres would have to be eliminated on grounds of incompetency or retrograde political views.

During 1949-1952, the new regime recruited almost 2.6 million new cadres. Only 2.2 percent were recruited from new university graduates. Fully 40 percent were recruited from demobilized soldiers, Communists, Youth League members, and progressive Kuomintang elements. The youth in particular played a significant role. And 57.7 percent of the new cadres were worker and peasant activists, who had demonstrated their organizational skill and revolutionary zeal in major campaigns ranging from land reform to *wufan*.[22]

The new regime thereby accomplished the major task of creating a new government bureaucracy, staffed heavily from the lower classes, from which corruption and favoritism had largely been eliminated. Other problems did remain, though. The overall level of competence of many officials was as low as their educational level. Conflicts between divergent groups—old Communists versus new Communists, Communists versus Kuomintang holdovers, more educated versus less educated—were inevitable. And the lack of a prior period of working together did harm effectiveness. But, the achievements clearly outweighed the problems.

GOVERNMENT PERFORMANCE

Now we turn to an analysis of the performance of the two governments. The Kuomintang government proved incapable of establishing and providing a strong and effective centralized authority ruling the provinces. Its actions reflected a weak and vacillating conservative force, hampered by rampant corruption. Although the country was at war with an enemy implacably determined to destroy its very national existence, the Kuomintang regime failed to carry out any serious popular mobilization against the war. It often deeply alienated the very people whom it sorely needed to mobilize.

Many of the government's problems during the Sino-Japanese War arose as a result of the way the Kuomintang had originally come to power in 1926 and 1927, and the way it ruled from Nanking from 1927 to 1937. During this period the Kuomintang chose to absorb and placate the regional warlords, utilizing money, arms and political maneuvers, rather than to challenge the warlords' power. To challenge their power through local reforms and political mobilization would have meant widespread rural change, to which Chiang was opposed. As a result, by 1936 the Kuomintang had strong influence in 2 provinces, some influence in 2 provinces, and minimal influence in 9 provinces. And its overall power was even further limited by serious factional divisions in the center itself. Overall, Ezra Vogel has commented:

> When Chiang Kai-shek rose to power, he was so heavily indebted to regional military leaders that he found it very difficult to exercise tight central control over them while keeping their allegiance. Indeed, it was only by a complicated system of supporting, persuading, cajoling,

threatening and exterminating his allies that he was able to maintain any semblance of central control.[23]

The Sino-Japanese War further weakened the center's tenuous hold over the provinces. The military balance shifted toward the regional warlords with the destruction of much of Chiang Kai-shek's elite forces in the disastrous campaigns of 1937 and 1938. The political balance shifted toward the warlords with the expulsion of the regime from its coastal strongholds to the remoteness of the southwest, itself a warlord bastion. And the loss of the coastal cities greatly diminished the economic resources available to the center. The Kuomintang government did not even have a firm base in Chungking, its capital in Szechwan, to which it fled from Wuhan in 1938. In December 1944 General Albert Wedemeyer reported to President Roosevelt that in light of Japanese advances he had recommended an evacuation of the government to Kunming. But Chiang had told him that "if he goes to the Kunming area, the Governor of Yunnan may kidnap him or at least place him under protective custody."[24]

Many regional warlords openly flouted Chungking's wishes. Shansi warlord, Yen Hsi-shan, maintaining his own ties with the Japanese and creating his own political party, did not even meet Chiang or make a single appearance in Chungking during the war. This was not totally atypical. Even worse, as the fortunes of Chungking waned throughout the war and approached disaster in 1944, those of the warlords waxed brightly. By late 1944 the Kwangsi-Kwangtung warlords revived ties with southwestern warlords to openly discuss a possible alternative government. Although Chiang Kai-shek remained in power in 1945 as the Americans won the war and the Japanese evacuated China, his rule was tenuous.

In this environment of strong domestic and foreign enemies, the Kuomintang tried to hang on to power through manipulation of elites rather than political mobilization of the masses. All efforts at reform were put off to the indefinite future after the end of the war. In the countryside there was no serious agrarian reform. Few efforts were made to modernize the backward countryside or encourage mass participation in the war effort. To the extent that the Communists did promote reforms, this only spurred the government in a more reactionary direction.

Inevitably such a government would prove inept in meeting serious emergencies that arose during the war. Two examples make this point clearly. Although China's greatest resources were located in her coastal cities, which were vulnerable to Japanese attack, the government made almost no plans for evacuation or destruction of valuable plants. Peking was lost so quickly that almost nothing was salvaged, while Shanghai, despite a three-month battle, sent less than 6 percent of its factories to the interior. Susan Marsh has trenchantly noted:

> Japan profited from the fact that the Nationalist government had not only virtually neglected to reorganize and evacuate industries to the hinterland, but had also failed to immobilize Shanghai, Nanking and other strategic cities as potential enemy war bases before they were abandoned. Japan was able to capture their resources and industrial plants, as well as employ the abundant Chinese labor supply of the coastal provinces.[25]

A second typical example came with the famine that struck millions of people in Honan province in 1943. Although the government appropriated adequate relief funds, millions of refugees received no aid. In February 1943 American Ambassador to China Gauss reported to the secretary of state that, despite the famine, the government was continuing to collect land taxes from farmers and forcing farmers to sell their land and even members of the families to escape starvation. By December 1943, Gauss reported to Washington that the famine continued as "the authorities are apparently doing little relief work at present; foreign relief organizations are doing excellent work but their efforts are limited by scarcity of funds."[26]

Ineptitude was mixed with widespread and official government corruption. Even Russian and American military and economic aid to China, so vital to the war effort, was repeatedly subjected to large-scale Chinese governmental corruption. In 1942 General Yang Chieh, Chinese ambassador to the Soviet Union, told John Paton Davies of "Russian disillusionment" when they "discovered that aircraft were misused and cracked up by inexperienced personnel and that other material seemed scarcely ever to find its way into combat against the Japanese. It disappeared and no accounting was given."[27] Things were even worse with the more bountiful American Lend-Lease aid. The Burma Road itself was "clogged with staggering corruption, thievery, appalling incompetence."[28]

This corruption in American Lend-Lease aid was endemic of a widespread corruption in Chinese society during the war. While Chiang Kai-shek himself was evidently incorruptible, many of his advisers and family members (as the Soongs and Kungs) greatly enriched themselves during the war. Many provincial and local warlords also profited from the war, often emulating Lung Yun, the Yunnan governor, who had an enormous traffic in opium guarded by his soldiers. By 1944 corruption was so widespread that John Service could report from Chungking that "the governmental and military structure is being permeated and demoralized from top to bottom by corruption, unprecedented in scale and openness."[29] By 1943 there were several provincial armed revolts, caused by corruption, conscription, enforced labor, requisitions, and taxation. By the spring of 1944, Honanese peasants, angered by Kuomintang military and civilian conduct, openly helped Japanese soldiers disarm Chinese soldiers. In June 1944 John Service reported from Chungking that a Kuomintang official recently admitted that in a free election the regime would not receive more than 20 percent of the votes.[30]

The same could hardly be said for the new Chinese Communist regime during the Korean War. Added to the enormous tasks of national integration and economic reconstruction, the Korean War intruded before the regime had been in power even one year. Under similar but less demanding conditions, the Kuomintang in 1937 had simply postponed all attempts at reform, national integration, and economic development until after the war. By contrast, the Communists in 1950 seized on the war as a vehicle to help achieve those very goals postponed by the Nationalists. The results were impressive as the Communists grew stronger, not weaker, during the war. By February 1951 American Consul General in Hong Kong Walter McConaughy reported to the secretary of state that "since the outbreak of the war Chinese Communist political control of the country has become stronger rather than weaker."[31] This pattern continued throughout the war. By October 1953, soon after the conclusion of the war, a top secret National Security Council Report no. 166 determined that "the Chinese Communists have established a strong, centralized political control over mainland China; they have so far succeeded in coping with their economic problems."[32]

How did they accomplish these feats? First, they created and solidified their organizational strength and penetration of the society. Before 1950 they had already created a powerful five-million-man Chinese Communist Party, strong People's Liberation Army and nascent decentralized government bureaucracy. During the Korean War, major changes occurred in all three organizations. The army was transformed from a sprawling primitive structure in 1950 to a more modernized and professionalized force in 1953. The Party organization was strengthened and reorganized through purges of unfit and corrupt elements and selective admission of new members fo the Party. Special attention went to strengthening the Party's weak base in urban areas.

The greatest area of concern was the governmental bureaucracy, which had been the weakest of the three major institutions before 1950. As we have seen, the Party recruited over 2.5 million new government cadres from 1950 to 1952. In this period the Party controlled the government through a series of rectification campaigns aimed at bureaucratism and commandism (1950), waste and corruption (1951-1952), and bureaucratism and commandism again (1953). The Party introduced a new control system with four organizations—the Party, Party control commissions, procuracy, and Ministry of Supervision—monitoring the government. In the area of personnel management, professionalism was the password, with a stress on upgrading cadre skills, introducing wage scales (1953), and directing the power of administrators and managers. Beginning in 1952, the government codified its organizational procedures and began replacing the six regional areas with a single unified government. The Communists emphasized a new bureaucratic work style, with emphasis on egalitarianism, austerity, and simplicity. Not all was nirvana. Problems persisted with eradicating the old habits of retained officials and the low levels of skills, experience, and education of veteran Communists. There was also a tendency toward swings between passivity and excessive zeal caused by too many campaigns. Overall, though, the government was "reasonably effective" in "maintaining high standards of organizational performance."[33]

The Communists sought to eliminate three major obstacles to a strong central government: corruption, localism, and foreign domination. The Communists in 1950 found corruption to be a very serious and dangerous problem. In Shanghai, many Communist officials were busy taking bribes, selling public property illegally to private individuals, and using public funds. In the 1951-1952 *sanfan* campaign, a major drive was launched against corrupt and wasteful government and Party cadres. Spectacular cases of graft were uncovered and over ten thousand officials were purged. In 1952 the government launched the *wufan* campaign against the bourgeoisie as the source of corruption. A. Doak Barnett could report of government bureaucrats that "their salaries have been kept low and corruption is reported to have been almost completely eliminated."[34]

A second traditional drain on effective central governance had been excessive localism. While corruption drained away the resources the center could mobilize, localism prevented the center from gaining access to key local resources. The Communists smashed the warlords and tried to build their own local networks. In so doing, they had to overcome their own decentralized guerrilla past. Primarily through the vehicle of land reform, the Communists destroyed local Communist networks and "transformed a semi-autonomous guerrilla organization into a disciplined local outpost of a strong central administration." In Kwangtung province, for example, the central government in 1952 used trained northern army cadres to bring radical land reform to the area against local wishes and purge the local organs.[35]

The third Chinese problem enduring for over a century had been foreign interference and even foreign imperialist intervention in Chinese affairs. Unlike the areas of corruption and localism, in the area of foreign interventionism the Kuomintang regime, which had focused on this problem, had made significant progress. The Communist regime completed this process. It ousted foreign businessmen and missionaries and attacked all forms of foreign influence. The Korean War, and the attendant "Resist America–Aid Korea" campaign, provided an excellent opportunity to castigate foreign enemies and their domestic allies and to promote Chinese patriotism. Thus, China could use the Korean War to extrude all foreign influence except limited Soviet influence.

Having eliminated these constraints, the Communists set out to mobilize far greater resources than hitherto used by the center. But one remaining obstacle remained—domestic enemies, now cut off from their foreign allies. The new regime openly used coercion to eliminate avowed enemies and isolate potential enemies. By 1952 the government created a nationwide system of public security committees in every village, factory, and institution. The government required the entire population to register and each household to sign a loyalty oath. In the urban "Punishment of Counterrevolutionaries" and rural agrarian reform campaigns, one to three million Chinese perished. Perhaps as many as 10 million other Chinese were sent to forced labor camps to undergo thought reform. Combined with vigorous "bandit-suppression campaigns" conducted by the army, these governmental moves completed the rout of domestic enemies left over from the civil war.

With a favorable environment, the Communists set out to actively mobilize the population and its resources for political ends. During the 1927–1949 period the Party had developed strong mobilization capacity in rural areas. Now it transferred these skills to an urban and national context. The government organized all sectors of the population, including workers, peasants, women, youth, students, and intellectuals in a series of mass organizations. These were supplemented by the creation of residents' committees in the cities and mutual-aid teams in rural areas. The results were most impressive. As A. Doak Barnett has concluded:

The myth, formerly accepted by many people, that no regime could effectively organize and discipline Chinese people seems to have been exploded . . . in three short years the Chinese Communists have in fact accomplished what must rank with the most phenomenal feats of social organization in history. . . . They have constructed an organizational apparatus that reaches deep into grass-roots levels of the country and into the privacy of people's lives.[36]

Making use of their strong organizational base, the Chinese Communists launched a series of mass movements with goals of political mobilization and attacking political and social issues and enemies. The land reform program from 1950 to 1952 destroyed the power and status of the landlords and mobilized peasants into peasant associations, which redistributed the land. The 1950 Marriage Law, which prohibited polygamy and arranged marriages and established the legal equality of the sexes and legal divorces, became the basis for a mass movement of oppressed women. The 1950 Campaign to Suppress Counterrevolutionaries eliminated many actual or potential enemies. The 1951 Democratic Reform Campaign successfully isolated and attacked powerful secret societies and labor gangs through a well-prepared mass campaign. A public campaign strongly reduced extortion, looting, and robbery and virtually eliminated gambling, prostitution, and opium. The *sanfan* and *wufan* campaigns eliminated public corruption and strongly reduced the power of the urban bourgeoisie. In all these campaigns the Chinese Communists moved carefully on a single front, thereby ensuring success through the mobilization of overwhelming pressure on a narrow, isolated target.

Finally, in addition to normative and coercive mechanisms of control, there were also positive utilitarian motivations for the people. By 1954 the government was spending almost five times more money on social welfare than in 1950. In 1951 the government introduced significant labor insurance regulations. Public health care, albeit of a low level, now reached a far greater proportion of the population. By 1953 the educational system had over twice as many students enrolled than in 1949.[37]

Sharp differences between Chinese governments in the two wars are therefore evident. In the Sino-Japanese War the Kuomintang government, hampered by localism and corruption, struggled to maintain the status quo. Unable and unwilling to mobilize China's vast resources, the government stumbled from defeat to defeat and was on the verge of disintegration. The Communist regime smashed localism and corruption and greatly enlarged the resources that it could mobilize. Carrying through the revolution that had swept it

into power, the Communists grew stronger throughout the course of
the war.

PARTIES

A short comparison of the role of the Kuomintang party in the Sino-
Japanese War and the Chinese Communist party in the Korean War
reiterates many of the themes elucidated above. The Kuomintang was
an incredibly weak party, which "became a shell with no substance,"
as it was "organizationally paralyzed as well as spiritually impoverished." Its base of power was so narrow and weak that some members of its Central Executive Committee were even jobless.[38] Chiang
Kai-shek's absolute veto over the decisions of party congresses and
the Central Executive Committee rendered the party impotent. The
military before and during the war became the final arbiter of intra-
party struggles. In many local areas, as Szechwan, local secret societies had penetrated the party and were more powerful than the
party.

The party's base was quite limited and it never attracted mass
support. Even in 1936, its membership represented .3 percent of the
population, mainly among the better-educated classes of the coastal
provinces. The war, by depriving the party of its coastal base, dealt it
a blow from which it never recovered. By 1939 the Kuomintang had
less than one-third of the members it possessed in 1936. Although by
1944 the party had 2.6 million members, many had been impressed
or routinely enrolled in the party. By 1944 the party had only
25,000 party workers. Work was suspended for lack of complete
cadres and minimal training.[39]

The major problem in attracting membership was the reactionary
ideology of the Kuomintang. An effective ideology needed to
account for the political weakness of the regime, set goals, integrate
the elite, and legitimize the political system. The neo-Confucianism
of Chiang Kai-shek did not provide an effective guide to action in the
Sino-Japanese War. The stress on traditional values, universal harmony, militarization of life, discipline, societal stability, personal
morality, and the blaming of all problems on foreigners and unequal
treaties did not accord with the need to resolve China's serious
domestic and foreign problems. Ignored in this ideology were such
basic needs as democracy, social justice, and mass participation in
government.

In this context the Kuomintang became a conservative faction-r⁻ den party lacking internal unity. Among the major factions were t.e Action Society of Whampoa graduates, the C.C. Clique of the Ch'en brothers, the Political Science Group of urban bureaucrats and intellectuals, the Western Hill Faction and the fading power of the Reorganized Faction of the renegade Wang Ching-wei. In addition the Soong family and Tai Li both played significant roles.

Lacking a reformist or revolutionary ideology and dynamic organization, the party was unable to mobilize a population aroused by the Japanese invasion. It also seemed curiously unwilling to do much effective mass mobilization work, perhaps because it would threaten the power of the warlords, upper classes, and conservative elements who played such a key role in the Kuomintang. In January 1941 American Ambassador in China Nicholas Johnson told the secretary of state that the "central authorities have done little to foster a popular movement in China. It may be because of fear . . . because of apathy or of a conscious shrinking from such a tremendous and momentous task."[40] In July 1943 a Chinese cabinet minister lamented to General Stilwell that "very few people know what it is all about. The mass of the people know only that Japan is fighting China."[41]

Once again, the Communists presented a very different picture. Many observers have commented on the strength, vitality, and dynamism of this revolutionary party. Praise for their dynamism even came from an unlikely source, the American consul general in Shanghai, Walter McConaughy, who wrote the following to the secretary of state in March 1950:

> Interesting to note that virtually all our sources, including the bitterest foes of the Communists, agree that in pursuance of their objectives, rank and file Communists definitely possess certain outstanding qualities. Such include: much greater vigor and thoroughness than KMT; general personal incorruptibility (as regards friends and 'squeeze') hither unknown in China; extraordinary capacity for hard work; eagerness to learn; Spartan austerity; fervent belief in propaganda fed them re America etc.; unswerving devotion to party objectives.[42]

The top leadership of the Chinese Communist party, including Mao Tse-Tung, Liu Shao-chi, and Chou En-lai, were experienced and gifted political veterans. For over two decades they had struggled together for the success of the revolution and achieved success against enormous odds. Their honesty, integrity, and devotion to the Party and revolution were unquestioned. While the Party had been repeatedly rent by harsh "two-line" struggles over time, it had shown strong recuperative powers. Most impressive was its ability to act decisively and rapidly once decisions had been made. The time period for deciding and implementing a major preemptive strike across the border must have been quite short. The Party leadership was flexible and pragmatic in adapting to changing realities. After the Chinese defeats in the spring of 1951, the old civil war tactics of fluid movement and guerrilla infiltration were discarded in favor of massive conventional defense. The political talents of the leadership, their incorruptibility, flexibility, pragmatism, and unity in action all set the Communists apart from the Nationalists.

The Party paid special attention to maintaining a strong and vital organization. During the Korean War the Party recruited 2 million new members, bringing its size to 6.1 million members by July 1953. It also heavily recruited new, better-educated cadres. In March 1951 it launched a major two- and one-half year long rectification campaign to correct problems of low standards, alien elements, and weak applicants. This campaign reregistered and reeducated Communists and, if necessary, expelled alien elements. Together with the 1952 *sanfan* campaign, these two campaigns purged over 500,000 Communists. The Party kept tight control of its membership through selection, screening, indoctrination, criticism, and self-criticism methods. The Party's creation of a disciplined party was "one of the Communists' most remarkable accomplishments, for they have succeeded where others in China have tried and failed."[43]

The Party used its organizational capabilities to vigorously mobilize the population for the war and to carry out major domestic functions. The Chinese Communist party was so successful in these tasks that by the end of the war the country was ready to embark on its First Five-Year Plan and continue movement toward full collectivization of agriculture in 1955.

* * *

Military performance to a great extent relies on the economic, social, and political institutions and capacities of a country. The Chinese Revolution greatly enhanced the capacity of the central government to wage war. The factors that had prevented the central government from utilizing China's vast resources—weak institutions, corruption, localism, foreign interference—were swept away in the revolution. A dynamic, unified, mobilizing Communist party displaced a weak, faction-ridden, conservative Kuomintang party. A new, relatively honest and strong government with deep local roots replaced a sprawling, corrupt, and ineffective government cut off from many regions by strong warlords. In the end, as in the French and Russian Revolutions, a new, more modern government emerged with greatly enhanced power from the revolutionary process.

PART 4
Conclusion

CHAPTER 12

On the Relationship Among Revolution, Armies, and War

Perhaps in few other areas has the impact of revolutionary change been as profound and dramatic as in the realms of state power and state capabilities in the international order. In international systems usually profoundly resistant to rapid changes, revolutions within a relatively short time have transformed states weak in power but rich in resources into strong and even feared members of the international system. The England of the Stuarts, so weak that it could not intervene in the Thirty Years' War, defeat Scotland, or even protect its own waters in the 1630s, was a distant historical memory by the 1650s when England had become a strong and even feared state after the English Revolution. The weakened France of Louis XV and Louis XVI, loser of many battles in the Seven Years' War and Anglo-French War (1778-1782) and passive in the face of Prussian invasion of Holland in 1787, became a powerful hegemonic state in Europe for almost two decades after the French Revolution. The Russian and Chinese Revolutions in this century have had a similar impact in transforming a weak and backward Russia into a great superpower by World War II and a divided and often humiliated China into a strong regional power by the Korean War.

The Soviet victory in World War II, reflecting the impact of the October Revolution and Stalin's revolution of the 1930s, was an historical event of great significance. It ended almost a century of Russian military impotence and defeats from the Crimean War (1853-1856) and Sino-Japanese War (1904-1905) to World War I (1914-1917) and the early defeats in World War II (1941-1942). It took Russia from being considered the weakest element in the Triple Entente in World War I and a state that could safely be excluded from the crucial 1938 Munich Conference to becoming a superpower that in 1945 occupied Berlin, Prague, Vienna, and Budapest. And in achieving this historic victory that echoed the glory of 1814, the Soviet state had destroyed in Nazi Germany the premier hegemonic European state, which had easily laid waste all the armies of Continental Europe, including the vaunted French army.[1]

In this work we have seen the vast improvement in Russian military capabilities between World War I and World War II. In World War I the Tsarist army, having been repeatedly humiliated by the Germany army, disintegrated in 1917. Against a far stronger German army and with an inferior geographic position and less Allied aid, the Red Army in World War II scored notable military victories that altered the whole balance of power in Europe. Rarely has the impact of revolution been so directly observable as in the contrasting fates of the Russian army in 1917 and 1945.

Perhaps a different comparison, this time between revolutionary Russia and prerevolutionary China in World War II, can illustrate the point in another way. The two mighty Axis powers, Germany and Japan, each respectively tried to conquer a large but traditionally weak power, Russia (1941-1945) and China (1937-1945), in the course of the war. In the first two years of the war the aggressors scored major victories in very bloody battles. The war became protracted resulting in huge losses of life (10 to 20 million people in each case) with the Axis powers resorting to widespread brutality. Yet, the latter phases of World War II saw very different outcomes. While the Red Army drove out the German army in 1944, liberated Eastern Europe, and occupied Berlin in 1945, the Kuomintang army was smashed by a weakening Japanese army in Operation ICHIGO in 1944 and awaited external salvation in 1945. The Red Army even went on to destroy the Japanese army in a lightning campaign in Manchuria in August 1945. One more fact makes this still more remarkable: the Russians faced a German invasion that had three times more men than the Japanese force that invaded China (3.2 million Germans compared with 1.0 million Japanese) and 5 to 10 times more tanks and firepower. United States General "Vinegar Joe" Stilwell recorded in his diary on January 19, 1943:

> What a fight the Russians have made. The nation has obviously found itself. Twenty years of work and struggle. Results: tough physique; unity of purpose; pride in their accomplishment; determination to win. . . . compare it with the Chinese cesspool.[2]

Similarly, the Chinese Revolution changed China from a weak

and often despised state to a strong and even feared regional power. The contrast between Chinese impotence in the Sino-Japanese War and Chinese power in the Korean War was especially telling. The rapid change reflecting the revolutionary impact of the Chinese Communist rise to power, shocked and deeply impressed American observers, who saw the East suddenly and successfully stand up to the West. Averell Harriman developed this argument at a conference on the Korean War.

> My impression was that MacArthur was impressed with the fact that the Chinese had never fought. He had seen the Chinese, and they had never fought during his experience in China. He did not place much confidence in their ability to fight, which was one of his great miscalculations. . . . General MacArthur's knowledge of the Chinese was obsolete.[3]

By the end of the Korean War (October 1953), a National Security Council Planning Board's secret report could conclude somberly:

> The emergence of a strong, disciplined and revolutionary Communist regime on the mainland of China has radically altered the power structure in the Far East. With the minor exceptions of Hong Kong and Macao, American, Japanese and European power and influence has been abruptly extruded from the whole vast area between the Amur, the Himalayas and Gulf of Tonkin. . . . The primary problem of U.S. foreign policy in the Far East is to cope with an altered structure of power which arises from the existence of a strong and hostile Communist China.[4]

The active participation of China at the 1954 Geneva Conference would confirm its new-found power and prestige.

Of course, in retrospect the rise of Communist China was far less sudden and more protracted than it seemed at the time. Already in the Sino-Japanese War, while the Kuomintang regime was slowly crumbling, the new Communist forces were vigorously expanding. From only 30,000 soldiers and a territory of 1 million people in 1937, the Communists by 1945 had 1 million soldiers and a territory with 95 million people. Similarly, although the Kuomintang army started the civil war in 1946 with 3.5 times more soldiers (4.3 million to 1.2 million) and far more heavy equipment than the People's Liberation Army, this advantage did not last long. By 1948 the Chinese Communists were sweeping across China, and in 1949 the devastated Kuomintang army was forced to flee to Taiwan. The rapidity of the Communist victory was based on the numerous factors of dynamism, cohesion, and organization that also prevailed in Korea.

My work, following in a tradition established earlier by such students of comparative revolutions as Crane Brinton, Barrington Moore, and Theda Skocpol, demonstrates the viability of analyzing the Russian and Chinese Revolutions in the broader sweep of revolutionary history.[5] The basic similarities between socialist revolutions and nonsocialist revolutions are quite striking. The greater power manifested by socialist revolutions and avoidance of restoration of the ancien regime testifies to the enhanced capabilities of such revolutionary states to use a conscious popular ideology and mass-mobilizing party to achieve results far greater than those achieved by earlier revolutions. Thus, my study demonstrates the revolutionary roots of Russian and Chinese Communism, the significant progressive aspects of these revolutions, and the strong correlation between revolution and power.

This work has a great deal to say implicitly about the validity of totalitarianism as a theoretical model for analyzing Stalinist Russia and Maoist China. Fundamentally I suggest the lack of any need for the use of such an exceptionalist theory that seeks to isolate Russia and China from their revolutionary roots. My analysis has emphasized precisely those aspects of Russian and Chinese experience— revolutionary dynamism, mass popular support, and progressive aspects of social change—that receive short shrift in totalitarian analyses. As Stephen Cohen has trenchantly critiqued the role of totalitarianism in Sovietology:

> The field's orthodox paradigm, 'totalitarianism,' was itself a constituent part of the American anti-Communist concensus, a scholarly concept used equally in official and popular discourse to explain contemporary history and rationalize policy. Like general Cold-War wisdom, for example, the totalitarian school now equated Stalin's Russia and Hitler's Germany, teaching that postwar Soviet Communism was a replay of Nazism in the 1930s or 'Red fascism,' and thus warning against any 'appeasement.'[6]

In addition, my analysis has also showed significant differences between the Soviet and Chinese experiences that vitiate any attempt to simplistically apply a monolithic totalitarian model to explain their developments. The success of Soviet Russia in World War II rested heavily on the great economic accomplishments of the 1930s, while the success of Maoist China rested primarily on political and social mobilization, not on economic development. Secondly, the time frame for development differed dramatically between the two countries. While Russia emerged as a weak power from the civil war in 1921 and required two more decades and Stalin's third "revolution from above" to become a major power, China emerged as a strong power from its final civil war in 1949. Finally, there were therefore very different gestation periods and paths to power, which had a profound influence on the evolution of politics in Russia and China. The rural militant egalitarian thrust of the "Yenan syndrome" differed radically from the urban, hypercentralized experience of "war communism."[7] Thus, totalitarian theory provides little guidance in understanding both the fundamental similarities and differences between the Russian and Chinese Revolutions.

Clearly, then, the correlation between revolution and enhanced power in the international system has been shown for these four great revolutions. But what about revolutions in lesser powers? Given the paucity of major revolutions and the inherent problems of dependency, it is hard to generalize; but it seems that the revolution/power relationship does hold. Cuba and Vietnam are notable examples. Although the Cuban army was relatively weak in 1959, the existence of a strong domestic and foreign counterrevolutionary threat led to emphasis on creation of a new revolutionary army. Having crushed internal opposition in the early 1960s, the army was sufficiently strong and capable to launch successful expeditions in Africa in the 1970s. In Vietnam, the Viet Minh developed from 1944 to 1954 into a cohesive force capable of driving the French from Vietnam and achieving victory at Dienbienphu. Especially after the destruction of South Vietnamese Communist forces in the 1968 Tet offensive, the regular North Vietnamese troops became the backbone of the Communist war effort. By 1973, despite heavy losses, they had forced American withdrawal from the war, and in 1975 the North Vietnamese army triumphantly entered Saigon and occupied South Vietnam. And in 1979 the army performed well against the limited Chinese incursion.

My emphasis on outcomes of revolution as opposed to the more common emphasis on causes of revolutions has also given us insights into the nature of military victory. My work clearly demonstrates the limits to the traditional view that wars are won preeminently by economic production and superior technology. In the four revolutions studied, only in Russia had there been an economic transformation to accompany the political revolution—and even there social factors were of great importance. Rather, my work has tended to show the critical role of political and social factors, in tandem with purely economic factors, in securing victory on the battlefield.[8]

From an analysis of these four revolutions it seems clear that armies have gone through four stages of development in relation to the revolution. First, in prerevolutionary states relatively traditional armies (and often navies), hampered by serious internal restrictions on their development and poorly supported by an inefficient state, have usually suffered serious military defeats. In the second stage a new revolutionary army emerges, either before the seizure of power (China, Cuba, Vietnam) or after the seizure of power (England, France, Russia) to defend the gains of the revolution. In the third stage the consolidated revolutionary army, now backed by a more capable and centralized government, sweeps aside remaining domestic foes (if any) and wins major victories over strong foreign enemies. Finally, in the fourth stage there is a tendency towards decline, as the revolutionary wave subsides in both the army and government. Let us look in detail at each of the four stages.

In the first stage of prerevolutionary France, England, Russia, and China, the traditionalist armies were intimately bound up in the old order and shared in and even accelerated its decline. Indeed the very creation of even a mildly effective armed forces had been an enormously difficult and problematic task for the state. The old order had to overcome its own limited financial base, opposition from an aristocracy seeking to retain its neofeudal control over arms, resistance from commoners to service in an alien and dangerous profession, and strong localism. So powerful were these constraints that only in France and Russia did the monarchs manage to create a truly national armed force (and even then with a significant foreign component). In England in the 1630s, Charles I had no standing army, while "as demonstrations of power in the game of international politics, the English fleets of the middle 1630s were little more than a joke."[9] In China, Chiang Kai-shek, even more so after he was forced into the hinterland following the 1937 and 1938 disasters, relied heavily on warlord armies over which his control was tenuous, and he directly controlled only 20 to 25 percent of his forces.

Ties between army and regime were extremely close. In wartime and often in peacetime the cost of supporting the army and navy and paying the interest on debts incurred through past wars was usually the single largest item in the budget. The military was typically the single most important element of the bureaucracy. The creation of the army was one of the first significant accomplishments of the state. During wartime no less than three of the four leaders of the prerevolutionary states (Charles I, Nicholas II, Chiang Kai-shek) directly assumed the post of commander in chief of the armed forces, even though two of them had no military experience or capabilities at all. By so doing, they gave visual expression to what was an obvious truth: that monarchs and governments and the bureaucracies they created were tied to their armies. The growth of the last meant an increase in the organs of government and in the decisions monarchies must make in terms of money and men of their subjects in the name of state imperatives and interests.[10]

With the officer corps dominated by the aristocracy and upper classes and the ranks dominated by the lower classes, the army was a faithful reflection of the old order in microcosm. The top military commanders were often not talented professional soldiers but courtiers in favor with the autocrat. Men such as Goring, Sukhomlimov, and Ho Ying-chin lacked any serious military talent, while those with talent were generally blocked from promotion by lack of patronage, money, or upper-class background. Not one of the most famous revolutionary army commanders—Oliver Cromwell, Napoleon Bonaparte, Georgi Zhukov, and Mao Tse-tung—based on old order qualifications, would have been allowed to lead the armies of the old order. Furthermore, having obtained their positions through influence, birth, and money, many officers exploited their positions for private gain and did little to prepare for battle. Although each army had its reformers with modern military views—from Prince Rupert and Guibert to Li Tsung-jen—they were almost invariably overshadowed by reactionary, privileged officers with antiquarian notions of warfare. And, always, the vast social gulf between aristocratic officers and commoner soldiers translated into a remote officer corps, which saw the use of brutal force as necessary to keep the soldiers in line.

As to the soldiers, in all these armies they served under duress and largely without enthusiasm. Abused by their officers, neglected by the state in terms of food, housing, and pay, ignored and feared by society, the lower-class soldiers had little to fight for in the old order and no hope of advancement into the officer corps. Given no political training, they felt little compunction in plundering the civilian population and deserted in droves when they had a chance.

As a consequence of these factors and restrictions inevitably placed on the army by the limited government capacity to serve its needs, the traditional army adopted a conservative style of warfare. The army inevitably eschewed an aggressive offensive style in favor of a passive defensive mentality. When the army did advance, it did so slowly and ponderously, moving in tight formations to avoid desertions and tied to its inadequate supply line. Their advances ended so often in disaster—whether the English invasions of Scotland (1639, 1640), the French moves into Germany (Seven Years' War), the Russian invasion of East Prussia (1914), or Chinese offensive at Shanghai (1937)—that passive defense seemed to be the trademark of all these armies.

The second stage of the emergence of a nascent revolutionary army (England 1642-1644), France 1792-1799, Russia 1918-1929, China 1927-1945) and the third stage of a consolidated revolutionary army (England 1645-1660, France 1800-1815, Russia 1930-1945, China 1946-1953) saw the creation of a totally new form of army. While in the second stage the hastily improvised armies defended the revolution against internal and external foes, in the third stage the consolidated army sallied forth to destroy strong foreign enemies. While in England, Russia, and China a new army was created, in France the old army was transformed. While in England, France, and China the creation of this new type of army was coterminous with the revolution, in Russia the weak base of the October Revolution necessitated Stalin's third revolution of the 1930s to create the new Red Army. And while the technical base of the French and Russian armies was quite strong, in England and China it was quite weak. Thus within the overall pattern considerable variation existed.

Overall, though, the new armies differed sharply from their predecessors and reflected the impact of revolution on society in general and the army as a total institution in particular. The officer corps was now uniformly open to talented men from all classes and strata in society. Promotion was based on merit, bravery, and experience. The result was that a galaxy of brilliant commanders rose to the fore—Cromwell, Ireton, Fleetwood, Monck, and Blake in England; Napoleon, Murat, Ney, and Soult in France; Zhukov, Konev, and Rokossovsky in Russia; and Chu Teh, Lin Biao, and Peng De-huai in China. Serving them were strong corps of battle-tested, loyal professional officers, many of whom had risen through the ranks. Uniformly these commanders were young (often in their 30s) and daring and innovative in style. The style of war concurrently became relentlessly offensive and aggressive. At the same time the soldiers had changed as well. Now they saw themselves as enfranchised citizens of a new state, defending it from rapacious enemies of the old order. This normative commitment was strongly stressed by chaplains (England) and commissars (France, Russia, and China). The army provided adequate food and shelter and possibility for advancement into the officer corps, all of which gave utilitarian reasons to fight. And in this environment, effective discipline could be maintained by officers who were closer to the men than officers of the old army.

At the same time professional ("expert") values increasingly overshadowed revolutionary ("red") values in all armies in stage three. In England in the 1650s, in France in the Napoleonic army (1799-1815), in Russia in World War II, and in China in the latter phases of the Korean War this new professional spirit became predominant. Rank and discipline became more important; advancement was more institutionalized, and professional soldiers predominated over revolutionary enthusiasts. These features enabled the revolutionary army to overcome strong enemies and endure very heavy casualties. By the end of this period of consolidation the armies stood triumphant—England at sea and on land, France (if tenuously) and Russia in Europe, and China in Asia.

These military changes paralleled and reflected broader changes in the nature of the revolutions. At this stage governments sought a reintegration of the polity through a broad synthesis of traditional values (such as nationalism) and revolutionary values.

Finally, in the fourth stage of the natural evolution of such armies is an often serious decline in their capabilities and importance. The process is closely linked to the passing of the revolutionary generation and reintegration of the nation into the international order as a "normal" member state. Furthermore, unless an economic transformation accompanies the political revolution (as in Russia), the great increase in taxes necessary to support the military creates popular discontent, laying the basis for restoration. This process was especially clear in England and France, less clear in China, and not evident in Russia. The restoration of the Stuarts in England in 1660 and Bourbons in France in 1814/1815 marked a definite end to the English and French Revolutions. After 1660, Charles II completely disbanded the 50,000 man army, eventually retaining only four regiments (Coldstream Guards, Grenadier Guards, Royal Horse Guards, and Royal Scots Guards) to serve as a nucleus for a future army. In France after 1815 the army was sharply reduced in size to 240,000 men by 1818. In both England and France the restored monarchs returned to small traditional professional armies dominated by aristocratic officers. The results were equally predictable. English land power went into sharp decline, and French land power went, in Charles de Gaulle's phrase, "from disaster to disaster," culminating in the rout in the 1870 Franco-Prussian War.[11]

As to the Communist states, the existence of a strong mass mobilizing party and conscious institutionalization of the revolution have prevented any direct restoration of the ancien regime. Continued adherence to Communist ideology has prevented any simple reintegration into the international order. And in Russia's case, the successful transformation of the country into a major industrial power and its continuing preoccupation with military affairs have prevented any serious deterioration in its military capabilities.

However a significant case can be made for China in the wake of the ascension of Deng Xiao-ping after Mao Tse-tung's death in 1976 (and the Hua Guo-feng interlude). Deng and his followers, deeply hostile to the Maoist radicalism so inherent in the Chinese revolution, have introduced elements of market socialism, purged the Maoists, and stripped the army of its remaining, aging revolutionary commanders. With the army's decrepitude already demonstrated by its poor performance in the 1979 Vietnamese incursion, the low priority on military spending and denigration of the army as a key force in society should ensure its existence as a relatively large but less than powerful force. The days of the revolutionary army sweeping the Party to power, driving the Americans from North Korea in 1950 and India from the border areas in 1962, are over, as is the revolution.

Now that we have clarified the evolution of armies over time, several remaining points need to be stressed. First, revolutionary armies are *not* invariably successful—witness the failures of Cromwell's Hispaniola campaign, Napoleon's Russian campaign and ultimate 1813-1815 demise, the Red Army in the civil war, 1920 Polish campaign, and early stages of World War II, and the People's Liberation Army in the 1951 Korean offensives. But what is impressive, in a world in which more powerful states nearly always defeat states lagging behind in development, is the great extent of these armies' victories, even more impressive compared to the failure of their predecessors.

Revolutionary armies are especially vulnerable to disaster in stage two, in the early years of their development. Hastily improvised on the battlefield under weak central command, often inadequately supported by nascent revolutionary regimes, frequently relying more on revolutionary enthusiasm than professional organization, these revolutionary armies are in danger of being defeated by stronger, more cohesive professional armies of the old order. The Parliamentary armies in 1643, the French armies in the early 1790s, the Red Army in the civil war, and the Chinese army by the time of the Fifth Encirclement Campaign of 1934 all seemed on the verge of extinction. And, in the Spanish Revolution of the 1930s this fate was not avoidable by 1939.

While revolutionary armies can fail, it is also important to see that revolutions are not the only pathway to military success. The secular processes of modernization, industrialization, and nation-building can build a strong base for a successful military. So too can successful, conservative reform from above, as in the Prussian military reforms after 1806 (which integrated revolutionary elements into the army and society while maintaining governmental control of the process) and in the creation of the vaunted Imperial Japanese Army.

Finally, a comparison between traditional states and revolutionary states, as seen in our four countries, is especially revealing. Traditional states seemed to have a paucity of everything—power, governmental roles, and most critically, tax revenues. Governmental functions were minimal and often carried out in a poor and corrupt manner. In the most basic sense, the traditional states were politically underdeveloped—their level of political modernization lagged behind their social and economic developments. As Samuel Huntington has argued:

> These countries lack many things. They suffer real shortages of food, literacy, education, wealth, income, health and productivity but most of them have been recognized and efforts made to do something about them. Beyond and behind these shortages, however, there is a greater shortage; a shortage of political community and of effective, authoritative legitimate government. The political community is fragmented against itself and where political institutions have little power, less majesty and no resiliency.[12]

A thicket of privileges—class, provincial, and regional—effectively bound the central government.

The problem in traditional governments started at the top, with the autocrat and the court or clique that surrounded him. Unlike in modern governments, there was no element of merit or concept of public service among these men. Rather the monarchs were chosen by the accident of birth or, as in the case of Chiang Kai-shek, through military skills. Furthermore, the political incompetence of all these men was legendary. So too was the predominant role of favoritism, patronage, high birth, and money among their advisers. Equally important was the widespread corruption and exploitation of public position for private interest. The inevitable result in all four countries was a remote and incompetent autocrat, surrounded by his family and a clique of well-connected and often corrupt officials, walled off and isolated from the population.

Under these conditions the quality of political leadership became a central problem in these traditional states. In all these states there were competent and capable bureaucrats and reformers who wanted to make the system work more efficiently. From Turgot and Necker in France to Stolypin and Witte in Russia there were men who clearly saw the defects of the system and strived to reform them. But, inevitably all their attempts came to naught. For all such attempts directly threatened the fundamental nature of the social system and the men (including the monarch) who gained such great financial and social rewards precisely from the system. The 121 peers of Charles I's England, the court nobles of Louix XVI's France, the Moscow and Petrograd aristocrats of Nicholas II's Russia, and the "Big Four" families of Chiang Kai-shek's China could hardly be expected not to strongly resist basic changes that threatened their power. Thus, even if reformers, or for that matter the autocrat himself, tried to make serious reforms, they would inevitably be sharply hampered by the system.

This modal, weak traditional government was invariably unable to mobilize the nation's resources for war. Politically, from fear of revolution, the government would desist from any serious attempt at popular mobilization. Economically it was strikingly unable to extract societal resources to use in war. In none of the four countries were the rudiments of a modern government bureaucracy created, although Russia came the closest. In England, France, and China there was not even a nascent central government bureaucracy and only minimal governmental penetration of local areas. Strong localism posed an insuperable obstacle to central control. In these countries government officials, recruited through birth, patronage, and purchase of office, often were openly corrupt in abusing their positions for private profit. These governments did not directly collect their taxes, rather farming out the taxes to wealthy individuals in return for leases from the government. Not one of the four governments was able to mobilize more than a meager 2 to 4 percent of national revenue for its own use—and even that was tainted by widespread corruption. All governments, seriously dominated by the upper classes, determinedly opposed serious reform.

By contrast, the revolutionary states smashed the fetters that had chained the traditional states and mobilized much more human and material resources to support their armies. The power of the upper classes was destroyed or significantly limited. The new leaders of the revolutionary states—Cromwell, Bonaparte, Lenin, Stalin, and Mao—were all very talented politicians and administrators, well aware of the need to mobilize the population on their behalf. The men who worked with them were generally equally talented and from diverse class backgrounds who had risen through merit and service to the revolution. The revolutions swept aside the crippling barriers of privilege and inequality and helped create a modern state with civic equality, national identity, and national ideology. It liberated provincial and individual resources from the bonds of the old order and put them at the disposal of the state.

The most striking aspect of the revolutionary states was the creation of a much stronger state bureaucracy, which was able to mobilize resources for governmental and military use. While in England and France the new states typically raised 2 to 3 times more revenue than their predecessor, in Russia and China the figure was 5 to 10 times more revenue. The corrupt, upper-class elite was ousted from the government, replaced by men chosen by merit from a broadened talent pool of all classes. The new nascent government bureaucracy usually was more efficient, honest, and rational, with a strong sense of representing the public interest. Corruption was generally sharply reduced through the elimination of purchase of office and creation of bureaucratic rules for procedures and salaries. Such a bureaucracy was capable of carrying out the political and economic mobilization of resources necessary for providing the supplies, manpower, weapons, and salaries so necessary to the army. In a word, the new governments provided far stronger and more modern political leadership.[13]

This result, of course, represents a classic example of the unanticipated consequences of social change. In these revolutions, fought in the name of justice and equality against oppressive states, it is truly ironic that the outcome was a state stronger and more effective in suppressing individual opposition. While the preceding traditional governments had claimed great powers but been unable to exercise them, the new governments were able to make good on their claims and promises in a very fundamental way.

In this context revolutions, then, are pathways to modernity, and revolutionary armies are important actors in that process. In the military sphere new social factors infuse the revolutionary army, which in turn creates a new and aggressive style of warfare. The basic changes wrought by the revolution provide the underpinnings for transformation of the army into a more modern institution capable of defending the revolutionary state. Samuel Huntington has assessed the relationship between revolution and modernization thus:

> More precisely, revolution is characteristic of modernization. It is one way of modernizing a traditional society. . . . Revolution is the ultimate

expression of a modernizing outlook, the belief that it is within the power of man to control and change his environment and that he has not only the ability but the right to do so.[14]

There are numerous other agents of modernization. Historically they have included worldwide trends of industrialization and commercialization, the rise of nation states, the expansion of the European state system, political upheavals, and socioeconomic changes. Furthermore, some states, as Germany and Japan, have successfully modernized and built powerful armies under the conservative aegis of the upper classes. Thus, multiple paths to modernity exist in recent history.[15]

Revolutions remain for nations one of the most distinctive paths to power in the international system. In the annals of military history many of the most famous pages were written by those revolutionary armies and their leaders—Cromwell at Naseby, Bonaparte at Austerlitz, Zhukov at Stalingrad, and Lin Biao in Korea. And through these military exploits the revolutionary armies, themselves prototypes of more modern institutions, helped propel England, France, Russia, and China from the ranks of secondary and degraded powers to becoming states of the first order in the international system. This, then, is the legacy of revolution, armies, and war.

Notes

CHAPTER 1

1. Charles Tilly, "Does Modernization Breed Revolution?" *Comparative Politics* vol. 5, no. 3 (April 1973), p. 446.

2. Theda Skocpol, *States and Social Revolution* (Cambridge: Cambridge University Press, 1979), p. 285. Similarly, Katharine Chorley has observed about the impact of war that "no other set of conditions seems likely to be able to produce those solvents" for the army. See Katharine Chorley, *Armies and the Art of Revolution* (London: Faber and Faber, 1943), p. 39. Furthermore, Walter Millis observed about war that "It challenges virtually every other institution of society—the justice and equity of its economy, the adequacy of its political system, the energy of its productive plant, the bases, wisdom, and purposes of its foreign policy. There is no aspect of our existence ... which is not touched, modified, perhaps completely altered by the imperatives of war." See Edward Meade Earle, "Introduction," in his edited work, *Makers of Modern Strategy* (Princeton: Princeton University Press, 1943), p. vii. Overall, then, war as the most concerted form of human interaction, forces men to examine their beliefs and reveals the adequacy of societal institutions most clearly.

3. Elbaki Hermassi, "Toward a Comparative Study of Revolutions," *Comparative Studies in Society and History* vol. 18, no. 2 (April 1976), p. 214.

4. Perhaps another reason for warfare is that revolutions in one country may provoke revolutions in other countries. Certainly the 1830 and 1848 French revolutions were highly contagious, as was the October Revolution and much later the 1949 Chinese Revolution.

5. With regard to the export of revolution by bayonets, Georges Lefebvre nicely summarized the French example, arguing that "wherever its armies had penetrated—Belgium, the Rhineland, Holland, Switzerland—the Revolution had undertaken the destruction of the Old Regime.... No nation imitated France

spontaneously; it was her armies that spread the principles of the Revolution."
See Georges Lefebvre, *Napoleon: From 18 Brumaire to Tilsit 1799-1807*, trans.
Henry Stockhold (New York: Columbia University Press, 1964), pp. 4-5.

6. Charles Firth, *Cromwell's Army* (London: Methuen and Company,
1902), p. vi.

7. Richard Hamilton, *Who Voted For Hitler?* (Princeton: Princeton University Press, 1982), p. 443. Theda Skocpol has similarly noted that structuralists
and Marxist scholars, with a focus on class, "virtually ignore the often much
more striking and immediate transformations that occur in the structure and
functions of state organizations, such as armies and administrations." See Theda
Skockpol, *States and Social Revolution*, p. 35.

8. A sampling of these include Katharine Chorley, *Armies and the Art of
Revolution*, Nicholas Timasheff, *War and Revolution* (New York: Sheed and
Ward, 1965), Kyung Hon Kim, *Revolution and the International System* (New
York: New York University Press, 1970), John Ellis, *Armies in Revolution* (London: Croom Helm, 1973), and Andre Corvisier, *Armies and Societies in Europe,
1494-1789*, trans. Abigail Siddall (Bloomington: Indiana University Press,
1979).

9. Theda Skocpol, *States and Social Revolutions*.

10. See, for example, Charles Firth, *Cromwell's Army*, Maurice Ashley,
Cromwell's Generals (New York: St. Martin's Press, 1955), Austin Woolrych,
Battles of the English Civil War (New York: Macmillan, 1961), Peter Young and
Richard Holmes, *The English Civil War* (London: Eyre Methuen, 1974), and
Mark Kishlansky, *The Rise of the New Model Army* (Cambridge: Cambridge
University Press, 1979).

11. For the pre-1789 period see Lee Kennett, *The French Armies in the
Seven Years' War* (Durham, N.C.: Duke University Press, 1967) and Samuel
Scott, *The Response of the Royal Army to the French Revolution* (Oxford:
Oxford University Press, 1978). For the revolutionary period see especially
David Chandler, *The Campaigns of Napoleon* (New York: Macmillan, 1966)
as well as Spenser Wilkinson, *The French Army Before Napoleon* (Oxford:
Oxford University Press, 1915), Colonel Ramsay Phipps, *The Armies of the
First French Republic* (Oxford: Oxford University Press, 1939), Henry
Lachouque, *Napoleon's Battles* (New York: E.P. Dutton, 1967) and Georges
Lefebvre, *Napoleon: From 18 Brumaire to Tilsit 1799-1807*, trans. Henry
Stockhold (New York: Columbia University Press, 1969) and his *Napoleon:
From Tilsit to Waterloo 1807-1815*, trans. J.E. Anderson (New York: Columbia
University Press, 1969).

12. For Western analysis of Russia in World War I, see Vasili Gourko, *War
and Revolution in Russia 1914-1917* (New York: Macmillan, 1919), Nicholas
Bolovine, *The Russian Army in the World War* (New Haven: Yale University
Press, 1931), Alfred Knox, *With the Russian Army 1914-1917* (London: Hutchinson and Company, 1921), Winston Churchill, *The Unknown War—The Eastern
Front* (New York: Charles Scribner's Sons, 1931), Norman Stone, *The Eastern*

Front 1914-1917 (New York: Charles Scribner's Sons, 1975) and Ward Rutherford, *The Russian Army in World War I* (London: Cremonesi Publishers, 1975) and Allan Wildman, *The End of the Russian Imperial Army* (Princeton: Princeton University Press, 1980). For Soviet analyses see N.A. Talenskii, *Pervaya mirovaya voina (1914-1918)* (Moscow: Gosizdat, 1944), G.I. Shigalin, *Voennaya ekonomika v pervuyu mirovuyu voinu (1914-1918)* (Moscow: Voenizdat, 1956, D.V. Verzhkhovski and V.F. Lyakhov, *Pervaya mirovaya voina* (Moscow: Voenizdat, 1964), I.I. Rostunov, *Russkoi front pervoi mirovoi voiny* (Moscow: Nauka, 1968) and *Istoriya pervoi mirovoi voiny*, 2 vols. (Moscow: Nauka, 1975). For World War II, see John Erickson, *The Road to Stalingrad* (London: Weidenfeld and Nicholson, 1975) and *The Road to Berlin* (Boulder, Colo.: Westview Press, 1984), Albert Seaton, *The Russo-German War 1941-45* (New York: Praeger, 1970) and *Istoriya vtoroi mirovoi voina 1939-1945* 12 vols. (Moscow: Voenydat, 1982).

On the Sino-Japanese War, see F.F. Liu, *A Military History of Modern China 1924-1949* (Princeton: Princeton University Press, 1956), John Boyle, *China and Japan at War 1937-1945* (Stanford: Stanford University Press, 1972), Frank Dorn, *The Sino-Japanese War, 1937-41* (New York: Macmillan, 1974), Takushiro Hattori, *Yaponiya v voine 1941-1945*, abridged translation from Japanese (Moscow: Voenizdat, 1973), Paul Sih, ed., *Nationalist China during the Sino-Japanese War, 1937-1945* (Hicksville, New York: Exposition Press, 1977) and Hsi-Sheng Ch'i, *Nationalist China at War* (Ann Arbor: University of Michigan Press, 1982). For American memoirs see Joseph Stilwell, *The Stilwell Papers* (New York: William Sloane Associates, 1948), General Albert Wedemeyer, *Wedemeyer Reports!* (New York: Henry Holt, 1958), John Paton Davies, Jr., *Dragon By the Tail* (New York: W.W. Norton, 1972) and Joseph Esherick, ed., *Lost Chances in China—The World War II Dispatches of John S. Service* (New York: Random House, 1974). For the official history see the three fine volumes by Charles Romanus and Riley Sunderland, *Stilwell's Mission to China* (1953), *Stilwell's Command Problems* (1956), and *Time Runs Out in CBI* (1959), all published by the Government Printing Office. For the Korean War see Allen Whiting, *China Crosses the Yalu* (New York: Macmillan, 1960), David Rees, *Korea: The Limited War* (Baltimore: Penguin Books, 1964), and Alexander George, *The Chinese Communist Army in Action* (New York: Columbia University Press, 1967). For memoirs see Mark Clark, *From the Danube to the Yalu* (New York: Harper and Brothers, 1960), Matthew Ridgway, *The Korean War* (Garden City, New York: Doubleday and Company, 1967) and J. Lawton Collins, *War in Peacetime* (Boston: Houghton Mifflin, 1969). For the official American history see Roy Appleman, *South to the Naktong, North to the Yalu* (1969), Walter Hermes, *Truce Tent and Fighting Front* (1966), and James Schnabel, *United States Army in the Korean War—Policy and Direction the First Year* (1972), all published by the Government Printing Office.

13. My stress on political, as opposed to social, revolution is due in part to my inclusion of the English case, which lacked the social radicalism of the other three revolutions. However, for its time the elimination of the monarchy and House of Lords and reformation of the Church and nature of government were quite radical. Perez Zagorin has recently written of the radicalism of the English Revolution in terms of "the magnitude of its political change; its destruction of a state church and its battles over religious liberty; the breadth and significance of its ideological debates, its stimulus to social and democratic aspirations; its

constitution making and republicanism; and its strong arousal of an insurgent radicalism from below." See Perez Zagorin, *Rebels and Rulers 1500-1660* (Cambridge: Cambridge University Press, 1982), vol. 2, p. 130.

14. See Bertrand de Jouvenel, *On Power*, trans. J.F. Huntington (Boston: Beacon Press, 1962), p. 218, and for Borkenau quote see Carl Friedrich, ed., *Revolution* (New York: Atherton, 1967), p. 131.

15. Stephen Cohen, *Rethinking the Soviet Experience* (New York: Oxford University Press, 1985), pp. 14-15. Overall this book is a provocative and illuminating work of the highest order, even though I find the need for greater balance in the discussion of Stalinism in the 1930s.

16. Theda Skocpol made this point nicely when she wrote, "The comparative historian's task—and potential scholarly contribution—lies not in the revealing new data about particular aspects of large time periods and diverse places, surveyed in comparative study, but rather in establishing interest and prima facie validity of an overall argument about causal regularities across various historical cases." See Theda Skocpol, *States and Social Revolution*, p. xiv, also pp. 38-39.

CHAPTER 2

1. Charles Firth, *Cromwell's Army* (London: Methuen and Company, 1902), p. 1.

2. J.R. Jones, "Britain and Europe in the Seventeenth Century," in W.R. Owens, ed., *Seventeenth Century England: A Changing Culture* (Totowa, N.J.: Barnes and Noble, 1981), p. 53.

3. Christopher Hill, *God's Englishman: Oliver Cromwell and the English Revolution* (London: Weidenfeld and Nicolson, 1970), p. 166.

4. See Wilbur Abbott, *The Writings and Speeches of Oliver Cromwell* (Cambridge: Harvard University Press, 1937), vol. 1 (1599-1649), p. 50, Maurice Ashley, *General Monck* (Totowa, N.J.: Rowman and Littlefield, 1977), pp. 5-12, and Conrad Russell, *Parliaments and English Politics, 1621-1629* (Oxford: Oxford University Press, 1979), pp. 243, 272-284.

5. See Christopher Hill, *God's Englishman: Oliver Cromwell and the English Revolution*, p. 166.

6. Maurice Ashley, *General Monck*, p. 21 and C.V. Wedgewood, *The King's Peace 1637-1641* (New York: Macmillan, 1955), pp. 13, 248-276.

7. See Peter Young and Richard Holmes, *The English Civil War* (London: Eyre Methuen, 1974), p. 22, Austin Woolrych, *Battles of the English Civil War* (New York: Macmillan, 1961), p. 29 and Maurice Ashley, *General Monck*, pp. 22-23.

8. Charles Firth, *Oliver Cromwell* (London: Putnam, 1947), pp. 387-388.

9. Ibid., p. 104, Peter Young and Richard Holmes, *The English Civil War*, pp. 195-203 and Austin Woolrych, *Battles of the English Civil War*, pp. 65-80.

10. Austin Woolrych, *Battles of the English Civil War*, p. 139.

11. Ibid., pp. 167-177, Peter Young and Richard Holmes, *The English Civil War*, pp. 289-290, and Charles Firth, *Oliver Cromwell*, pp. 196-200, 472.

12. For the Irish campaign, see Godfrey Davis, *The Early Stuarts 1603-1660* (Oxford: Oxford University Press, 1937), pp. 159-162, Wilbur Abbott, *The Writings and Speeches of Oliver Cromwell* (Cambridge: Harvard University Press, 1939), vol. 2 (1649-1653), pp. 137-180, 381, 495-496.

13. Peter Young and Richard Holmes, *The English Civil War*, p. 314, Maurice Ashley, *Cromwell's Generals* (New York: St. Martin's Press, 1955), pp. 36-44, 59-60 and Wilbur Abbott, *The Writings and Speeches of Oliver Cromwell*, vol. 2 (1649-1653), pp. 312-320, 456-465.

14. See G.M.D. Howat, *Stuart and Cromwellian Foreign Policy* (New York: St. Martin's Press, 1974), pp. 90-91.

15. Ibid., p. 74, Charles Firth, *Oliver Cromwell*, pp. 308-309, 371, Godfrey Davies, *The Early Stuarts 1603-1660*, p. 229, and Maurice Ashley, *Cromwell's Generals*, pp. 128-129.

16. Peter Young and Richard Holmes, *The English Civil War*, pp. 335-338 and J.R. Jones, "Britain and Europe in the Seventeenth Century," in W.R. Owens, ed., *Seventeenth Century England: A Changing Culture*, pp. 95-97.

17. Brian Manning, *The English People and the English Revolution 1640-1649* (London: Heinemann, 1976), p. 72.

18. William McNeill, *The Pursuit of Power: Technology, Armed Force and Society Since A.D. 1000* (Chicago: University of Chicago Press, 1982), p. 160.

19. Peter Young and Richard Holmes, *The English Civil War*, p. 107.

20. Wilbur Abbott, *The Writings and Speeches of Oliver Cromwell*, vol. 1, p. 261.

21. Ibid., vol. 1, p. 278.

22. For Cromwell's officers, see Charles Firth, *Cromwell's Army*, pp. 40-55, and Maurice Ashley, *Cromwell's Generals*, vol. 1 (1599-1649), pp. 192, 702, 727.

23. See Charles Firth, *Cromwell's Army*, p. 4, and Donald Pennington, "The War and the People" in John Morrill, ed., *Reactions to the English Civil War 1642-1649* (New York: St. Martin's Press, 1982), p. 130.

24. Charles Firth, *Cromwell's Army*, p. 4.

25. Maurice Ashley, *General Monck*, p. 9.

26. Ibid., pp. 11-12.

27. Mark Kishlansky, *The Rise of the New Model Army* (Cambridge: Cambridge University Press, 1979), p. 66, Christopher Hill, *God's Englishman: Oliver Cromwell and the English Revolution*, p. 64, Charles Firth, *Cromwell's Army*, pp. 37, 66, and Peter Young and Richard Holmes, *The English Civil War*, p. 107.

28. J.S. Morrill, *The Revolt of the Provinces* (London: George Allen and Unwin, 1976), p. 63, Mark Kishlansky, *The Rise of the New Model Army*, p. 70, and Charles Firth, *Oliver Cromwell*, p. 247.

29. Lord Clarendon, quoted in Charles Firth, *Oliver Cromwell*, p. 408. It should be noted, though, all rapacious behavior by English soldiers was not eliminated. During the Irish campaign Cromwell sanctioned several massacres that in the long run enflamed Irish opinion against the British. But these massacres resulted from the deliberate policy of the New Model Army and not random acts by soldiers.

30. Peter Young and Richard Holmes, *The English Civil War*, p. 274.

31. C.V. Wedgewood, *The King's War 1641-1647* (London: Collins, 1958), p. 513 and Mark Kishlansky, *The Rise of the New Model Army*, pp. 73-75, 200-218.

32. Wilbur Abbott, *The Writings and Speeches of Oliver Cromwell*, vol. 1, p. 703.

33. Murray Tolmie, *The Triumph of the Saints* (Cambridge: Cambridge University Press, 1977), p. 157.

34. Austin Woolrych, *Battles of the English Civil War*, p. 137 and Brian Manning, *The English People and the English Revolution 1640-1649*, p. 251.

35. Michael Walzer, *The Revolution of the Saints* (New York: Atheneum, 1972), p. 295, John Ellis, *Armies in Revolution* (London: Croom Helm, 1973), pp. 14-40 and Katharine Chorley, *Armies and the Art of Revolution* (London: Faber and Faber, 1943), pp. 25-71.

36. Michael Walzer, *The Revolution of the Saints*, pp. 278-290.

37. Frederick Dietz, *English Public Finance 1558-1641* (New York: Barnes and Noble, 1964), pp. 446-447.

38. Katharine Chorley, *Armies and the Art of Revolution*, pp. 129-131.

39. In Charles Firth, *Oliver Cromwell*, p. 14.

40. Frederick Dietz, *English Public Finance 1558-1641,* p. 240 and Charles Firth, *Cromwell's Army,* p. 3.

41. G.E. Aylmer, *The King's Servants: The Civil Service of Charles I 1625-1642* (New York: Columbia University Press, 1961), p. 66.

42. Charles Firth, *Oliver Cromwell,* p. 247.

43. Wilbur Abbott, *The Writings and Speeches of Oliver Cromwell,* vol. 1 (1599-1649), p. 358 and Peter Young and Richard Holmes, *The English Civil War,* pp. 333-334.

44. Michael Oppenheim, *A History of the Administration of the Royal Navy and of Merchant Shipping in Relation to the Navy From MDIX to MDCLX* (Ann Arbor: Shoestring Press, 1961), pp. 241, 185-194, 285-287.

45. Charles Firth, *Oliver Cromwell,* p. 387 and Godfrey Davis, *The Early Stuarts 1603-1660,* p. 233.

46. For a recent biographical study of Charles I, see the fine work by Charles Carlton, *Charles I: The Personal Monarch* (London: Routledge and Kegan Paul, 1983).

47. Perez Zagorin, *The Court and the Country,* p. 59. In recent years a series of biographies on the main figures in the Court of Charles I have significantly revised the previously almost wholly negative view of the Court. Even Buckingham has received a more sympathetic hearing. However, these works, while improving and sharpening knowledge of the Court, cannot change the general picture of a Court pursuing policies that deeply alienated the country and set the stage for civil war. See H.R. Trevor-Roper, *Archbishop Laud 1573-1645* (London: Macmillan and Company, 1962), Martin Havram, *Caroline Courtier: The Life of Lord Cottington* (London: Macmillan, 1973), Michael Alexander, *Charles I's Lord Treasurer* (Chapel Hill: University of North Carolina Press, 1975), Roger Lockyer, *Buckingham* (London: Longman, 1981), and Charles Carlton, *Charles I: The Personal Monarch* (London: Routledge and Kegan Paul, 1983).

48. Lawrence Stone, *The Crisis of the Aristocracy 1558-1641* (Oxford: Oxford University Press, 1965), pp. 413, 421-423, 465-494.

49. See G.E. Aylmer, *The King's Servants: The Civil Service of Charles I 1625-1642,* pp. 248, 331-333.

50. G.E. Aylmer, *The King's Servants: The Civil Service of Charles I 1625-1642,* pp. 64, 331.

51. Charles Wilson, *England's Apprenticeship 1603-1763* (London: Longmans, Green and Company, 1965), pp. 97-106, 107.

52. G.E. Aylmer, *The King's Servants: The Civil Service of Charles I 1625-*

1642, pp. 62-67 and Perez Zagorin, *The Court and the Country*, pp. 41-55.

53. Charles Firth, *Cromwell's Army*, p. 200. See also Charles Wilson, *England's Apprenticeship 1603-1763*, pp. 108, 130-131, G.E. Aylmer, *The King's Servants: The Civil Service of Charles I 1625-1642*, pp. 435-437, and Antonia Fraser, *Cromwell: The Lord Protector* (New York: Alfred A. Knopf, 1973), p. 627.

54. Charles Firth, *Oliver Cromwell*, p. 246. See also G.E. Aylmer, *The King's Servants: The Civil Service of Charles I 1625-1642*, p. 433 and Christopher Hill, *God's Englishman: Oliver Cromwell and the English Revolution*, p. 206. The county committees were often run by a new group of active and zealous people recruited from local lawyers, former army officers from the lower classes, and gentry from minor manorial farms. See D.H. Pennington, "The County Community at War," in E.W. Ives, ed., *The English Revolution* (London: Edward Arnold, 1968), p. 72.

CHAPTER 3

1. David Ogg, *Europe of the Ancien Regime 1715-1783* (New York: Harper and Row, 1965), pp. 151-167.

2. *The Cambridge Modern History* (Cambridge: Cambridge University Press, 1925, vol. 6, p. 272, also xiv-xvi, 342, 426.

3. Olwen Hufton, *Europe: Privilege and Protest 1730-1789* (Ithaca: Cornell University Press, 1980), p. 124.

4. *The Cambridge Modern History*, vol. 6, p. 347. See also, Olwen Hufton, *Europe: Privilege and Protest 1730-1789*, pp. 65-176.

5. *The Cambridge Modern History*, vol. 6, p. 393, also 376-379, 452-454.

6. Jean Egret, *The French Prerevolution 1787-1788* trans. Wesley Camp (Chicago: University of Chicago Press, 1977), pp. 40-41.

7. For a good survey, see Gunther Rothenberg, *The Art of Warfare in the Age of Napoleon* (London: B.T. Batsford, 1977), pp. 33-42.

8. For the best account of the Napoleonic campaigns, see David Chandler's massive work, *The Campaigns of Napoleon* (New York: Macmillan, 1966), pp. 403-588. For other good accounts see Michael Glover, *The Napoleonic Wars* (New York: Hippocrene Books, 1978), pp. 83-89 and especially Georges Lefebvre, *Napoleon: From 18 Brumaire to Tilsit 1799-1807* trans. Henry Stockhold (New York: Columbia University Press, 1969), pp. 257-273.

9. See David Chandler, *The Campaigns of Napoleon*, pp. 599, 622, 656-660, 696-730, Theodore Ropp, *War in the Modern World* (New York: Collier

Books, 1962), pp. 125-130, and Gunther Rothenberg, *The Art of Warfare in the Age of Napoleon*, pp. 48-52.

10. David Chandler, *The Campaigns of Napoleon*, pp. 781-1092, Gunther Rothenberg, *The Art of Warfare in the Age of Napoleon*, pp. 54-55, and Louis Bergeron, *France Under Napoleon*, trans. R.R. Palmer (Princeton: Princeton University Press, 1981), pp. 228-260.

11. Charles de Gaulle, *France and Her Army*, trans. F.L. Dash (London: Hutchinson and Company, n.d.), p. 57. See also David Chandler, *The Campaigns of Napoleon*, pp. xxxii, 982-1092, and Georges Lefebvre, *Napoleon: From 18 Brumaire to Tilsit 1799-1807*, p. 221.

12. Lee Kennett, *The French Armies in the Seven Years' War* (Durham, N.C.: Duke University Press, 1967), pp. 139-141.

13. See Michael Howard, *War in European History* (London: Oxford University Press, 1976), p. 75 and Hans Rothfels, "Clausewitz" in Edward Mead Earle, ed., *Makers of Modern Strategy* (Princeton: Princeton University Press, 1943), p. 97, and Andre Corvisier, *Armies and Societies in Europe 1494-1789*, trans. Abigail Siddall (Bloomington: Indiana University Press, 1979), pp. 166-169.

14. Jean Egret, *The French Prerevolution 1787-1788*, p. 51. See also Spenser Wilkinson, *The French Army Before Napoleon* (London: Oxford University Press, 1915), p. 94 and Samuel Scott, *The Response of the Royal Army to the French Revolution* (Oxford: Oxford University Press, 1978), pp. 22-23.

15. John Lynn, *The Bayonets of the Republic* (Urbana: University of Illinois Press, 1984), pp. 91-92. See also Samuel Scott, *The Response of the Royal Army to the French Revolution*, pp. 20-21, 30-34 and Jean Egret, *The French Prerevolution 1787-1788*, pp. 46-49. It should be noted that, under Napoleon, marshals once again gained inordinate wealth as compensation for their contributions to the state.

16. Basil Liddell-Hart, *The Ghost of Napoleon* (New Haven: Yale University Press, 1935), p. 87. See also Spenser Wilkinson, *The French Army Before Napoleon*, pp. 87-88, Lee Kennett, *The French Armies in the Seven Years' War*, pp. 16-19 and Andre Corvisier, *Armies and Societies in Europe*, pp. 150-152.

17. Charles de Gaulle, *France and Her Army*, p. 31, Andre Corvisier, *Armies and Societies in Europe*, p. 102, and Spenser Wilkinson, *The French Army Before Napoleon*, p. 102.

18. See Hew Strachan, *European Armies and the Conduct of War* (London: Allen and Unwin, 1983), p. 38, Katharine Chorley, *Armies and the Art of Revolution*, p. 145, and Samuel Scott, *The Response of the Royal Army to the French Revolution*, pp. 203-204.

19. Georges Lefebvre, *Napoleon: From 18 Brumaire to Tilsit 1799-1807*, p. 219. See also Louis Bergeron, *France Under Napoleon*, p. 65, David Chandler,

The Campaigns of Napoleon, pp. 335-338, and John Lynn, *The Bayonets of the Republic*, pp. 67-76, 88, 96, and 283.

20. David Chandler, *The Campaigns of Napoleon*, pp. 335-338.

21. Lee Kennett, *The French Armies in the Seven Years' War*, pp. 81-82. By his estimate fully 84 percent of all soldiers came from the "popular classes" (p. 75). The French War Minister Comte de St. Germain stated, "In the present state of things, armies can only be composed of the slime of the nation and of all that is useless to society." See John Lynn, *The Bayonets of the Republic*, p. 63.

22. Charles de Gaulle, *France and Her Army*, p. 23.

23. John Ellis, *Armies in Revolution* (London: Croom Helm, 1973), p. 83. See also Samuel Scott, *The Response of the Royal Army to the French Revolution*, pp. 43-44.

24. Lee Kennett, *The French Armies in the Seven Years' War*, pp. 76-84 and Andre Corvisier, *Armies and Societies in Europe, 1494-1789*, pp. 180-183.

25. Gunther Rothenberg, *The Art of Warfare in the Age of Napoleon*, pp. 98, 134-135.

26. Katharine Chorley, *Armies and the Art of Revolution*, p. 146.

27. Gunther Rothenberg, *The Art of Warfare in the Age of Napoleon*, p. 61 and Georges Lefebvre, *Napoleon: From 18 Brumaire to Tilsit 1799-1807*, pp. 228-229.

28. Gunther Rothenberg, *The Art of Warfare in the Age of Napoleon*, p. 61.

29. Michel Vovelle, *The Fall of the French Monarchy 1787-1792*, trans. Susan Burke (Cambridge: Cambridge University Press, 1984), p. 32.

30. Olwen Hufton, *Europe: Privilege and Protest 1730-1789*, p. 67. See also Michel Vovelle, *The Fall of the French Monarchy 1787-1792*, pp. 31-32. Perhaps Bertrand de Jouvenel best summed up the limits on the power of the traditional government, quoting Soulavie that power, "found itself checked at every turn by the respect which it had to pay to our rights and usages. When it asked its subjects for gratuities, gifts, taxes and grants in aid, it had, in order to get them, to make representation to the clergy of France and call them together. It negotiated for entry into force of a fiscal edict with parlement. It asked for jurisdiction in the state of Langvedoc. It commanded it in Burgundy. In Brittany it generally had to buy it, more or less indirectly. It took it by force of arms in the provincial administrations." See Bertrand de Jouvenel, *On Power*, trans. J.F. Huntington (Boston: Beacon Press, 1962), pp. 222-223, and Jean Egret, *The French Prerevolution 1787-1788*, pp. xiii-xiv.

31. *The Cambridge Modern History*, vol. 6, p. 360.

32. For an excellent study of French government, see J.F. Bosher, *French*

Finances 1770-1795 (Cambridge: Cambridge University Press, 1970), pp. 278-284.

33. Ibid., p. 26 and Olwen Hufton, *Europe: Privilege and Protest 1730-1789*, pp. 314-316.

34. Michel Vovelle, *The Fall of the French Monarchy 1787-1792*, pp. 31, 58.

35. Ibid., pp. 75-76 and Jean Egret, *The French Prerevolution 1787-1788*, p. 43.

36. Georges Lefebvre, *Napoleon: From 18 Brumaire to Tilsit 1799-1807*, pp. ix-x.

37. Alfred Cobban, *A History of Modern France* (Harmondsworth, England: Penguin Books, 1961, vol. 2, pp. 2026, 38.

38. For a good study, see Louis Bergeron, *France Under Napoleon*, pp. 53-76, 133.

39. J.F. Bosher, *French Finances 1770-1795*, pp. 295-317.

40. Ibid., p. 313.

41. Louis Bergeron, *France Under Napoleon*, p. 50.

42. Ibid., p. 40 and Georges Lefebvre, *Napoleon: From Tilsit to Waterloo 1807-1815*, trans. J.E. Anderson (New York: Columbia University Press, 1969), pp. 171-172.

43. See David Chandler, *The Campaigns of Napoleon*, pp. 312-319.

44. Robert Holtmann, *The Napoleonic Revolution* (Philadelphia and New York: J.B. Lippincott Company, 1967), p. 178.

CHAPTER 4

1. Due to poor record keeping and political sensitivities, casualty and prisoner-of-war figures for the Russian army remain highly tentative and conflicting for both wars. For World War I, estimates of Russian war deaths range from 1.65 million (Golovine) and 1.7 million (Gilbert) to 2.3 million (Ferro, *Sovetskaya voennaya entsiklopediya*) and 2.5 million (Shigalin). Estimates of Russian POWs range from 2.4 million (Golovine) to 2.9 million (Knox). For World War II, sources are even worse. Only one Soviet source even lists a figure for Red Army dead *(Sovetskaya voennaya entsiklopediya)* and one Western source (Seaton) gives broad categories of numbers (8 million dead and wounded, 6.0 million prisoners) from which further deductions may be drawn. Overall, the picture is quite unsatisfactory. For Soviet sources see G.I. Shigalin, *Voennaya ekonomika*

v peruvuyu mirovuyu voinu (1914-1918) (Moscow: Voenizdat, 1956), p. 243 and *Sovetskaya voennaya entsiklopediya* (Moscow: Voenizdat, 1982), vol. 2, p. 65, vol. 6, p. 275. For Western sources see Nicholas Golovine, *The Russian Army in the World War* (New Haven: Yale University Press, 1931), pp. 93, 99; Marc Ferro, *The Great War, 1914-1918* (London: Routledge and Kegan Paul, 1973) and Martin Gilbert, *First World War with the Russian Army (1914-1917)* (London: Hutchinson and Company, 1921), p. 542.

2. Albert Seaton, *The Russo-German War 1941-1943* (New York: Praeger, 1970), p. 586, Lieutenant-General Nicholas Golovine, *The Russian Army in the World War*, pp. 74, 92; and G.I. Shigalin, *Voennaya ekonomika v pervuyu mirovuyu voinu (1914-1918)*, p. 243.

3. Geoffry Evans, *Tannenberg: 1410: 1914* (London: Hamish Hamilton, 1970), pp. 78-84, 156-57.

4. Lieutenant-General Nicholas Golovine, *The Russian Army in the World War*, p. 222. As a result of these repeated defeats, the belief grew in the Tsarist army that "the Germans could do anything." See Major-General Sir Alfred Knox, *With the Russian Army 1914-1917*, p. 349. Winston Churchill could write that in World War I "the Germans fight with army corps and the Russians with armies thrice their number; and the battle is still obstinate.... German troops were equal to two or three times the number of Russians." See Winston Churchill, *The Unknown War—the Eastern Front* (New York: Charles Scribner's Sons, 1931), p. 247.

5. *Sovetskaya voennaya entsiklopediya*, vol. 2, p. 59.

6. The capabilities of the Austro-Hungarian army were even less than those of the Russian army. Its economic base was weak and its political base weaker. Although German and Austrian officers dominated the officer corps, the ranks were heavily composed of Czechs, Croats, and Slovenes who wanted independence from the empire.

7. Winston Churchill, *The Unknown War—the Eastern Front*, p. 1.

8. In response to German and Austrian military modernization, the Tsarist Defense Minister Sukhomlinov in 1913 drew up a "Great Program" for preparing the army for war by 1917. Moving ever so slowly, the Tsarist government did not have a detailed program ready until February 1914, and the Duma passed the four-year plan only in May 1914, three months before the start of World War I. Similarly, the Red Army in 1939 launched a major military modernization program that would be completed only in 1943. The leading Soviet economic planner at that time, N.A. Voznesensky, later admitted that "the war caught Soviet war industry in the process of assimilating a new technology; the mass production of modern military equipment was not yet organized." See Seweryn Bialer, ed., *Stalin and His Generals* (London: Souvenir Press, 1970), p. 60 and Bernard Pares, *The Fall of the Russian Monarchy* (London: Jonathan Cape, 1939), p. 194.

9. Albert Seaton, *The Russo-German War 1941-45*, p. 586.

10. *Istoriya pervoi mirovoi voiny* (Moscow: Nauka, 1975), vol. 2, pp. 307, 309.

11. Ibid., vol. 2, pp. 313, 319, and Ward Rutherford, *The Russian Army in World War I* (London: Cremonesi Publishers, 1975), pp. 250-53.

12. Rutherford, *The Russian Army in World War I*, p. 254.

13. Florinsky, *The End of the Russian Empire* (New Haven: Yale University Press, 1931), p. 261.

14. *Istoriya pervoi mirovoi voiny*, vol. 2, pp. 428-30.

15. Marc Ferro, *The Great War 1914-1918*, p. 209.

16. *Istoriya pervoi mirovoi voiny*, vol. 2, p. 434.

17. Alexander Werth, *Russia at War 1941-1945* (New York: E.P. Dutton and Company, 1964), p. 858.

18. See *Sovetskaya voennaya entsiklopediya*, vol. 1, p. 273, vol. 2, p. 143; D.V. Verzhkhovski and V.F. Lyakhov, *Pervaya mirovaya voina* (Moscow: Voenizdat, 1964), p. 45; G.I. Shigalin, *Voennaya ekonomika v pervuyu mirovuyu voinu (1914-1918)*, p. 301; and Albert Seaton, *The Russo-German War 1941-45*, p. 518.

19. Albert Seaton, *The Russo-German War 1941-45*, p. 305.

20. This is not to denigrate the Allied war effort, which helped Russia to fight on against Germany before June 1944. The engagement and defeat of Japan by the United States prevented a dangerous Japanese invasion of the Soviet Far East. Allied actions drew off nearly all the German navy and much of the German air force from 1941 to 1944. Allied actions in Africa, the Middle East, and Italy prevented German occupation of vital areas. However, it is still a fact that no significant number of German divisions were directly engaged by the Allies before June 1944. Even the July 1943 invasion of Sicily brought 160,000 Allied troops face to face with 10 Italian divisions and just 2 German armored divisions. See R. Ernest Dupuy, *World War II: A Compact History* (New York: Hawthorn Books, 1969), p. 147.

21. V.D. Sokolovsky, ed., *Soviet Military Strategy*, trans. Herbert Dinerstein, Leon Goure, and Thomas Wolfe (Santa Monica, California: Rand, 1963), p. 112, *Istoriya vtoroi mirovoi voiny 1939-1945* (Moscow: Voenizdat, 1982), vol. 12, p. 141 and A.A. Strokov, *Vooruzhennye sily: Voennoe iskusstvo v pervoi morovoi voine* (Moscow: Voenizdat, 1974), p. 558.

22. G.I. Shigalin, *Voennaya ekonomika v pervuyu mirovuyu voinu (1914-1918)*, pp. 170-72, 174, 179.

23. Major-General Sir Alfred Knox, *With the Russian Army, 1914-1917*, p. 293.

24. *Istoriya velikoi otechestvennoi voiny Sovetskogo Soyuza 1941-1945* (Moscow: Voenizdat, 1960), vol. 6, p. 48.

25. Albert Seaton, *The Russo-German War 1941-1945*, p. 589.

26. See Frank Dorn, *The Sino-Japanese War, 1937-41* (New York: Macmillan, 1974), p. 266.

CHAPTER 5

1. B.H. Liddell-Hart, *History of the Second World War* (London: Cassell, 1970), and Major-General J.F.C. Fuller, *The Second World War 1939-45* (New York: Duell, Sloane and Pearce, 1949).

2. Adam Ulam, *Expansion and Coexistence—the History of Soviet Foreign Policy 1917-67* (New York: Praeger, 1968), p. 315, and B.H. Liddell-Hart, *History of the Second World War*, p. 41.

3. Albert Seaton, *The Russo-German War 1941-45*, p. 221.

4. J.F.C. Fuller, *The Second World War 1939-45*, p. 125.

5. James Lucas, *War on the Eastern Front 1941-1945* (New York: Bonanza Books, 1982), p. 89.

6. Albert Seaton, *The Russo-German War 1941-45*, pp. 225, 243, 306, 334, 341; B.H. Liddell-Hart, *History of the Second World War*, pp. 241, 480.

7. Albert Seaton, *The Russo-German War 1941-45*, pp. 412-21, 534-38; B.H. Liddell-Hart, *History of the Second World War*, p. 570-73, 663, 667.

8. James Lucas, *War on the Eastern Front 1941-1945*, pp. 84, 104 and B.H. Liddell-Hart, *History of the Second World War*, p. 478.

9. Albert Seaton, *The Russo-German War 1941-1945*, p. 421.

10. It is important to note the variability of winter in Russia over the years and by regions. While 3 to 12 inches of snow and frost is common in the south for four months, 3 feet of snow lasting for six to seven months is typical in the north. German General von Greiffenberg went so far as to say that "climate in Russia is a series of natural disasters." See James Lucas, *War on the Eastern Front 1941-1945*, pp. 78, 95 and Albert Seaton, *The Russo-German War 1941-1945*, p. 43.

11. Adam Ulam, *Expansion and Coexistence*, p. 330, and B.H. Liddell-Hart, *History of the Second World War*, p. 257.

12. R. Ernest Dupuy, *World War II: A Compact History*, p. 108.

13. Alexander Werth, *Russia at War 1941-1945*, p. 496 and Albert Seaton, *The Russo-German War 1941-1945*, pp. 504, 588.

14. Alfred Knox, *With the Russian Army 1914-1917*, pp. 509-11; *Istoriya grazhdanskoi voiny v SSSR* (Moscow: Gosizdat, 1958), vol. 1, p. 28.

15. Bernard Pares, *The Fall of the Russian Monarchy*, p. 335.

16. Adam Ulam, *Expansion and Coexistence*, p. 325.

17. Field Marshal Erich von Manstein, *Lost Victories*, ed. and trans. Anthony G. Powell (Chicago: Henry Regnery Company, 1958), pp. 260-90.

18. B.H. Liddell-Hart, *History of the Second World War*, p. 710. R. Ernest Dupuy has gone so far as to argue that in August 1941, "by shifting his main effort from the center (to the north and south), where Russian armies were in a state of collapse, and by asking more of men and machines than was possible, the Fuhrer had thrown away almost certain victory and had assured his own eventual defeat." Similarly for 1942 Dupuy finds that "Hitler, by his fantastic changes of objectives and stupid insistence on holding territory had wrecked his Eastern armies." See R. Ernest Dupuy, *World War II: A Compact History*, pp. 74, 108.

19. Alexander Dallin, *German Rule in Russia 1941-1945* (Boulder, Colo: Westview Press, 1981), p. 660.

20. See Charles Tilly's fine work, *The Rebellious Century*.

21. See Adam Ulam, *Stalin* (New York: Viking, 1973), pp. 557-58, 576, 614.

22. See respectively Alfred Knox, *With the Russian Army 1914-1917*, p. xxxii, and Alexander Werth, *Russia at War 1941-1945*, p. xvi.

23. See Theodore von Laue, "Problems of Industrialization" in Theofanis Stavrou, ed., *Russia Under the Last Tsar* (Minneapolis: University of Minnesota Press, 1969), p. 126.

24. Indeed in the first ten months of the war the Red Army mobilized 1.2 million non-Slavs into its ranks. See Teresa Rakowska-Harmstone and Christopher Jones, *Warsaw Pact: The Question of Cohesion*, unpublished manuscript, pp. 108-110.

25. Robert Tucker, "Stalinism as Revolution from Above," Robert Tucker ed., *Stalinism—Essays in Historical Interpretation* (New York: W.W. Norton, 1977), p. 80.

CHAPTER 6

1. See respectively Stanley Cohn, "The Soviet Economy: Performance and Growth," in William Blackwell, ed., *Russian Economic Development from Peter the Great to Stalin* (New York: New Viewpoints, 1974), p. 324 and I.I. Mints, *Istoriya velikogo Oktyabrya* (Moscow: Nauka 1977), vol. 1, pp. 38–39.

2. General Vasili Gourko, *War and Revolution in Russia 1914–1917* (New York: Macmillan Company, 1919), p. 4; and G.I. Shigalin, *Voennaya ekonomika v pervuyu mirovuyu voinu (1914–1918)*, pp. 113, 136 and Alex Nove, *An Economic History of the USSR* (Harmondsworth, England: Penguin Books, 1925), p. 29.

3. *Istoriya vtoroi mirovoi voiny 1939–1945*, vol. 2, p. 183.

4. Ibid., vol. 2, pp. 159, 184, vol. 3, pp. 391–92, vol. 12, p. 155, and William Blackwell, ed., *Russian Economic Development from Peter the Great to Stalin*, p. 356.

5. Nicholas Golovine, *The Russian Army in the World War*, p. 31.

6. Vasili Gourko, *War and Revolution in Russia 1914–1917*, pp. 118, 20. Indeed, some military plants were actually closed in 1914 since current requirements had been met! (p. 10).

7. G.I. Shigalin, *Voennaya ekonomika v pervuyu mirovuyu voinu (1914–1918)*, p. 170; Alfred Knox, *With the Russian Army 1914–1917*, pp. xxiv, xxv; Ward Rutherford, *The Russian Army in World War I*, p. 23; and I.I. Rostunov, *Ruskii front pervoi mirovoi voiny* (Moscow: Nauka, 1976), p. 386.

8. Joseph Stalin, *Problems of Leninism* (Moscow: Foreign Language Publishing House, 1947), p. 213.

9. David Holloway, *The Soviet Union and the Arms Race* (New Haven: Yale University Press, 1983), p. 7.

10. There is, of course, the hoary question of whether Tsarist Russia, had there been no war, could have made similar progress. First, of course, it is important to stress that there *was* a war and revolution. The assumption of no European military conflict when there were two such gigantic occurrences in the first half of this century is highly unrealistic. Second, even granting such an improbable occurrence, anachronistic, repressive Tsarist Russia would probably, with its severe internal political problems, not have remained immune from revolution. Third, even if war and revolution had miraculously been averted, stagnation rather than great progress would have been the most likely outcome. Any economic gains made in the 1920s would have been more than destroyed in the worldwide depression of the 1930s. Its heavy dependence on foreign capital would have led to enormous problems then. It likely would have suffered a fate similar to Poland. In 1939 Polish production of cast iron, steel, coal, and oil was 7 to 50 percent *lower* than in 1913. And even an advanced country such as Germany showed only incremental progress in military production during this

period. Overall, then, it is highly unlikely that the Tsarist system could have adapted to modern economic and political systemic needs and given Russia the breakthrough it so urgently needed. For Polish statistics, see *Istoriya vtoroi mirovoi voiny*, vol. 2, p. 349.

11. G.I. Shigalin, *Voennaya ekonomika v pervuyu mirovuyu voinu (1914–1918)*, pp. 169–70.

12. Nicholas Golovine, *The Russian Army in the World War*, p. 127, vol. 2, p. 9, and Frank Golder, ed., *Documents of Russian History 1914-1917* (New York: Century Company, 1927), p. 193.

13. Vasili Gourko, *War and Revolution in Russia 1914-1917*, p. 125; Alfred Knox, *With the Russian Army 1914-1917*, p. 220.

14. *Istoriya pervoi mirovoi voiny*, vol. 2, p. 542; Norman Stone, *The Eastern Front, 1914-1917*, p. 12; and G.I. Shigalin, *Voennaya ekonomika v pervuyu mirovuyu voinu (1914-1918)*, p. 243.

15. *Sovetskaya voennaya entsiklopediya*, vol. 6, p. 273, and Nicholas Golovine, *The Russian Army in the World War*, pp. 135, 142.

16. G.I. Shigalin, *Voennaya ekonomika v pervuyu mirovuyu voinu (1914–1918)*, p. 243.

17. Heinz Guderian, *Panzer Leader*, p. 179.

18. Alec Nove, *An Economic History of the USSR*, p. 274.

19. Erich von Manstein, *Lost Victories*, p. 521.

20. Alec Nove, *An Economic History of the USSR*, p. 171, and Alexander Werth, *Russia at War 1941-1945*, pp. 220-23.

21. *Istoriya vtoroi mirovoi voiny*, vol. 12, p. 161, and *Istoriya velikoi otechestvennoi voiny Sovetskogo Soyuza 1941-1945*, vol. 6, p. 45.

22. Alec Nove, *An Economic History of the USSR*, p. 273. By contrast German mobilization was quite slow. In 1942 only 26 percent of the German GNP went for the war. This figure reached 50 percent only in 1944. See V.D. Sokolovsky, ed., *Soviet Military Strategy*, p. 105.

23. *Istoriya velikoi otechestvennoi voiny Sovetskogo Soyuza 1941-1945*, vol. 6, p. 45.

24. Michael Florinsky, *The End of the Russian Empire*, p. 208.

25. Michael Florinsky, *The End of the Russian Empire*, p. 215.

26. Frank Golder, ed., *Documents of Russian History 1914-1917*, pp. 217–19, 226 and Ward Rutherford, *The Russian Army in World War I*, p. 156.

228 CHAPTER 6 NOTES

27. Alfred Knox, *With the Russian Army 1914-1917*, p. 331; Alexander Solzhenitsyn, *August 1914*, p. 586; and Ward Rutherford, *The Russian Army in World War I*, p. 29.

28. *Istoriya grazhdanskoi voiny v SSSR*, vol. 1, p. 24; S.S. Oldenburg, *Last Tsar: Nicholas II, His Reign and His Russia*, trans. Leonid I. Mihalap and Patrick J. Rollins (Gulf Breeze, Florida: Academic International Press, 1978), vol. 4, p. 78; and Alfred Knox, *With the Russian Army 1914-1917*, p. 221.

29. Vasili Gourko, *War and Revolution in Russia 1914-1917*, p. 228, and Alfred Knox, *With the Russian Army 1914-1917*, p. 193.

30. Bernard Pares, *The Fall of Russian Monarchy*, p. 327.

31. Michael Florinsky, *The End of the Russian Empire*, p. 72; Frank Golder, ed., *Documents of Russian History 1914-1917*, p. 188; and Alfred Knox, *With the Russian Army 1914-1917*, p. 222.

32. Hugh Seton-Watson, *The Decline of Imperial Russia 1855-1914* (New York: Praeger, 1962), p. 360; Norman Stone, *The Eastern Front 1914-1917*, p. 225; and Alexander Solzhenitsyn, *August 1914*, translated by Michael Glenny (New York: Farrar, Straus and Giroux, 1971), pp. 274, 381.

33. Alexander Solzhenitsyn, *August 1914*, p. 381.

34. Michael Florinsky, *The End of the Russian Empire*, p. 220.

35. *Istoriya pervoi mirovoi voiny*, vol. 1, p. 100 and I.I. Mints, *Istoriya velikogo Oktyabrya*, vol. 1, p. 357.

36. Vasili Gourko, *War and Revolution in Russia 1914-1917*, p. 165, and Alexander Solzhenitsyn, *August 1914*, p. 431.

37. Alexander Solzhenitsyn, *August 1914*, pp. 77-78, 307, 382.

38. Ward Rutherford, *The Russian Army in World War I*, p. 24.

39. Nicholas Golovine, *The Russian Army in the World War*, p. 100, and S.S. Oldenburg, *Last Tsar: Nicholas II, His Reign and His Russia*, p. 95.

40. See *The Letters of the Tsar to the Tsaritsa, 1914-1917*.

41. Seweryn Bialer, ed., *Stalin and His Generals*, pp. 43-44.

42. Ibid., p. 343, David Holloway, *The Soviet Union and the Arms Race*, p. 12, and B.H. Liddell-Hart, *History of the Second World War*, p. 260.

43. Albert Seaton, *The Russo-German War 1941-1945*, p. 85.

44. Seweryn Bialer, ed., *Stalin and His Generals*, p. 407.

45. Ibid., pp. 628–640.

46. See *Istoriya kommunisticheskii partiya Sovetskogo Soyuza* (Moscow: Politizdat, 1970), vol. 5, bk. 1 (1938–1948), p. 313.

CHAPTER 7

1. In August 1914 Tsarist Russia had 180 million people compared to 187 million people in Soviet Russia in June 1941. But due to higher war casualties and greater territory occupied by the enemy, Soviet Russia in 1942 had 126 million people compared to 155 million people in Tsarist Russia at the end of 1915. By 1945 the Russian population was roughly 170 million people compared to 150 million in 1917.

2. See *Sovetskaya voennaya entsiklopediya*, vol. 6, p. 273, and *Istoriya vtoroi mirovoi voiny 1939–1945*, vol. 12, p. 269.

3. *Istoriya vtoroi mirovoi voiny 1939–1945*, vol. 12, p. 218.

4. See table 3, Marc Ferro, *The Great War 1914–1918*, p. 129, and M.M. Kir'yan, *Voenno-tekhnicheskii progress i vooruzhennye sily SSSR* (Moscow: Voenizdat, 1982), p. 174.
The Tsarist machinery was hampered by the lack of popular support, backwardness of the economy, and rampant illiteracy. Unable and unwilling to institute universal military training, the Tsarist army annually had exempted 48 percent of liable males from service, compared to 3 percent in Germany and 0 percent in France. Until 1916 Russia's front line strength was less than France's, despite having four times the population. Furthermore, Russia could not effectively use its military manpower. At the end of 1916 General Vladimir Guorko in a memorandum to the tsar observed that while the French had a healthy 2 to 1 front to rear ratio, the Russians had a terrible 1 to 2.25 front to rear ratio, which was deteriorating rapidly. See Nicholas Golovine, *The Russian Army in the World War*, p. 65; B.M. Liddell-Hart, ed., *The Red Army* (New York: Harcourt Brace and Company, 1956), p. 20; and Norman Stone, *The Eastern Front 1914–1917*, pp. 212–13.

5. G.I. Shigalin, *Voennaya ekonomika v pervuyu mirovuyu voinu (1914–1918)*, p. 149.

6. Ibid., pp. 147–50, and Alfred Knox, *With the Russian Army 1914–1917*, p. 291.

7. Frank Golder, ed., *Documents of Russian History 1914–1917*, p. 181.

8. *Sovetskaya voennaya entsiklopediya*, vol. 2, p. 57; *Istoriya vtoroi mirovoi voiny 1939–1945*, vol. 4, pp. 136–40.

9. *Istoriya vtoroi mirovoi voiny 1939–1945*, vol. 4, pp. 137–40, vol. 12,

p. 158; *Istoriya velikoi otechestvennoi voiny Sovetskogo Soyuza*, vol. 6, pp. 45–46; and Alec Nove, *An Economic History of the USSR*, p. 270.

10. B.H. Liddell-Hart, *History of the Second World War*, p. 245. A classic example was the Kharkov tractor factory. Evacuated to the Urals in October 1941, this factory already sent its first 25 tanks to the front by December 1941. See *Istoriya vtoroi mirovoi voiny 1939–1945*, vol. 8, p. 153.

11. Hugh Seton-Watson, *The Decline of Imperial Russia*, p. 347.

12. Of course in the long run he had miscalculated German military capabilities and the date of the invasion. In the first arena he had much company, in the second he was largely culpable.

13. John Erickson, *The Road to Berlin* (Boulder, Co.: Westview Press, 1984), p. 345.

14. Donald Treadgold, *Lenin and His Rivals: The Struggle for Russia's Future* (New York: Praeger, 1955), pp. 17–30.

15. See *Letters of the Tsaritsa to the Tsar 1914–1916*, trans. A.L. Haynes (Hattiesburg, Miss.: Academic International Press, 1970), p. 455.

16. Bernard Pares, *The Fall of Russian Monarchy*, p. 321.

17. Frank Golder, ed., *Documents of Russian History 1914–1917*, p. 189. The tsar clearly listened to the tsarina. In a September 1916 letter to her, the tsar wrote, "Yes, truly, you ought to be my eyes and ears there in the capital, while I have to stay here. It rests with you to keep peace and harmony among the Ministers. Now I shall naturally be calm and at least need not worry over internal affairs." See *The Letters of the Tsar to the Tsaritsa 1914–1917*, p. 269.

18. Alfred Knox, *With the Russian Army 1914–1917*, p. 334; Bernard Pares, *The Fall of Russian Monarchy*, pp. 157, 243; and Michael Florinsky, *The End of the Russian Empire*, p. 75. Serge Sazonov, Russia's Foreign Minister in 1914, called Goremykin a "decrepit old man, only half alive" who was "obviously unfit." See his *Fateful Years: 1909–1916* (New York: Frederick A. Stokes Company, 1928), p. 272.

19. Bernard Pares, *The Fall of Russian Monarchy*, p. 318, and Frank Golder, ed., *Documents of Russian History 1914–1917*, pp. 105, 107, 161.

20. Bernard Pares, *The Fall of the Russian Monarchy*, pp. 380, 155–58; Theofanis Stavrou, ed., *Russia Under the Last Tsar*, p. 109; Frank Golder, ed., *Documents of Russian History 1914–1917*, pp. 113, 255; and Michael Florinsky, *The End of the Russian Empire*, pp. 91–92.

21. Bernard Pares, *The Fall of the Russian Monarchy*, p. 376; Hugh Seton-Watson, *The Decline of the Imperial Russia 1885–1914*, p. 362; and Frank Golder, ed., *Documents of Russian History 1914–1917*, pp. 166–68.

22. P.A. Zaionchkovsky, *Pravitel'stvennyi apparat samoderzhavnoi Rossii V XIX v.* (Moscow: Mysl', 1978, pp. 222-24.

23. Merle Fainsod, "Bureaucracy and Modernization: The Russian and Soviet Case" in Joseph La Palombara, ed., *Bureaucracy and Political Development* (Princeton: Princeton University Press, 1971), p. 248.

24. See Stephen Sternheimer, "Administration for Development: The Emerging Bureaucratic Elite, 1920–1930," in Walter Pinter and Don Rowney, eds., *Russian Officialdom* (Chapel Hill: University of North Carolina Press, 1980), pp. 316–351 and Kendall Bailes, *Technology and Society Under Lenin and Stalin* (Princeton: Princeton University Press, 1980, pp. 202, 204.

25. *Sostav rukovoyashchikh rabotnikov i spetsialistov Soyuza SSR* (Moscow: Soyuzorguchet', 1939), pp. 8, 10, and Merle Fainsod, "Bureaucracy and Modernization: The Russian and Soviet Case," in Joseph La Palombara, ed., *Bureaucracy and Political Development*, pp. 255–56.

26. Ward Rutherford, *The Russian Army in World War I*, pp. 25, 42, and Alfred Knox, *With the Russian Army 1914–1917*, p. 421.

27. Ward Rutherford, *The Russian Army in World War I*, pp. 24, 26, 58; Bernard Pares, *The Fall of the Russian Monarchy*, p. 221; and Geoffrey Evans, *Tannenberg: 1410:1914*, p. 79.

28. For the best account of Sorge's mission, see Charles Willoughby, *Shanghai Conspiracy—the Sorge Spy Ring* (New York: E.P. Dutton and Company, 1952), and Chalmers Johnson, *An Instance of Treason—Ozaki Hotsumi and the Sorge Spy Ring* (Stanford: Stanford University Press, 1964).

29. Alexander Foote, *Handbook for Spies* (Garden City, New York: Doubleday, 1949), pp. 92–95.

30. Albert Seaton, *The Russo-German War 1941-45* (New York: Praeger, 1970), pp. 43–45, 64; James Lucas, *War on the Eastern Front 1941–1945*, pp. viii, 3, 6, 10, 12, 17; B.H. Liddell-Hart, *History of the Second World War*, p. 169; and J.F.C. Fuller, *The Second World War 1939–45*, p. 122.

31. B.H. Liddel-Hart, *History of the Second World War*, p. 169.

32. Thomas Riha, "Constitutional Developments in Russia" in Theofanis Stavrou, ed., *Russia Under the Last Tsar*, p. 112. As Ward Rutherford put it, the government was "anxious to stifle all expressions of patriotism as inimical to what they considered the true interests of the nation." See Ward Rutherford, *The Russian Army in World War I*, p. 137.

33. The major exceptions were 1.5 million small nationality minorities, including the Volga Germans, Kalmyks, Karuchai, Chechen, Ingush, and Crimean Tatars, falsely accused of treason and deported to Siberia. For the best account of these sad events see Robert Conquest, *The Nation Killers—The Soviet Deportation of Nationalities* (New York: Macmillan, 1960).

34. M.M. Kir'yan, *Voenno-tekhnicheskii progress i vooruzhennye sily SSR*, p. 156; *Sovetskaya voennaya entsiklopediya*, vol. 2, p. 68; *Istoriya vtoroi miro-voi voiny 1939-1945*, vol. 12, pp. 71, 78; *Istoriya velikoi otechestvennai voiny Sovetskogo Soyuza*, vol. 6, pp. 342-66, and *Istoriya kommunisticheskoi partii Sovetskogo Soyuza*, vol. 5, bk. 1, p. 596. Indeed, 74 percent of all heroes of the Soviet Union during the war were Communists and another 11 percent were Komsomolites. See *50 let vooruzhennykhsil SSSR* (Moscow: Voenizdat, 1968), p. 469.

35. Frederick Barghoorn, "Soviet Russia: Orthodoxy and Adaptiveness," in Lucian Pye and Sidney Verba, eds., *Political Culture and Political Development* (Princeton: Princeton University Press, 1965), p. 450.

36. Winston Churchill, *The Hinge of Fate* (London: Houghton Mifflin, 1951), p. 613.

37. Issac Deutscher, *Stalin* (London: Oxford Unversity Press, 1949), p. 568.

CHAPTER 8

1. Samuel Griffith II, *The Chinese People's Liberation Army* (New York: McGraw-Hill, 1967), p. 206.

2. T.R. Fehrenbach, *This Kind of War* (New York: Macmillan, 1963), p. 636. Indeed, in one battle in April 1953 the United States Army expended over 130,000 rounds of artillery ammunition in one day (p. 632). For other cases see F.F. Liu, *A Military History of Modern China, 1924-1949* (Princeton: Princeton University Press, 1956), p. 136; John Gittings, *The Role of the Chinese Army* (London: Oxford Univerity Press, 1967), p. 76; Robert Leckie, *Conflict—The History of the Korean War* (New York: G. Putnam's Sons, 1962), pp. 195, 364 and 387; and Alvin Coox, "Recourse to Arms: The Sino-Japanese Conflict 1937-1945," in Alvin Coox and Hilary Conroy, eds., *China and Japan: Search for Balance Since World War I* (Santa Barbara, Calif.: ABC-Clio Press, 1978), pp. 304-306.

3. Alexander George, *The Chinese Communist Army in Action* (New York: Columbia University Press, 1967), p. 83.

4. F.F. Liu, *A Military History of Modern China, 1924-1949*, p. 209; Takushiro Hattori, *Yaponiya v voine 1941-1945*, abridged translation (Moscow: Voenizdat, 1973), p. 582; Alvin Coox, "Recourse to Arms: The Sino-Japanese Conflict, 1937-1945," in Alvin Coox and Hilary Conroy, eds., *China and Japan: Search for Balance since World War I*, p. 304; James Sheridan, *China in Disintegration* (New York: Free Press, 1975), p. 269. Also see the December 19, 1950 memo by Dean Rusk in *Foreign Relations of the United States, 1950* (Washington, D.C.: Government Printing Office, 1976), vol. 7, p. 1574.

5. Douglas MacArthur, *Reminiscences* (New York: McGraw-Hill Book Company, 1964), p. 362 and Hsiang-Hsiung Wu, "Total Strategy Used by China and

Some Major Engagements in the Sino-Japanese War of 1937-1945," in Paul Sih, ed., *Nationalist China During the Sino-Japanese War, 1937-1945* (Hicksville, N.Y.: Exposition Press, 1977), p. 38.

6. Frank Dorn, *The Sino-Japanese War, 1937-41* (New York: Macmillan, 1974), pp. 8, 231.

7. David Bergamini, *Japan's Imperial Conspiracy* (New York: Pocket Books, 1972), p. 897. In the last nine months of the war, 897,000 Japanese died compared to 32,000 American deaths. In the battles of 1945 as many as 24 Japanese soldiers died for each American military fatality, as in the Philippines (pp. 1090-1091). As for Admiral King's statement, see Tang Tsou, *America's Failure in China, 1941-1950* (Chicago: University of Chicago Press, 1963), p. 66. Even in December 1942 the Allies had deployed only 350,000 troops in the Pacific (p. 60).

8. For descriptions of these battles, see John Boyle, *China and Japan At War 1937-1945* (Stanford: Stanford University Press, 1972), p. 57; O. Edmund Clubb, *Twentieth Century China* (New York: Columbia University Press, 1964), p. 228, David Bergamini, *Japan's Imperial Conspiracy*, pp. 742-744 and Takushiro Hattori, *Yaponiya v voine 1941-1945*, abridged translation, pp. 591-592.

9. This is not to disparage Japan's military capabilities. Japan did remarkably well with its limited economic resources. But its great victories were achieved against less developed countries (as China) or the colonial possessions of Western Europe in Asia. Very few European troops—by one count 75,000 soldiers—were in Malaya, the Philippines, and East Indies at the time of Japan's great triumphs of 1941 and 1942. See David Bergamini, *Japan's Imperial Conspiracy*, p. 916.

10. *Foreign Relations of the United States, 1952-1954*, vol. 15, p. 650.

11. Hsu Long-hsuen and Chang Ming-kai, *History of the Sino-Japanese War (1937-1945)* (Taipei, Taiwan: Chung Wu Publishing Company, 1971), pp. 266-271; Alvin Coox, "Recourse to Arms: The Sino-Japanese Conflict 1937-1945," in Alvin Coox and Hilary Conroy, eds., *China and Japan: Search for Balance Since World War I*, p. 304; and F.F. Liu, *A Military History of Modern China 1924-1949*, p. 209.

12. Walter Hermes, *Truce Tent and Fighting Front* (Washingtong, D.C.: Government Printing Office, 1966), pp. 338, 352, and David Rees, *Korea: The Limited War* (Baltimore, Md.: Penguin Books, 1964), p. 194.

13. Alvin Coox, "Recourse to Arms: The Sino-Japanese Conflict 1937-1945," in Alvin Coox and Hilary Conroy, eds., *China and Japan: Search for Balance Since World War I*, pp. 309-310. At the end of the war the Japanese forces in China had but 305 tanks. See Tang Tsou, *America's Failure in China, 1941-1950* (Chicago: University of Chicago Press, 1963), p. 331.

14. *Foreign Relations of the United States, 1950* (Washington, D.C.: Government Printing Office, 1976), vol. 7, pp. 1261-1262.

15. *Declassified Documents Series*, 1980, no. 381A.

16. *Foreign Relations of the United States, 1952-1954* (Washington, D.C.: Government Printing Office, 1984), vol. 15, pp. 826-827.

17. *Foreign Relations of the United States, 1950* (Washington, D.C.: Government Printing Office, 1976), vol. 6, p. 66. The number of Japanese troops in Manchuria rose from 300,000 in 1937 to 700,000 in 1941 to 1,100,000 in 1942. For Johnson quote, see Walter Hermes, *Truce Tent and Fighting Front*, p. 564.

18. David Rees, *Korea: The Limited War*, p. 94 and Joseph Goulden, *Korea— The Untold Story of the War* (New York: Times Books, 1982), p. 277 and Walter Hermes, *Truce Tent and Fighting Front*, p. 499. One major advantage for South Korea over North Korea in expanding its army was that there were 21 million South Koreans to only 9 million North Koreans. A second advantage was that Syngman Rhee was a far more prominent Korean nationalist leader than Kim Il-sung. Finally, the United States could and did provide far more aid in the south than Russia and China provided in the north.

19. Chalmers Johnson, *Peasant Nationalism and Communist Power* (Stanford: Stanford University Press, 1962), and John Boyle, *China and Japan at War 1937-1945* (Stanford: Stanford University Press, 1972), p. 294.

20. George Taylor, *The Struggle for North China* (New York: Institute of Pacific Relations, 1940), p. 150, Hsu Long-hsuen and Chang Ming-kai, *History of the Sino-Japanese War 1937-1945)*, p. 571 and *Foreign Relations of the United States, 1939* (Washington, D.C.: Government Printing Office, 1955), pp. 277– 280.

21. Frank Dorn, *The Sino-Japanese War, 1937-41* (New York: Macmillan, 1974), pp. 93, 109; Dick Wilson, *When Tigers Fight* (New York: Viking Press, 1982), p. 53; and John Toland, *The Rising Sun* (New York: Random House, 1970), p. 50.

22. *Foreign Relations of the United States, 1943, China* (Washington, D.C.: Government Printing Office, 1957), p. 159 and David Bergamini, *Japan's Imperial Conspiracy*, p. 963.

23. Saburo Ienaga, *Japan's Last War* (Canberra, Australia: Australian National University Press, 1979), p. 282. In addition 32,000 Japanese were killed in Korea.

24. There is considerable evidence on this point. As Harold Sunoo has observed, "There is no evidence that China participated in planning the war." See Harold Sunoo, *America's Dilemma in Asia: The Case of South Korea* (Chicago: Nelson-Hall, 1979), p. 98. As late as May Day 1950, Liu Shao-chi was optimistic about the future "very good" conditions for peaceful reconstruction and did not see the United States as a major threat to world peace. See John Gittings, *The Role of the Chinese Army*, p. 44. Of particular interest is that China did not intervene in the Korean War at the most propitious times—in June 1950 when the North Korean army drove the South Korean army into the Pusan

pocket and in September 1950 when the American army was vulnerable after the Inchan landing. It intervened only when the American army surged toward the Yalu.

25. *Foreign Relations of the United States, 1950* (Washington, D.C.: Government Printing Office, 1976), vol. 6, p. 815.

26. Indeed, on January 26, 1950 the American consul general in Shanghai, Walter McConaughy, reported to the secretary of state that, "the new regime faces an extremely serious situation. . . . Since the takeover of Shanghai JMP currency has depreciated fifteen times. The nation's food situation is serious; much distress in the interior." See *Foreign Relations of the United States, 1950* (Washington, D.C.: Government Printing Office, 1976), vol. 6, p. 297. See also Edgar O'Ballance, *Korea: 1950-1953*, p. 57 and Ho Kan-chih, *A History of the Modern Chinese Revolution*, p. 551.

27. *Foreign Relations of the United States, 1950,* vol. 7, p. 934.

28. A.M. Halpern, "China in the Postwar World," *China Quarterly*, no. 21 (January-March, 1965), p. 29; Allen Whiting, *China Crosses the Yalu* (New York: Macmillan, 1960), p. 122; and Robert Simmons, *The Strained Alliance* (New York: Free Press, 1975), p. 183. Fighting abroad also made it considerably more difficult to motivate the average Chinese peasant soldier than in a war for defense of the homeland.

29. O. Edmund Clubb, *Twentieth Century China* (New York: Columbia University Press, 1964), p. 226 and Hsi-Sheng Chi, *Nationalist China At War* (Ann Arbor: University of Michigan Press, 1982), p. 43 and Samuel Griffith II, *The Chinese People's Liberation Army*, p. 293.

30. David Rees, *Korea: The Limited War* (Baltimore, Md.: Penguin Books, 1964), pp. 176, 1978. Indeed, by late December many American military leaders thought a total evacuation from Korea would be necessary. On December 29, 1950 the Joint Chiefs of Staff sent General Douglas MacArthur a telegram stating that "the Chinese Communists possess the capability of forcing United Nations forces out of Korea. . . . Since developments may force our withdrawal from Korea, it is important . . . to determine, in advance, our last reasonable opportunity for an orderly evacuation." See *Foreign Relations of the United States, 1950* (Washington, D.C.: Government Printing Office, 1976), vol. 7, pt. 2, p. 1513.

31. *Foreign Relations of the United States, 1951* (Washington, D.C.: Government Printing Office, 1983), vol. 7, pt. 2, p. 1513.

32. Walter Hermes, *Truce Tent and Fighting Front*, p. 34.

33. Hsi-Sheng Chi, *Nationalist China at War*, pp. 91-92.

34. Frank Dorn, *The Sino-Japanese War, 1937-1941*, pp. 329-331, 357-361; John Paton Davies, Jr., *Dragon By The Tail* (New York: W.W. Norton, 1972), p. 239; and Hsi-Sheng Ch'i, *Nationalist China At War*, p. 62.

35. *Foreign Relations of the United States, 1951*, vol. 7, pt. 1, p. 1263.

36. *Foreign Relations of the United States, 1952-1954*, vol. 15, p. 549.

37. *Declassified Documents Series*, no. 80, 345A, p. 5.

38. Walter Hermes, *Truce Tent and Fighting Front*, pp. 194-195, 383.

39. During Operation ICHIGO, most Japanese troops with battle experience in China were sent to the Pacific Ocean and southwest front. In their place the bulk of Japanese troops were men "yet not trained, not possessing military experience, poorly equipped with personal weapons." The "extreme lack of ships" led to primary reliance on vulnerable railroad lines. See Takushiro Hattori, *Yaponiya v Voine 1941-1945*, abridged translation, p. 434. Furthermore during the operation the army ran out of supplies and no new supplies were sent after November 1944. See Dick Wilson, *When Tigers Fight*, p. 242.

40. *Foreign Relations of the Untied States, 1944* (Washington, D.C.: Government Printing Office, 1967), vol. 6, p. 100.

41. *United States Relations With China* (Washington, D.C.: Government Printing Office, 1949), p. 66. It is true that in May and June of 1945 the Kuomintang armies did manage to recapture a few key cities, including Nanning, Kweilin, and Luchow. But, this seizure of 52,000 square kilometers occurred only *after* they had been abandoned by the Japanese army, which was then preparing for a final stand in Japan against the advancing American military.

42. See Joseph Goulden, *Korea—The Untold Story of the War* (New York: Times Books, 1982), p. 641.

43. See David Rees, *Korea: The Limited War*, p. 428.

44. Samuel Griffith II, *The Chinese People's Liberation Army*, pp. 170-171. United Nations commander General Mark Clark concurred that in three years the Chinese army "had become much smarter and more effective." See Mark Clark, *From the Danube to the Yalu* (New York: Harper and Brothers, 1960), p. 316. At a National Security Council meeting late in July 1953, Secretary of State John Foster Dulles "was worried about the situation because the Chinese Communists could so easily provoke an incident, even after the armistice, and could launch a strong attack against us." See *Foreign Relations of the United States 1952-1954*, vol. 15, p. 1421. These improvements were across the board. While the Chinese air force in June 1950 lacked any operational MIG-15s and was relatively weak, by July 1953 the air force was using 2,000 jet fighters. In April 1953 National Intelligence Estimate no. 80 concluded that by American standards, Chinese "fighter units are believed to be reaching a fairly high standard of combat efficiency." See David Rees, *The Limited War*, pp. 382-383 and *Foreign Relations of the United States, 1952-1954*, vol. 15, p. 868. While Chinese artillery fire was relatively weak in 1950, Walter Hermes has concluded that "artillery fire in June and July 1953 was both heavy and accurate in support of their final offensives." See Walter Hermes, *Truce Tent and Fighting Front*, p. 510. Finally, while the PLA prior to 1950 had little defensive experience and

none in static warfare, the National Intelligence Estimate no. 80 in April 1953 found that "a highly organized, well integrated defensive zone extends possibly 15 to 20 miles to the rear of present battle positions. Many fortified areas have been constructed in the rear of this zone and are being improved and expanded." See *Foreign Relations of the United States, 1952-1954*, vol. 15, p. 865.

CHAPTER 9

1. Cited in J. Lawton Collins, *War in Peacetime* (Boston: Houghton Mifflin, 1969), p. 211. Similarly General Matthew Ridgway argued that "the Chinese greatly outnumbered U.N. forces." See General Matthew Ridgway, *The Korean War* (Garden City, N.Y.: Doubleday and Company, 1967), p. 88.

2. See Alexander George, *The Chinese Communist Army in Action* (New York: Columbia University Press, 1967), p. 6; Allen Whiting, *China Crosses the Yalu* (New York: Macmillan, 1960), p. 122; and Edgar O'Ballance, *Korea: 1950-1953* (Hamden, Conn.: Archon Books, 1969), p. 71 for estimates of a PLA of 300,000 men.

3. Reginald Thompson, *Cry Korea* (London: Macdonald Company, 1951), pp. 246-247.

4. See Frank Dorn, *The Sino-Japanese War 1937-41* (New York: Macmillan, 1974), p. 180 and Dick Wilson, *When Tigers Fight* (New York: Viking Press, 1982), p. 36.

5. See L. Montross et al., *United States Marine Operations in Korea 1950-1953: The East-Central Front* (Washington, D.C.: Government Printing Office, 1962), vol. 4, p. 35. About the only time the PLA seemed truly indifferent to casualties came in the Fifth-Phase Chinese offensive when the PLA took 70,000 casualties. See James McGovern, *To the Yalu* (New York: William Morrow and Company, 1972), pp. 191-192.

6. See George Paloczi Horvath, *Mao Tse-tung, Emperor of the Blue Arts* (Garden City, N.Y.: Doubleday, 1963), pp. 231-232. Ironically, in more recent years Soviet scholarship has taken to decrying Maoist militarism as responsible for many Chinese problems since 1958. See, for example, G. Apalin, *Militarism in Peking's Policies* (Moscow: Progress Publishers, 1980).

7. *Declassified Documents Series*, 1980, no. 372A, p. 17.

8. John Gittings, *The World and China, 1922-1972* (New York: Harper and Rowe, 1974), p. 185. Chinese displeasure at minimal Soviet aid could be seen in the fact that Chinese Army Day messages in August barely referred to Stalin or the Soviet Union (p. 186). What is especially interesting here is that Chinese complaints about Soviety military deliveries in the early 1950s sound very similar to Egyptian complaints about Soviet weapons transfers in the late 1960s and early 1970s. In both cases this dissatisfaction later helped fuel a break in the alliance with the Soviet Union. Indeed, in 1950 the most common Chinese weap-

ons were American arms seized during the civil war. See Robert Simmons, *The Strained Alliance* (New York: Free Press, 1975), p. 181.

9. See Robert Simmons, *The Strained Alliance,* pp. 181-182. It is interesting to note that the area in which the Russians provided the most equipment—airplanes—was also the one force that was never used in an offensive mode in the Korean War. The National Intelligence Estimate no. 32, in July 1951 estimated there were 10,000 Soviet advisers in China. See *Foreign Relations of the United States, 1951* (Washington, D.C.: Government Printing Office, 1983), vol. 7, pt. 2, p. 1742. The American Ambassador in Korea Muccio reported from Pusan in June 1951 that "no Soviets are reported with CCF units in Korea." See *Foreign Relations of the United States, 1951,* vol. 7, pt. 1, p. 549.

10. Hsi-Sheng Ch'i, *Nationalist China At War* (Ann Arbor: University of Michigan Press, 1982), pp. 57-59, 63-64; *Sovetskaya voennaya entsiklopediya* (Moscow: Voenizdat, 1978), vol. 5, 541; and *Foreign Relations of the United States, 1939* (Washington, D.C.: Government Printing Office, 1955), p. 261.

11. United States Army, *American Military History* (Washington, D.C.: Government Printing Office, 1969), p. 548 and James Schnabel, *United States Army in the Korean War—Policy and Direction: The First Year* (Washington, D.C.: Government Printing Office, 1972), pp. 43, 60.

12. Saburo Ienaga, *Japan's Last War* (Canberra, Australia: Australian National University Press, 1979), pp. 85-86.

13. James Schnabel, *United States Army in the Korean War—Policy and Direction: The First Year,* pp. 283-284. As in Vietnam, the Communists in Korea did possess an important sanctuary, this time in Manchuria.

14. General Matthew Ridgway, *The Korean War* (Garden City, N.Y.: Doubleday and Company, 1967), p. 157.

15. *Foreign Relations of the United States, 1950* (Washington, D.C.: Government Printing Office, 1976), vol. 7, pp. 1041-1042.

16. *Foreign Relations of the United States, 1950,* vol. 7, pp. 1242, 1248. Lieutenant Col. Robert Rigg foresaw "carnage" if the Chinese used their airpower for "we, not they, are most vulnerable to air attack ... the Chinese ... air force has available to it more profitable targets, proportionately, than are open to us." See Lieutenant Colonel Robert Rigg, *Red China's Fighting Hordes* (Harrisburg, Pa.: Military Service Publishing Company, 1952), p. 320.

17. *Foreign Relations of the United States, 1951,* vol. 7, pt. 1, p. 291.

CHAPTER 10

1. *Foreign Relations of the United States, 1944* (Washington, D.C.: Government Printing Office, 1967), vol. 6, pp. 288-289.

2. Ibid.

3. The situation in Shanghai even in March 1950 was still sufficiently serious that the American consul general there, Walter McConaughy, could wire the Secretary of State on March 16, 1950 that there was a "critical near catastrophic economic situation, bringing misery to people at an accelerating rate. Attested to from all sides." See *Foreign Relations of the United States, 1950* (Washington, D.C.: Government Printing Office, 1976), vol. 6, p. 318. See also Allen Whiting, *China Crosses the Yalu* (New York: Macmillan, 1960), pp. 15-16 and A. Doak Barnett, *Communist China: The Early Years, 1949-55* (New York: Praeger, 1966), p. 236.

4. Arthur Young served as financial adviser to the Kuomintang government from 1929 to 1947. See his *China's Wartime Finance and Inflation, 1937-1945* (Cambridge: Harvard University Press, 1965), p. 63. See also Chi-Ming Hou, "Economic Development and Public Finance in China, 1937-1945," in Paul Sih, ed., *Nationalist China During the Sino-Japanese War, 1937-1945* (Hicksville, N.Y.: Exposition Press, 1977), p. 233.

5. Colin Clark, "Economic Growth in Communist China," *China Quarterly* no. 21 (January-March 1965), p. 164; Jurgen Domes, *The Internal Politics of China, 1949-1972*, trans. Rudiger Machetzki (New York: Praeger, 1973), p. 71; and Alexander Eckstein, *China's Economic Development* (Ann Arbor: University of Michigan Press, 1975), p. 14.

6. *Foreign Relations of the United States, 1943, China* (Washington, D.C.: Government Printing Office, 1957), p. 234 and Chi-Ming Hou, "Economic Development and Public Finance in China, 1937-1945," in Paul Sih, ed., *Nationalist China During the Sino-Japanese War, 1937-1945*, pp. 226-227.

7. *Foreign Relations of the United States, 1945* (Washington, D.C.: Government Printing Office, 1969), vol. 7, p. 1073 and Arthur Young, *China's Wartime Finance and Inflation, 1937-1945*, pp. 320-321.

8. A. Doak Barnett, *Communist China: The Early Years 1949-1955* (New York: Praeger, 1966), p. 223. As Arthur Young has stated, "China's wartime inflation was caused chiefly by monetary excesses and to a much less extent by non-monetary factors." See Arthur Young, *China's Wartime Finance and Inflation, 1937-1945*, p. 299. For details of Communist efforts to tame inflation, see Alexander Eckstein, *China's Economic Development*, pp. 198-199.

9. Alexander Eckstein, *China's Economic Development,* pp. 197-198.

10. *Foreign Relations of the United States, 1941* (Washington, D.C.: Government Printing Office, 1956), vol. 4, p. 87 and Arthur Young, *China's Wartime Finances and Inflation, 1937-1945*, p. 53.

11. *Foreign Relations of the United States, 1941*, vol. 4, pp. 86-87.

12. *Foreign Relations of the United States, 1945* (Washington, D.C.: Government Printing Office, 1969), vol. 7, p. 110; Barbara Tuchman, *Stilwell and the*

American Experience in China (New York: Macmillan, 1970), p. 456; and John Service, *The Amerasia Papers: Some Problems in the History of US-China Relations* (Berkeley: University of California Press, 1970), pp. 202–203.

13. Alexander Eckstein, *China's Economic Development*, pp. 201–203.

14. *The Memoirs of Li Tsung-jen* (Boulder, Colo.: Westview Press, 1979), p. 330. Although Li Tsung-jen was a rival of Chiang, his memoirs are quite interesting, as befitted a distinguished military commander.

15. This is not to suggest that Mao was ever-victorious. His forces were defeated in the Autumn Harvest Uprising (1972), Fifth Encirclement Campaign (1934), and New Fourth Army Incident (1940). But these incidents were overshadowed by far more significant victories and ultimate attainment of power in 1949 against all odds.

16. Joseph Stilwell, *The Stilwell Papers* (New York: William Sloane Associates, 1948), p. 151. In another diary entry that same year (1942) Stilwell wrote of Ho, "He pays no attention whatsoever to preparations of the Chinese Army for a vital campaign (Burma) but gets eloquent because a bottle of iodine is spilled in India" (p. 177).

17. Mark Clark, *From the Danube to the Yalu* (New York: Harper and Brothers, 1950), pp. 87, 89.

18. Frank Dorn, *The Sino-Japanese War, 1937–41*, pp. 130–131.

19. Tang Tsou, *America's Failure in China, 1941–1950* (Chicago: University of Chicago Press, 1963), p. 50. A Russian observer of a Japanese bombing of a Chinese headquarters, which contained more than one faction, tells an interesting story. According to him, there were many casualties and one of the first to be dug out of the rubble was a general. As he was being dug out, a senior officer arrived, took one look at the rescued general, and yelled, "Bury him! He's not one of ours." Only Russian intervention saved the life of the general, who later went mad. Dick Wilson, who recorded this story, comments that "the bad feeling among Chinese was almost as great as between Chinese and Japanese." See Dick Wilson, *When Tigers Fight* (New York: Viking Press, 1982), p. 10.

20. Lloyd Eastman, "Regional Politics and Central Government," in Paul Sih, ed., *Nationalist China During the Sino-Japanese War, 1937–1945* (Hicksville, N.Y.: Exposition Press, 1977), p. 346–347.

21. *Foreign Relations of the United States 1943, China*, pp. 27–28. Two European Red Cross doctors after two years on the Ichang front reported in January 1943 that the officers were selling much surplus rice on the black market by registering more soldiers than they had and by giving each soldier four ounces less rice daily than he was supposed to receive. See Arthur Young, *China's Wartime Finance and Inflation, 1937–1945* (Cambridge: Harvard University Press, 1965), pp. 319–320; *The Memoirs of Li Tsung-jen*, pp. 423–424; and Joseph Esherick, ed., *Lost Chance in China: The World War II Dispatches of*

John S. Service (New York: Random House, 1974), p. 13. These statements were contained in telegrams of the American Ambassador in China Gauss to the secretary of state in December 1943 and January 1944. See *Foreign Relations of the United States, 1943, China,* pp. 27-28, 191 and *Foreign Relations of the United States, 1944, China,* p. 8.

22. Frank Dorn, *The Sino-Japanese War, 1937-41,* p. 185.

23. See *Foreign Relations of the United States, 1943, China,* p. 234. In another telegram in December 1944, Everett Drumright complained that "the Chinese strategy is entirely defensive in character," that the Chinese soldier has "from an offensive standpoint . . . no value" and that "the Chinese wish to maintain the status quo in this area, not desiring to arouse the Japanese." See *Foreign Relations of the United States, 1944, China,* p. 6.

24. See Barbara Tuchman, *Stilwell and the American Experience in China, 1911-1945,* pp. 457-458. In November 1944 General Albert Wedemeyer wrote in despair to General George Marshall that "the disorganization and muddled planning of the Chinese is beyond belief." See *Foreign Relations of the United States, 1944, China,* p. 191.

25. Joseph Stilwell, *The Stilwell Papers* (New York: William Sloane Associates, 1948), pp. 316-318.

26. Ibid., p. 68. As John Boyles stated, "Troop strength measured the wealth of a commanding general and determined not just his military status but also his political stature. With his armies intact he was wealthy and influential." It was "a short-sighted general who dissipated his force" in combat. See John Boyle, *China and Japan At War 1937-1945* (Stanford: Stanford University Press, 1972), p. 318.

27. *The Memoirs of Li Tsung-jen,* pp. 409, 428.

28. *Foreign Relations of the United States, 1942,* China, p. 223 and Frank Dorn, *The Sino-Japanese War, 1937-41,* p. 169.

29. See respectively Charles Romanus and Riley Sunderland, *Stilwell's Mission to China* (Washington, D.C.: Government Printing Office, 1953), p. 153; Charles Romanus and Riley Sunderland, *Time Runs Out in CBI* (Washington, D.C.: Government Printing Office, 1959), p. 231; and Frank Dorn, *The Sino-Japanese War, 1937-41,* p. 100.

30. Joseph Stilwell, *The Stilwell Papers,* p. 117 and Lloyd Eastman, "Who Lost China? Chiang Kai-shek Testifies," research note in *China Quarterly* no. 88 (December, 1981), p. 659.

31. *Declassified Documents Series,* no. 79, 267B, p. 2.

32. Samuel Griffith II, *The Chinese People's Liberation Army* (New York: McGraw-Hill Book Company, 1967), pp. 129, 131.

33. Roy Appleman, *South to the Naktong, North to the Yalu* (Washington, D.C.: Government Printing Office, 1960), p. 770 and James McGovern, *To the Yalu* (New York: William Morrow and Company, 1972), p. 131.

34. Mark Clark, *From the Danube to the Yalu* (New York: Harper and Brothers, 1950), p. 96.

35. For General Wedemeyer's report see Charles Romanus and Riley Sunderland, *Time Runs Out in CBI*, p. 369 and for John Service's report see John Service, *The Amerasia Papers: Some Problems in the History of US-China Relations* (Berkeley: University of California Press, 1971), p. 204. As Service went on to say, "military service is regarded in the minds of the people as a sentence of death."

36. See David Barrett, *Dixie Mission: The United States Army Observer Group in Yenan* (Berkeley: Chinese Research Monograph no. 6, Center for Chinese Studies, 1970), p. 86 and Charles Romanus and Riley Sunderland, *Time Runs Out in CBI*, p. 370.

37. Barbara Tuchman, *Stilwell and the American Experience In China, 1911–45*, p. 363 and Anthony Tang, "Comments" and Lawrence Shyu, "China's Wartime Parliament," in Paul Sih, ed., *Nationalist China During the Sino-Japanese War, 1937-1945*, pp. 196, 295.

38. See Joeseph Esherick, ed., *Lost Chance in China: The World War II Dispatches of John S. Service* (New York: Random House, 1974), p. 11 and *Foreign Relations of the United States, 1942, China*, p. 243.

39. Barbara Tuchman, *Stilwell and the American Experience in China, 1911–45*, p. 264 and Charles Romanus and Riley Sunderland, *Time Runs Out in CBI*, p. 243.

40. Hsi-Sheng Ch'i, *Nationalist China at War*, pp. 94–98 and Dick Wilson, *When Tigers Fight*, p. 167.

41. Joseph Stilwell, *The Stilwell Papers*, p. 142 and *Foreign Relations of the United States, 1944, China*, p. 416.

42. Lloyd Eastman, "Facets of an Ambivalent Relationship: Smuggling, Puppets and Atrocities During the War, 1937–1945," in Akira Iriye, ed., *The Chinese and the Japanese*, p. 299; Hsi-Sheng Ch'i, *Nationalist China at War*, p. 97; George Taylor, *The Struggle for North China* (New York: Institute of Pacific Relations, 1940), p. 99; and Paul Sih, ed., *Nationalist China During the Sino-Japanese War, 1937-1945*, p. 309.

43. See Robert Leckie, *Conflict—The History of the Korean War* (New York: G.P. Putnam's Sons, 1962), p. 216.

44. Samuel Griffith II, *The Chinese People's Liberation Army*, p. 181 and Alexander George, *The Chinese Communist Army in Action* (New York: Columbia University Press, 1967), p. 130.

45. For number, see Franz Schurmann, *Ideology and Organization in Communist China* (Berkeley and Los Angeles: University of California Press, 1968), p. 135 and John Gittings, *The Role of the Chinese Army* (London: Oxford University Press, 1967), p. 111.

46. See Alexander George, *The Chinese Communist Army in Action*, p. 225. As George said further, "The fighting qualities of the Chinese soldier are not in question. His toughness and battlefield courage were amply proven in Korea."

CHAPTER 11

1. For figures on the PLA, see James Townsend, *Politics in China*, 2nd edition (New York: Little, Brown and Company, 1980), p. 254 and John Gittings, *The World and China, 1922-1972* (New York: Harper and Row, 1974), p. 189.

2. *Foreign Relations of the United States, 1944, China*, p. 799. These Chinese intelligence failures occurred despite the strong presence of Tai Li's powerful and feared secret police.

3. *Foreign Relations of the United States, 1943, China*, p. 194. See also Harold Quigley, *Far Eastern War 1937-1941* (Boston: World Peace Foundation, 1942), p. 111; *Foreign Relations of the United States, 1942, China* (Washington, D.C.: Government Printing Office, 1956), p. 222; *Foreign Relations of the United States, 1945, China* (Washington, D.C.: Government Printing Office, 1969), p. 192; and Frank Dorn, *The Sino-Japanese War, 1937-41*, pp. 341-342.

4. Lyman Van Slyke, *Enemies and Friends—The United Front in Chinese Communist History* (Stanford: Stanford University Press, 1967), p. 128 and *Foreign Relations of the United States, 1944, China*, p. 583.

5. Joseph Stilwell, *The Stilwell Papers* (New York: William Sloane Associates, 1948), pp. 118-121; *Foreign Relations of the United States, 1943, China*, pp. 4, 477; and O. Edmund Clubb, *Twentieth Century China* (New York: Columbia University Press, 1964), p. 240.

6. John Paton Davies, Jr., *Dragon By the Tail* (New York: W.W. Norton, 1972), pp. 296-298.

7. See F.F. Liu, *A Military History of Modern China, 1924-1949* (Princeton: Princeton University Press, 1956), p. 225. It should be noted, though, that Kuomintang ineptitude did not prevent the Soviet Union from signing a pact with China in August 1945 and the United States from providing significant economic and military assistance to China in the 1945-1948 period. See also Joseph Esherick, ed., *Lost Chance in China: The World War II Dispatches of John S. Service*, pp. 57-59; Charles Romanus and Riley Sunderland, *Time Runs Out in CBI* (Washington, D.C.: Government Printing Office, 1959), pp. 9-10; Edmund Clubb, *Twentieth Century China* (New York: Columbia University Press, 1964), pp. 234, 275-283; and *Foreign Relations of the United States, 1943, China*, p. 495.

8. *Foreign Relations of the United States, 1950* (Washington, D.C.: Government Printing Office, 1976), vol. 7, p. 1104.

9. James McGovern, *To the Yalu* (New York: William Morrow and Company, 1972), pp. 38–39; John Gittings, *The World and China, 1922–1972* (New York: Harper and Row, 1974), pp. 181–182; and *Foreign Relations of the United States, 1950*, vol. 7, pp. 852, 914.

10. Walter Zelman, *Chinese Intervention in the Korean War*, UCLA Security Studies Paper no. 11 (1967), p. 3.

11. *Foreign Relations of the United States, 1950*, vol. 7, p. 1194.

12. Ibid., p. 1086.

13. Ibid., pp. 1104–1105.

14. John Gittings, *The World and China, 1922–1972*, p. 188.

15. *Foreign Relations of the United States, 1941* (Washington, D.C.: Government Printing Office, 1956), vol. 4, p. 82.

16. See Chiang Kai-shek, *China's Destiny* (New York: Roy Publishers, 1947), pp. 44, 105, 298–299, Hsi-Sheng Ch'i, *Nationalist China at War*, pp. 27, 31.

17. See Barbara Tuchman, *Stilwell and the American Experience in China, 1911–45* (New York: Macmillan, 1970), p. 321.

18. *Foreign Relations of the United States, 1944, China*, p. 242.

19. *Foreign Relations of the United States, 1938* (Washington, D.C.: Government Printing Office, 1954), vol. 3, p. 320.

20. *Foreign Relations of the United States, 1944, China*, p. 496 and Joseph Stilwell, *The Stilwell Papers*, p. 177.

21. Hsi-Sheng Ch'i, *Nationalist China At War*, p. 140.

22. See Harry Harding, *Organizing China—The Problem of Bureaucracy, 1949–1976* (Stanford: Stanford University Press, 1981), p. 35; Ezra Vogel, "From Revolutionary to Semi-Bureaucrat: The 'Regularisation' of Cadres," *China Quarterly* no. 29 (January–March 1967), p. 54; James Townsend, *Politics in China*, 2nd edition (New York: Little, Brown and Company, 1980), p. 251 and Victor Funnell, "The Chinese Communist Youth Movement 1949–1966," *China Quarterly* no. 42 (April–June 1970), p. 114.

23. Ezra Vogel, "Land Reform in Kwangtung 1951–1953: Central Control and Localism," *China Quarterly* no. 38 (April–June 1969), p. 27. For a detailed review of provinces controlled by the center, see Hung-Mao Tien, *Government and Politics in Kuomintang China 1927–1937* (Stanford: Stanford University Press, 1972), p. 5.

24. Charles Romanus and Riley Sunderland, *Time Runs Out in CBI*, p. 166.

25. Susan Marsh, "Chou Fo-hai: The Making of a Collaborator," in Akira Iriye, ed., *The Chinese and the Japanese* (Princeton: Princeton University Press, 1980), p. 318 and Hsi-Sheng Ch'i, *Nationalist China at War*, pp. 166, 221.

26. *Foreign Relations of the United States, 1943, China*, pp. 208, 396.

27. John Paton Davies, Jr., *Dragon By the Tail*, pp. 248-249.

28. Frank Dorn, *The Sino-Japanese War, 1937-41* (New York: Macmillan, 1974), pp. 377-378.

29. Barbara Tuchman, *Stilwell and the American Experience in China, 1911-45*, p. 377.

30. *Foreign Relations of the United States, 1943, China*, p. 261. Similarly Representative Mike Mansfield told President Roosevelt, after a trip to China, in January 1945 that "China's house has a leaky roof and a shaky foundation." See *Foreign Relations of the United States, 1945* (Washington, D.C.: Government Printing Office, 1969), vol. 7, p. 11. For other references, see John Service, *The Amerasia Papers: Some Problems in the History of U.S.–China Relations*, p. 207; Joseph Esherick, ed., *Lost Chance in China—The World War II Dispatches of John S. Service*, p. 19, *Foreign Relations of the United States, 1943, China*, p. 383; and *Foreign Relations of the United States, 1944, China*, vol. 6, p. 289.

31. *Foreign Relations of the United States, 1951* (Washington, D.C.: Government Printing Office, 1983), vol. 7, pt. 2, p. 1572.

32. *Declassified Documents Series*, 1980, no. 37A, p. 2.

33. For an excellent discussion of Chinese government, see Harry Harding, *Organizing China—The Problem of Bureaucracy, 1949-1976*, pp. 63-64, 70-78.

34. A. Doak Barnett, *Communist China: The Early Years, 1949-55* (New York: Praeger, 1966), p. 224.

35. Ezra Vogel, *Canton Under Communism* (New York: Harper and Row, 1971), pp. 95, 123.

36. A. Doak Barnett, *Communist China: The Early Years, 1949-55*, p. 45.

37. Joyce Kallgren, "Social Welfare and China's Industrial Workers," in A. Doak Barnett, ed., *Chinese Communist Politics in Action*, pp. 541-546; Martin Whyte, "Inequality and Stratification in China," *China Quarterly* no. 64 (December 1975), p. 694; and A. Doak Barnett, *Communist China: The Early Years, 1949-55*, p. 227.

38. Hsi-Sheng Ch'i, *Nationalist China At War*, pp. 193-217.

39. Ibid., pp. 194–204 and James Sheridan, *China in Disintegration* (New York: Free Press, 1975), pp. 212–214.

40. *Foreign Relations of the United States, 1940* (Washington, D.C.: Government Printing Office, 1955), vol. 4, p. 480. Ambassador Johnson further reported that the Kuomintang was "not overtly enthusiastic" over efforts to mobilize the population, which "have not been rewarded by any concrete success."

41. Joseph Stilwell, *The Stilwell Papers*, p. 214.

42. *Foreign Relations of the United States, 1950* (Washington, D.C.: Government Printing Office, 1976), p. 321.

43. A. Doak Barnett, *Communist China: The Early Years 1949–1955*, pp. 7–8, 46.

CHAPTER 12

1. Of course, as we have already discussed in the section on Russia, this was achieved with considerable Allied aid. Nevertheless, it is a fact that the bulk of German casualties were suffered on the eastern front. It is also true that for three long years, from June 1941 to June 1933, there was no effective second western front in Europe to drain off German forces from the eastern front. And by June 1944, at the time of the Normandy invasion, the Russians had driven the Germans out of nearly all of Russia and were moving into Poland.

2. Joseph Stilwell, *The Stilwell Papers* (New York: William Sloane Associates, 1948), p. 190.

3. See Francis Heller, ed., *The Korean War—A 25 Year Perspective* (Lawrence, Kans.: The Regents Press of Kansas, 1977), p. 33.

4. *Declassified Documents Series*, 1980, no. 372A, p. 1. Tang Tsou has spoken of "the emergence of China as a powerful nation in Asia" during the Korean War, whose first phases marked "the first great victory won by Chinese forces over a major power which had a lasting effect on the outcome of an international war since the Opium War opened the modern era in China." See Tang Tsou, *America's Failure in China 1941–1950* (Chicago: University of Chicago Press, 1963), p. 589.

5. See Crane Brinton, *The Anatomy of Revolution* (New York: Prentice Hall, 1952); Barrington Moore, *Social Origins of Dictatorship and Democracy* (Boston: Beacon Press, 1967); and Theda Skocpol, *States and Social Revolution* (Cambridge: Cambridge University Press, 1979).

6. Stephen Cohen, *Rethinking the Soviet Experience* (London: Oxford University Press, 1985), p. 13.

7. See especially my article, "The Impact of Civil Wars on Communist Political Culture: The Russian and Chinese Cases," *Studies in Comparative Communism*, vol. 16, nos. 1 and 2 (Spring/Summer 1983), pp. 25-48.

8. See also Elbaki Hermassi, "Toward a Comparative Study of Revolutions," *Comparative Studies in Society and History*, vol. 18, no. 2 (April 1976), p. 175.

9. Frederick Dietz, *English Public Finance 1558-1641* (New York: Barnes and Noble, 1964), p. 448. It should be noted that while the English navy had been a powerful force under Elizabeth, the English army had been a modest force.

10. Olwen Hufton, *Europe: Privilege and Protest 1730-1789* (Ithaca, N.Y.: Cornell University Press, 1980), p. 95.

11. See Charles de Gaulle, *France and Her Army*, trans. F.L. Dash (London: Hutchinson and Company, n.d.), p. 61. For England after the Restoration see Peter Young and Richard Holmes, *The English Civil War* (London: Eyre Methuen, 1974), pp. 331-333 and Maurice Ashley, *General Monck* (Totowa, N.J.: Rowman and Littlefield, 1977), pp. 218-221. For France see John Ellis, *Armies in Revolution* (London: Croom Helm, 1973), pp. 138-153.

12. Samuel Huntington, *Political Order in Changing Societies* (New Haven: Yale University Press, 1968), pp. 1-2, 264.

13. See Theda Skocpol, *States and Social Revolutions*, p. 41. Similarly almost 50 years ago Crane Brinton wrote, "Politically the revolution ends the worst abuses, the worst inefficiencies of the old regime . . . the machinery of government works more smoothly after than immediately before the revolution. . . . The achievement of governmental efficiency is really the most striking uniformity we can note in estimating political changes effected by our revolutions." See Crane Brinton, *The Anatomy of Revolution* (New York: Prentice-Hall, 1952), p. 266.

14. See Samuel Huntington, *Political Order in Changing Societies* (New Haven: Yale University Press, 1968), p. 264. Huntington has defined the characteristics of modernity as including strong, adaptable, and coherent political parties, a high degree of popular participation in public affairs, civilian control of the military, extensive government activity in the economy, effective procedures to regulate political conflict, command of the political loyalty of citizens, and capacity to tax resources, conscript citizens, and innovate and execute policy (p. 1).

15. For a fascinating, if seriously flawed, discussion of the Japanese and German paths see Barrington Moore, Jr., *Social Origins of Dictatorship and Democracy* (Boston: Beacon Press, 1966). For a discussion of pathways to modernity see Theda Skocpol, *States and Social Revolutions*, p. 4.

Bibliography

This bibliography is not intended to be comprehensive, but rather to serve as a guide to books in the field. The entries are organized in five categories: Armies and Revolution, The English Revolution, The French Revolution, The Russian Revolution, and The Chinese Revolution.

ARMIES AND REVOLUTION

Adelman, Jonathan. *The Revolutionary Armies.* Westport, Conn.: Greenwood Press, 1980.

————, ed. *Communist Armies in Politics.* Boulder, Colo.: Westview Press, 1982.

Brinton, Crane. *The Anatomy of Revolution.* New York: Prentice-Hall, 1952.

Chorley, Katharine. *Armies and the Art of Revolution.* London: Faber and Faber, 1943.

de Jouvenel, Bertrand. *On Power.* Translated by J. S. Huntington. Boston: Beacon Press, 1962.

Ellis, John. *Armies in Revolution.* London: Croom Helm, 1973.

Friedrich, Carl, ed. *Revolution.* New York: Atherton, 1967.

Fuller, J.F.C. *The Conduct of War 1789-1961.* New Brunswick: Rutgers University Press, 1961.

Howard, Michael. *War in European History.* London: Oxford University Press, 1976.

Huntington, Samuel. *Political Order in Changing Societies.* New Haven: Yale University Press, 1968.

Johnson, Charles. *Revolutionary Change.* Boston: Little, Brown, 1966.

Kim, Kyung Hon. *Revolution and the International System.* New York: New York University Press, 1970.

LaPalombara, Joseph, ed. *Bureaucracy and Political Development.* Princeton: Princeton University Press, 1971.

McNeill, William. *The Pursuit of Power: Technology, Armed Forces and Society Since A.D. 1000.* Chicago: University of Chicago Press, 1982.

Montgomery, Field Marshal Viscount. *A History of Warfare.* Cleveland: World Publishing, 1968.

Moore, Barrington, Jr. *Social Origins of Dictatorship and Democracy.* Boston: Beacon Press, 1967.

Ropp, Theodore. *War and the Modern World.* New York: Colliers, 1962.

Skocpol, Theda. *States and Social Revolution.* Cambridge: Cambridge University Press, 1979.

Strachan, Hew. *European Armies and the Conduct of War.* London: George Allen and Unwin, 1983.

Tilly, Charles, ed. *The Formation of National States in Western Europe.* Princeton: Princeton University Press, 1975.

Timasheff, Nicholas. *War and Revolution.* New York: Sheed and Ward, 1965.

Turner, Gordon, ed. *A History of Military Affairs in Western Society Since the Eighteenth Century.* New York: Harcourt Brace, 1953.

THE ENGLISH REVOLUTION

Abbott, Wilbur. *The Writings and Speeches of Oliver Cromwell.* 3 vols. Cambridge: Harvard University Press, 1937, 1939, 1945.

Alexander, Michael. *Charles I's Lord Treasurer.* Chapel Hill: University of North Carolina Press, 1975.

Ashley, Maurice. *Cromwell's Generals.* New York: St. Martin's Press, 1955.

_____. *General Monck.* Totowa, N.J.: Rowman and Littlefield, 1977.

Aylmer, G.E. *The King's Servants: The Civil Service of Charles I 1635-1642.* New York: Columbia University Press, 1961.

The Cambridge Modern History. Vol. 6. Cambridge: Cambridge University Press, 1925.

Carlton, Charles. *Charles I: The Personal Monarch.* London: Routledge and Kegan Paul, 1983.

Davis, Godfrey. *The Early Stuarts 1603-1660.* Oxford: Oxford University Press, 1937.

Dietz, Frederick. *English Public Finance 1558-1641.* New York: Barnes and Noble, 1964.

Firth, Charles. *Cromwell's Army.* London: Methuen and Company, 1902.

_____. *Oliver Cromwell.* London: Putnam, 1907/1947.

Fisher, F.J. ed. *Essays in the Economic and Social History of Tudor and Stuart England.* Cambridge: Cambridge University Press, 1961.

Fraser, Antonia. *Cromwell: The Lord Protector.* New York: Alfred A. Knopf, 1973.

Gardiner, Samuel. *Oliver Cromwell.* New York: Collier Books, 1962.

Havran, Martin. *Caroline Courtier: The Life of Lord Cottington.* London: Macmillan, 1973.

Hill, Christopher. *God's Englishman: Oliver Cromwell and the English Revolution.* London: Weidenfeld and Nicolson, 1970.

Howat, G.M.D. *Stuart and Cromwellian Foreign Policy.* New York: St. Martin's Press, 1974.

Ives, E.W. ed. *The English Revolution, 1640-1660.* London: Edward Arnold, 1968.

Kishlansky, Mark. *The Rise of the New Model Army.* Cambridge: Cambridge University Press, 1979.

Lockyer, Roger. *Buckingham.* London: Longman, 1981.

_____. *Tudor and Stuart Britain 1471-1714.* New York: St. Martin's Press, 1964.

Manning, Brian. *The English People and the English Revolution 1640-1649.* London: Heinemann, 1976.

Morrill, John, ed. *Reactions to the English Civil War 1642-1649.* New York: St. Martin's Press, 1982.

_____. *The Revolt of the Provinces.* London: George Allen and Unwin, 1976.

Ollard, Richard. *The Image of the King.* New York: Atheneum, 1979.

Oppenheim, Michael. *A History of the Administration of the Royal Navy and of Merchant Shipping in Relation to the Navy from MDIX to MDCLX.* Ann Arbor, Mich.: Shoe String Press, 1961.

Owens, W.R. ed. *Seventeenth Century England: A Changing Culture.* Totowa, N.J.: Barnes and Noble, 1981.

Perry, R.H., ed. *The English Civil War and After, 1642-1658.* Berkeley and Los Angeles: University of California Press, 1970.

Roseveare, Henry. *The Treasury.* New York: Columbia University Press, 1969.

Russell, Conrad. *Parliaments and English Politics, 1621-1629.* Oxford: Oxford University Press, 1979.

Stone, Lawrence. *The Crisis of the Aristocracy 1558-1641.* Oxford: Oxford University Press, 1965.

Tolmie, Murray. *The Triumph of the Saints.* Cambridge: Cambridge University Press, 1977.

Trevor-Roper, H.R. *Archbishop Land 1573-1645.* London: Macmillan, 1962.

Walzer, Michael. *The Revolution of the Saints.* New York: Atheneum, 1972.

Wedgewood, C.V. *The King's Peace 1637-1641.* New York: Macmillan, 1955.

_____. *The King's War 1641-1647.* London: Collins, 1958.

Wilson, Charles. *England's Apprenticeship 1603-1763.* London: Longmans, Green, 1965.

Woolrych, Austin. *Battles of the English Civil War.* New York: Macmillan, 1961.

Young, Peter, and Holmes, Richard. *The English Civil War.* London: Eyre Methuen, 1974.

Zagorin, Perez. *The Court and the Country.* New York: Atheneum, 1970.

_____. *Rebels and Rulers, 1500-1660.* Cambridge: Cambridge University Press, 1982.

THE FRENCH REVOLUTION

Alger, John. *The Quest for Victory.* Westport, Conn.: Greenwood Press, 1982.

Bergson, Louis. *France Under Napoleon.* Translated by R.R. Palmer. Princeton: Princeton University Press, 1981.

Basher, J.F. *French Finances 1770-1795.* Cambridge: Cambridge University Press, 1970.

Chandler, David. *The Campaigns of Napoleon.* New York: Macmillan, 1966.

Cobban, Alfred. *A History of Modern France*. Vol. 2 (1799-1945). Harmonds-worth, England: Penguin Books, 1961.

————. *France since the Revolution*. New York: Barnes and Noble, 1970.

Corvisier, Andre. *Armies and Societies in Europe, 1494-1789*. Translated by Abigail Siddal. Bloomington: Indiana University Press, 1979.

DeGaulle, Charles. *France and Her Army*. Translated by F.L. Dash. London: Hutchinson and Company, n.d.

Egret, Jean. *The French Prerevolution 1787-1788*. Translated by Wesley Camp. Chicago: University of Chicago Press, 1977.

Glover, Michael. *The Napoleonic Wars*. New York: Hippocrene Books, 1978.

Holtmann, Robert. *The Napoleonic Revolution*. Philadelphia and New York: J.B. Lippincott Company, 1967.

Hufton, Olwen. *Europe: Privilege and Protest 1730-1789*. Ithaca, N.Y.: Cornell University Press, 1980.

Kennett, Lee. *The French Armies in the Seven Years' Wars*. Durham, N.C.: Duke University Press, 1967.

Knapton, Ernest. *France: An Interpretive History*. New York: Charles Scribner's Sons, 1971.

Lachouque, Henry. *Napoleon's Battles*. New York: E.P. Dutton, 1967.

Lefebvre, Georges. *Napoleon: From 18 Brumaire to Tilsit 1799-1807*. Trans-lated by Henry Stockhold. New York: Columbia University Press, 1969.

————. *Napoleon: From Tilsit to Waterloo 1807-1815*. Translated by J.E. Anderson. New York: Columbia University Press, 1969.

Liddell-Hart, Basil. *The Ghost of Napoleon*. New Haven: Yale University Press, 1935.

Lynn, John. *The Bayonets of the Republic*. Urbana: University of Illinois Press, 1984.

McElwee, William. *The Art of War: Waterloo to Mons*. Bloomington: Indiana University Press, 1974.

Ogg, David. *Europe of the Ancien Regime 1715-1783*. New York: Harper and Row, 1965.

Phipps, Ramsay. *The Armies of the First French Republic*. Vol. 5. Oxford: Oxford University Press, 1939.

Quimby, Robert. *The Background of Napoleonic Warfare*. New York: Columbia University Press, 1957.

Rothenberg, Gunther. *The Art of War in the Age of Napoleon*. London: B.T. Batsford, 1977.

Scott, Samuel. *The Response of the Royal Army to the French Revolution*. Oxford: Oxford University Press, 1978.

Vovelle, Michel. *The Fall of the French Monarchy 1787-1792*. Translated by Susan Burke. Cambridge: Cambridge University Press, 1984.

THE RUSSIAN REVOLUTION

Adams, Arthur. *Imperial Russia After 1861*. Boston: D.C. Heath, 1965.

Amann, Ronald; Cooper, Julian; and Davies, R.W., eds. *The Technological Level of Soviet Industry*. New Haven: Yale University Press, 1977.

Bailes, Kendall. *Technology and Society Under Lenin and Stalin*. Princeton: Princeton University Press, 1978.

Bialer, Seweryn, ed. *Stalin and His Generals.* London: Souvenir Press, 1970.
————. *Stalin's Successors.* Cambridge: Cambridge University Press, 1979.
Blackwell, William, ed. *Russian Economic Development From Peter the Great to Stalin.* New York: New Viewpoints, 1974.
Carr, E.H. *The October Revolution: Before and After.* New York: Vintage Books, 1971.
Cohen, Stephen. *Rethinking the Soviet Experience.* New York: Oxford University Press, 1985.
Churchill, Winston. *The Unknown War—The Eastern Front.* New York: Charles Scribner's Sons, 1931.
Dallin, Alexander. *German Rule in Russia, 1941-1945.* 2nd edition. Boulder, Colo.: Westview Press, 1981.
Dupuy, R. Ernest. *World War II: A Compact History.* New York: Hawthorne Books, 1969.
Edelman, Robert. *Gentry Politics on the Eve of the Russian Revolution.* New Brunswick: Rutgers University Press, 1980.
Erickson, John. *The Road to Berlin.* Boulder, Colo.: Westview Press, 1984.
————. *The Road to Stalingrad.* Boulder, Colo.: Westview Press, 1979.
Eroshkin, N.P. *Istoriya gosudarstvennykh v chrezhdenii do revolyutsionnoi Rossi.* Moscow: Vyshaya Shkola, 1983.
Evans, Geoffrey. *Tannenberg: 1410:1914.* London: Hamish Hamilton, 1970.
Ferro, Marc. *The Great War 1914-1918.* Translated by Nicole Stone. London: Routledge and Kegan Paul, 1973.
Florinsky, Michael. *The End of the Russian Empire.* New Haven: Yale University Press, 1931.
Fuller, J.F.C. *The Second World War 1939-45.* New York: Duell, Sloan and Pearce, 1949.
Gilbert, Martin. *First World War Atlas.* New York: Macmillan, 1970.
Golder, Frank, ed. *Documents of Russian History 1914-1917.* New York: Century, 1927.
Golovine, Nicholas. *The Russian Army in the World War.* New Haven: Yale University Press, 1931.
Gourko, Vasili. *War and Revolution in Russia 1914-1917.* New York: Macmillan, 1919.
Grechko, Andrei. *The Armed Forces of the Soviet State.* Yuri Sviridov. Moscow: Voenizdat, 1975.
Guderian, Heinz. *Panzer Leader.* New York: Ballantine Books, n.d.
Holloway, David. *The Soviet Union and the Arms Race.* New Haven: Yale University Press, 1983.
Istoriya grazhdanskoi voiny v SSSR. Vol. 1. Moscow: Gosizdat, 1958.
Istoriya kommunisticheskoi partii Sovetskogo Soyuza, vol. 5., bk. 1 (1938-1945). Moscow: Partizdat, 1980.
Istoriya pervoi mirovoi voiny. 2 vols. Moscow: Nauka, 1975.
Istoriya velikoi otechestvennoi voiny Sovetskogo Soyuza 1941-1945. 6 vols. Moscow: Voenizdat, 1960.
Istoriya vtoroi mirovoi voina 1939-1945. 12 vols. Moscow: Voenizdat, 1982.
Kiryan, M.M. *Voenno-tekhnicheskii progress i vooruzhennye sily SSSR.* Moscow: Voenizdat, 1982.
The Letters of the Tsar to the Tsaritsa 1914-1917. Translated by A.L. Hynes. Hattiesburg, Miss.: Academic International Press, 1970.
The Letters of the Tsaritsa to the Tsar 1914-1916. Translated by A.L. Hynes.

Hattiesburg, Miss.: Academic International Press, 1970.

Liddell-Hart, Basil. *History of the Second World War*. London: Cassell, 1970.

_____, ed. *The Red Army*. New York: Harcourt, Brace, 1956.

Lucas, James. *War on the Eastern Front 1941-1945*. New York: Bonanza Books, 1982.

Mints, I.I., *Istoriya velikogo Oktyabrya*. Vol. 1. Moscow: Nauka, 1977.

Nikitinskii, I.N. and Sofinov, P. *Nemetskii shpionazh v Rossii vo vremya voiny 1914-1918 g.g.* Moscow: Gosizdat, 1942.

Nove, Alec. *An Economic History of the U.S.S.R.* Hammondsworth, England: Penguin Books, 1975.

Oldenburg, S.S. *Last Tsar: Nicholas II, His Reign and His Russia*. Vol. 4. Translated by Leonid Mihalap and Patrick Rollins. Gulf Breeze, Fla.: Academic International Press, 1978.

Out of My Past—The Memoirs of Count Kokovtsov. Stanford: Stanford University Press, 1935.

Pares, Bernard. *Day by Day With the Russian Army 1914-1915*. New York: Houghton Mifflin, 1915.

_____. *The Fall of the Russian Monarchy*. London: Jonathan Cape, 1939.

Pearson, Raymond. *The Russian Moderates and the Crisis of Tsarism 1914-1917*. New York: Barnes and Noble, 1977.

Pervaya mirovaya voina 1914-1918. Moscow: Nauka, 1968.

Pinter, Walter, and Rouney, Don, ed. *Russian Officialdom*. Chapel Hill: University of North Carolina Press, 1980.

Randall, Francis. *Stalin's Russia*. New York: Free Press, 1965.

Rigby, T.H. ed. *Stalin*. Englewood Cliffs, N.J.: Prentice Hall, 1966.

Rodzianko, M.V. *The Reign of Rasputin: An Empire's Collapse*. Translated by Catherine Zvegintzoff. London: A.M. Philpot, 1927.

Rossiya v mirovoi voine 1914-1918 goda (v trifrakh). Moscow: Central Statistical Administration, 1925.

Rostunov, I.I. *Russkii front pervoi mirovoi voiny*. Moscow: Nauka, 1976.

Rutherford, Ward. *The Russian Army in World War I*. London: Cremonesi Publishers, 1975.

Sazonov, Serge. *Fateful Years 1909-1916*. New York: Frederick A. Stokes, 1928.

Seaton, Albert. *The Russo-German War 1941-45*. New York: Praeger, 1970.

Seton-Watson, Hugh. *The Decline of Imperial Russia 1855-1914*. New York: Praeger, 1970.

Shifman, M.S. *Voina i ekonomika*. Moscow: Voenizdat, 1964.

Shigalin, G.I. *Voennaya ekonomika v pervuyu mirovuyu voinu (1914-1918)*. Moscow: Voenizdat, 1956.

Solzhenitsyn, Alexander. *August 1914*. Translated by Michael Glenny. New York: Farrar, Straus and Giroux, 1971.

Sovetskaya voennaya entsiklopediya. Vols. 5 and 6. Moscow: Voenizdat, 1978.

Stalin, Joseph. *The Great Patriotic War of the Soviet Union*. Translation. New York: International Publishers, 1945.

Stavrov, Theofanis, ed. *Russia Under the Last Star*. Minneapolis: University of Minnesota Press, 1969.

Stone, Norman. *The Eastern Front, 1914-1917*. New York: Charles Scribner's Sons, 1975.

Strokov, A.A. *Vooruzhennye sily i voennoe iskusstvo v pervoi mirovoi voine*. Moscow: Voenizdat, 1974.

Talenskii, N.A. *Pervaya mirovaya voina (1914-1918 g.g.)*. Moscow: Gosizdat, 1944.

Tucker, Robert, ed. *Stalinism—Essays in Historical Interpretation*. New York: W.W. Norton, 1977.

Ulam, Adam. *Expansion and Coexistence—The History of Soviet Foreign Policy 1917-67*. New York: Praeger, 1968.

_____. *The Rivals—America and Russia since World War II*. New York: Viking Press, 1971.

Verzhkhovskii, D.V., and Lyakhov, V.F. *Pervaya mirovaya voina*. Moscow: Voenizdat, 1964.

von Manstein, Erich. *Lost Victories*. Edited and translated by Anthony G. Powell. Chicago: Henry Regnery, 1958.

Werth, Alexander. *Russia at War 1941-1945*. New York: E.P. Dutton, 1964.

White, D. Fedotoff. *The Growth of the Red Army*. Princeton: Princeton University Press, 1944.

Wildman, Aaron. *The End of the Russian Imperial Army*. Princeton: Princeton University Press, 1980.

Zaionchkovsky, A.M. *Mirovaya voina, 1914-1918*. Moscow: Voenizdat, 1981.

THE CHINESE REVOLUTION

Appleman, Roy. *South to the Naktong, North to the Yalu*. Washington, D.C.: Government Printing Office, 1960.

Barnett, A. Doak. *China on the Eve of Communist Takeover*. New York: Praeger, 1963.

_____, ed. *Chinese Communist Politics in Action*. Seattle and London: University of Washington Press, 1969.

_____. *Communist China: The Early Years 1949-55*. New York: Praeger, 1966.

Barrett, David. *Dixie Mission: The United States Army Observer Group in Yenan*. Berkeley: Chinese Research Monograph no. 6, Center for Chinese Studies, 1970.

Bergamini, David. *Japan's Imperial Conspiracy*. New York: Pocket Books, 1972.

Boyle, John. *China and Japan at War 1937-1945*. Stanford: Stanford University Press, 1972.

Chi, Hsi-sheng. *Nationalist China at War*. Ann Arbor: University of Michigan Press, 1982.

Chiang Kai-shek. *China's Destiny*. New York: Roy Publishers, 1947.

Ch'ien Tuan-sheng. *The Government and Politics of China*. Cambridge: Harvard University Press, 1950.

China Handbook 1937-1945. New York: Macmillan, 1947.

Clark, Mark. *From the Danube to the Yalu*. New York: Harper and Brothers, 1950.

Clubb, O. Edmund. *Twentieth Century China*. New York: Columbia University Press, 1964.

Collins, J. Lawton. *War in Peacetime*. Boston: Houghton Mifflin, 1969.

Coox, Alvin, and Conroy, Hilary, eds. *China and Japan: Search for Balance Since World War I*. Santa Barbara, Calif.: ABC-Clio Press, 1978.

Davies, John Paton. *Dragon by the Tail.* New York: W.W. Norton, 1972.

Domes, Jurgen. *The Internal Politics of China 1949-1972.* Translated by Rudiger Machetzki. New York: Praeger, 1973.

Dorn, Frank. *The Sino-Japanese War, 1937-41.* New York: Macmillan, 1974.

Eckstein, Alexander. *China's Economic Development.* Ann Arbor: University of Michigan Press, 1975.

Esherick, Joseph, ed. *Lost Chance in China: The World War II Dispatches of John S. Service.* New York: Random House, 1974.

Fehrenback, T.R. *This Kind of War.* New York: Macmillan, 1963.

Foreign Relations of the United States, 1937. Vols. 3 and 4. Washington, D.C.: Government Printing Office, 1954.

Foreign Relations of the United States, 1938. Vol. 3. Washington, D.C.: Government Printing Office, 1954.

Foreign Relations of the United States, 1939. Vol. 3. Washington, D.C.: Government Printing Office, 1955.

Foreign Relations of the United States, 1940. Vol. 4. Washington, D.C.: Government Printing Office, 1955.

Foreign Relations of the United States, 1941. Vol. 5. Washington, D.C.: Government Printing Office, 1956.

Foreign Relations of the United States, 1942, China. Washington, D.C.: Government Printing Office, 1956.

Foreign Relations of the United States, 1943, China. Washington, D.C.: Government Printing Office, 1967.

Foreign Relations of the United States, 1944. Vol. 6. Washington, D.C.: Government Printing Office, 1967.

Foreign Relations of the United States, 1945. Vol. 7. Washington, D.C.: Government Printing Office, 1969.

Foreign Relations of the United States, 1950. Vols. 6 and 7. Washington, D.C.: Government Printing Office, 1976.

Foreign Relations of the United States, 1951. Vol. 7, pts. 1 and 2. Washington, D.C.: Government Printing Office, 1983.

Foreign Relations of the United States, 1952-1954. Vol. 15. Washington, D.C.: Government Printing Office, 1984.

Gardner, Lloyd, ed. *The Korean War.* New York: Quadrangle Books, 1972.

George, Alexander. *The Chinese Communist Army in Action.* New York: Columbia University Press, 1967.

Gittings, John. *The Role of the Chinese Army.* London: Oxford University Press, 1967.

————. *The World and China, 1922-1972.* New York: Harper and Row, 1974.

Goulden, Joseph. *Korea—The Untold Story of the War.* New York: Time Books, 1982.

Griffith, Samuel. *The Chinese People's Liberation Army.* New York: McGraw-Hill, 1967.

Guttman, Allen, ed. *Korea and the Theory of Limited War.* Boston: D.C. Heath, 1967.

Harding, Harry. *Organizing China—The Problem of Bureaucracy, 1949-1976.* Stanford: Stanford University Press, 1981.

Hattori, Takushiro. *Yaponiya v voine 1941-1945.* Abridged translation. Moscow: Voenizdat, 1973.

Heller, Francis, ed. *The Korean War—A 25 Year Perspective.* Lawrence, Kans.: Regents Press of Kansas, 1977.

Hermes, Walter. *Truce Tent and Fighting Front*. Washington, D.C.: Government Printing Office, 1966.

Ho Kan-chih. *A History of the Modern Chinese Revolution*. Peking: Foreign Languages Press, 1960.

Ho, Ping-ti, and Tsou, Tang, eds. *China's Heritage and the Communist Political System*. Chicago: University of Chicago Press, 1968.

Hsu, Long-hsuen, and Chang, Ming-kai. *History of the Sino-Japanese War (1937–1945)*. Taipei: Chung Wu Publishing Company, 1971.

Ienaga, Saburo. *Japan's Last War*. Canberra: Australian National University Press, 1979.

Iriye, Akira, ed. *The Chinese and the Japanese*. Princeton: Princeton University Press, 1980.

Jansen, Marius. *Japan and China: From War to Peace, 1894–1972*. Chicago: Rand McNally, 1974.

Jencks, Harlan. *From Muskets to Missiles: Politics and Professionalism in the Chinese Army, 1945–1981*. Boulder, Colo.: Westview Press, 1982.

Joffe, Ellis. *Party and Army: Professionalism and Political Control in the Chinese Officer Corps, 1949–1964*. Harvard East Asia Monograph no. 19, 1964.

Johnson, Chalmers. *Peasant Nationalism and Communist Power*. Stanford: Stanford University Press, 1962.

Kahn, E.J. *The Peculiar War*. New York: Random House, 1952.

Lebra, Joyce, ed. *Japan's Greater East Asia Co-Prosperity Sphere in World War II*. Kuala Lumpur: Oxford University Press, 1975.

Leckie, Robert. *Conflict—The History of the Korean War*. New York: G.P. Putnam's Sons, 1962.

Liu, F.F. *A Military History of Modern China 1924–1949*. Princeton: Princeton University Press, 1956.

Liu, Ta-Chung, and Yeh, Kung-Chia. *The Economy of the Chinese Mainland: National Income and Economic Development, 1933–1959*. Princeton: Princeton University Press, 1965.

Long, Gavin. *MacArthur as Military Commander*. London: B.T. Batsford, Ltd., 1969.

Lu, David. *From Marco Polo Bridge to Pearl Harbor*. Washington, D.C.: Public Affairs Press, 1961.

MacArthur, Douglas. *Reminiscences*. New York: McGraw-Hill Book Company, 1964.

Marshall, S.L.A. *The River and the Gauntlet*. Westport, Conn.: Greenwood Press, 1970.

McGovern, James. *To the Yalu*. New York: William Morrow, 1972.

The Memoirs of Li Tsung-jen. Boulder, Colo.: Westview Press, 1979.

Morley, James, ed. *The China Quagmire: Japan's Expansion on the Asian Continent 1933–1941*. New York: Columbia University Press, 1983.

O'Ballance, Edgar. *Korea: 1950–1953*. Hamden, Conn.: Archon Books, 1969.

Pye, Lucian. *China: An Introduction*. Boston: Little, Brown, 1978.

Quigley, Harold. *The Far Eastern War 1937–1941*. Boston: World Peace Foundation, 1942.

Rees, David. *Korea: The Limited War*. Baltimore: Penguin Books, 1964.

Ridgway, Matthew. *The Korean War*. Garden City, N.Y.: Doubleday, 1967.

Rigg, Robert. *Red China's Fighting Horde*. Harrisburg, Pa.: Military Service Publishing Company, 1952.

Romanus, Charles, and Sunderland, Riley. *Stilwell's Command Problems*.

Washington, D.C.: Government Printing Office, 1956.
————. *Stilwell's Mission to China*. Washington, D.C.: Government Printing Office, 1953.
————. *Time Runs Out in CBI*. Washington, D.C.: Government Printing Office, 1959.
Schaller, Michael. *The U.S. Crusade in China 1938-1945*. New York: Columbia University Press, 1979.
Schnabel, James, *The United States Army in the Korean War—Policy and Direction: The First Year*. Washington, D.C.: Government Printing Office, 1972.
Schurmann, Franz. *Ideology and Organization in Communist China*. Berkeley and Los Angeles: University of California Press, 1968.
————, and Schell, Orville, eds. *Republican China*. New York: Random House, 1967.
Service, John. *The Amerasia Papers: Some Problems in the History of U.S.-China Relations*. Berkeley: University of California Press, 1971.
Sheridan, James. *China in Disintegration*. New York: Free Press, 1975.
Sih, Paul, ed. *Nationalist China During the Sino-Japanese War 1937-1945*. Hicksville, N.Y.: Exposition Press, 1977.
Simmons, Robert. *The Strained Alliance*. New York: Free Press, 1975.
Solinger, Dorothy. *Regional Government and Political Integration in Southwest China, 1949-1954*. Berkeley: University of California Press, 1977.
Stilwell, Joseph. *The Stilwell Papers*. New York: William Sloane Associates, 1948.
Sunoo, Harold Hakwon. *America's Dilemma in Asia: The Case of South Korea*. Chicago: Nelson-Hall, 1979.
Taylor, George. *The Struggle for North China*. New York: Institute of Pacific Relations, 1940.
Thompson, Reginald. *Cry Korea*. London: Macdonald, 1951.
Tien, Hung-Mao. *Government and Politics in Kuomintang China 1927-1937*. Stanford: Stanford University Press, 1972.
Toland, John. *The Rising Sun*. New York: Random House, 1970.
Townsend, James. *Politics in China*, 2nd edition. New York: Little Brown, 1980.
Tsou, Tang. *America's Failure in China 1941-1950*. Chicago: University of Chicago Press, 1963.
Tuchman, Barbara. *Stilwell and the American Experience in China, 1911-45*. New York: Macmillan, 1970.
United States Army. *American Military History*. Washington, D.C.: Government Printing Office, 1969.
United States Relations With China. Washington, D.C.: Government Printing Office, 1949.
Van Slyke, Lyman. *Enemies and Friends—The United Front in Chinese Communist History*. Stanford: Stanford University Press, 1967.
Vogel, Ezra. *Canton Under Communism*. New York: Harper and Row, 1971.
Wedemeyer, Albert. *Wedemeyer Reports!* New York: Henry Holt, 1958.
Whiting, Allen. *The Chinese Calculus of Deterrence*. Ann Arbor: University of Michigan Press, 1975.
————. *China Crosses the Yalu*. New York: Macmillan, 1960.
Whitson, William. *The Chinese High Command*. New York: Praeger, 1973.
Wilson, Dick. *When Tigers Fight*. New York: Viking Press, 1982.
Young, Arthur. *China's Wartime Finances and Inflation, 1937-1945*. Cambridge: Harvard University Press, 1965.

Zelman, Walter. *Chinese Intervention in the Korean War.* UCLA Security Studies Paper no. 11, 1967.
In addition, the issues of *China Quarterly* and *The Declassified Documents Reference System* were especially helpful with regard to China.

Index